Date Due

Demco

W/D

COLUMBIA UNIVERSITY STUDIES IN ENGLISH
AND COMPARATIVE LITERATURE

NUMBER 121

GEORGIC TRADITION
IN ENGLISH POETRY

GEORGIC TRADITION IN ENGLISH POETRY

BY

DWIGHT L. DURLING

KENNIKAT PRESS, INC./PORT WASHINGTON, N. Y.

GEORGIC TRADITION IN ENGLISH POETRY

Copyright 1935, 1963 Columbia University Press
This Edition published in 1964 by KENNIKAT PRESS

Library of Congress Catalog Card No: 64-15536

Manufactured in the United States of America

To

ROBERT

CONTENTS

Converse of the "historical estimate." The didactic motive in eighteenth-century poetry. Plan of the book. Significance of the types of poetry to be discussed.

Didactic poetry in general. Certain classes of medieval and Renaissance English didactic verse. The humanistic tradition and ancient genres. Influences in Renaissance Italy which brought the revival of classical didactic forms. Expression of these influences in Fracastoro. The "defense of poetry" among English critics, tending to enforce a didactic theory of poetic function. Reasons for English interest in didactic poetry of other tongues. Sprat's recommendation of the new science to poets. "Imitation" as a copying of models in English literary practice, and the English reflection of Renaissance Maronolatry. Dryden's Vergil and Addison's essay on the Georgics. Trapp's Praelectiones poeticae. Tickell's De poesi didactica. Joseph Warton's Reflections on Didactic Poetry.
Translations which show the growth of English interest in didactic forms.

Moufat, Dennys, Philips, Gay, and others who helped to "naturalize" georgic verse in England.

Vergil and Thomson as fountainheads of the European didactic-descriptive tendency in verse. Thomson and his predecessors in English. Hinchliffe's Seasons of 1718. Thomson and "physico-theological" verse. Thomson's Seasons and the genre of descriptive verse he popularized, as based upon the form of the Georgics. Elements in the Georgics which became stock materials among didactic and descriptive poets. Thomson's expansions of these materials and additions to them. Theology and moral philosophy in The Seasons. Thomson's method in description. His extraordinary popularity as a poet broadly representative of the tendencies of his century.

Mingling of didactic and descriptive forms. Question of the artistic congruity of the georgic genre. Types of verse to be discussed in the present chapter. Examples of these types from 1726 to 1750. The growth of country verse from 1750 to 1775. 1775 onward: influence of the growing interest in science; further history of types to 1810 and their gradual decline thereafter. Twentieth-century georgics. The place of the tradition as a whole.

Poems related to the georgic genre, but treating subjects of other kinds, from 1730 onward. These poems as a group.

Divisions of time in English poetry before Thomson. The "descriptive poem" as a genre. What the descriptive poets learned from Thomson. Plan of the present chapter. Immediate contemporaries of The Seasons. Thomson's influence on poets in shorter lyrical forms. Slow growth of the descriptive form up to the 1770's. Aikin's Essay on the Application of Natural History to Poetry, and Pennant's recommendation of science to descriptive poets, in British Zoölogy.

Increased interest in science shown by publications of Newbery and Dodsley and by the multiplication of popularizers and amateurs. Gilbert White and descriptive poetry. Growth of the genre in the later eighteenth and early nineteenth centuries. The further spread of interest in natural history, and the development of a prose literature of nature and country life, which tended to displace descriptive verse. Later examples of the genre, and its decline after 1835. Extraordinary longevity of Thomson as a literary " original " and of the descriptive poem as a type.

The " loco-descriptive poem " influenced by didactic and descriptive forms. Kinds of local verse and purpose of the present note. Early examples of the type. Mixture of genres and debt of local poets to originally distinct didactic and descriptive forms. Decline of local verse in its old forms.

Place of the descriptive and didactic school in the developing knowledge and understanding of nature, country life, and the man of the country. Its relation to other social factors tending toward these ends. Extent of observation of nature in these poets. Influences which brought the decline of old descriptive genres. Wordsworth as heir of the tradition of country-and-nature verse. Natural science and nature worship in poetry before Wordsworth: new synthesis of old elements in his philosophy of nature.

INTRODUCTION

THERE was reason for Matthew Arnold's warning against the " historical estimate ": there is a real danger in the tendency to exaggerate the artistic importance of a work because of its distance from us in time. Arnold did not speak of a converse tendency, equally real. The historical importance of a work may be minimized because it has fallen radically out of line with current concepts in taste and art. Perhaps it is especially easy to minimize the historical importance of didactic and descriptive poetry. Lessing's objections against the descriptive form seem to have permanent validity, rooted as they are in psychological law. What Warton, Bowles, Arnold and others said of Pope tended to discredit all the didactic forms of the eighteenth century. " Not doctrine, but inspiration " became the accepted definition of the aim and method of poetry. Since the first triumph of romanticism there has been little evidence of tendency to bring back "mankind" rather than individual man as the primary subject matter of English poetry. We still explore paths and by-ways of romantic individualism, even into artistic caprice and idiosyncrasy. It is necessary to break away from contemporaneity to examine without prejudice an age when the didactic function in general was assumed as a premise of poetic art.

Almost all poets of the eighteenth century were didactic poets. The practical impulse of the rising middle class merged with the practical impulse which underlay the great models of Roman literature; even the forms of Roman poetry — satire, epistle, philosophical and moral verse, didactic epic — came into vogue. It is not easy to differentiate the kinds of didactic poetry. Addison, Tickell, Joseph Trapp, and Joseph Warton all differ in their attempts to classify such verse into definite categories according to subject matter, agreeing only in accepting the Horatian canon of " delight and instruction " for poetry in general. Perhaps the most reasonable classification would be based on form rather than subject matter. Many poets of the period adopted the forms of Horatian or Juvenalian satire for ethical instruction. Many used the informal epistle or the Horatian " ode " for a similar purpose. The informality and " artful negligence " of the *Ars poetica* attracted many writers on the theory and practice of various arts. The epic of

Lucretius influenced a number of poets utterly unlike Lucretius in intention, supporters of religion (whether orthodox or unorthodox), who often strove for his manner and imitated his artistic form, poets like Blackmore, Henry Brooke, Moses Browne, Lofft, Sotheby, and others. The Ovidian didactic poems on love, with their tone of cool flippancy and wit, were unsuited to the general taste of the period and had few imitators excepting humorous adapters, though the *Heroides* had a different fate. The eclectic form of the *Georgics* of Vergil, drawn from Hesiod, Lucretius, and the Alexandrians, had many imitators. Lucretius came to be more fully appreciated in the nineteenth century. Earlier his philosophy was a heavy count against him, and the Renaissance critics had set an example in condemning his lack of finish in contrast with their idol, Vergil. Horatian style and forms were more easily imitated, and after Pope the century is full of minor Horatians. The Vergil of the *Georgics* was difficult to follow with success; but many poets made the attempt, and one, James Thomson, became perhaps the strongest single force in the century in extending the province of poetry and bringing it more closely into touch with nature and the life of the country.

Apart from moral ideas, there were two primary subjects in the *Georgics:* the occupations of country life and the phenomena of nature. In the eighteenth century there were two types of verse strongly influenced by the georgic genre: poems on country occupations and poems on typical, unlocalized appearances of nature. A third type of verse, the poem of local description, quite separate in origin, showed after 1750 important features drawn from the other two genres. These three broadly defined poetic types, with a few scattered poems showing georgic characteristics but unrelated in subject, form the material of the chapters to follow. It is to be understood, however, that the discussion is not limited to poems directly or indirectly derived from the *Georgics* of Vergil.

After Gay's *Shepherd's Week* and Ramsay's *Gentle Shepherd*, the pastoral eclogue contributed little to realistic treatment of country life. It continued its affectation of Arcadian unreality, its quasi-dramatic presentation of unnatural shepherds and other countrymen. A realistic treatment of the country turned rather to the tradition of the *Georgics*. In this treatment Philips, Gay, and Thomson led the way for many followers. Imitation of Vergil, especially of his didactic manner, led to grotesqueries of style which are easy to ridicule; but it would be uncritical to conclude that

poems which fall into such excesses of imitative zeal in a tongue
inhospitable to the Latin "magisterial manner" are therefore
poems to be ignored. It was in poets like Gay, Thomson, Smart,
Dodsley, Dyer, Ralph, Stevenson, Hurdis, and Cowper, that the
English country tradition expressed itself strongly and realistically
in the eighteenth century. Within the limits of forms usually influenced by the Georgics, English taste for the country and for nature, and English interest in the countryman, were expressed with
growing fullness and reality. The taste for landscape, encouraged
by many influences, grew constantly. Increased closeness of observation, minute faithfulness and precision — a very different thing
from appreciation of broad, general scenes — became a conscious
end, striven for by poets of the later eighteenth century, usually
through the discipline of natural history, an element present from
the first in poets who emulated the Vergil of the Georgics. The
poets of a georgic tradition were also those who first and most
clearly in the eighteenth century expressed the elements of the
philosophical attitude of the romanticists toward nature, an attitude already clearly announced in the ideas of Thomson, Mallet,
Akenside, Cowper, Thomas Gisborne, and others. In spite of obvious faults, these poets were leaders in assimilating knowledge of
nature and a philosophy of nature into poetry. Wordsworth and
Shelley combine descriptive skill with philosophical range, but
before this comprehensiveness was possible many poets had worked
toward similar ends. During the century the scope of English
poetry was broadened by a new knowledge of nature, a new re-
ceptivity to science, a wider interest in the country and the countryman, a new philosophical relationship to nature as a whole. Humanitarian sentiment, a new ethics independent of supernatural
revelation, middle-class economic and social interests, concern with
foreign lands and other peoples, were further extensions of the
province of poetry during the century. All these elements appear
in poets cited in the following chapters. No single poet, except perhaps Thomson, who is an extraordinary summation of the tendencies of his time, reflects all these changes; but the humblest and
most derivative of them may express something important in the
life of his period.

    This seems a fitting place to speak of the method of the following
chapters. I have chosen a chronological order in the main and have
discussed individual poems at least briefly, in the hope that the
book could thus be more generally useful, many of the poems be-

ing difficult of access. Such a method seemed adapted also to review of new tendencies developing within the forms discussed.

It is a pleasure to acknowledge many debts of gratitude incurred in writing this book. I have availed myself of results of the researches of Miss M. C. Lilly in *The Georgic*, a work treating some of the material I have used, but different in scope and purpose. I have built in some cases on her foundations. Otto Zippel's critical edition of *Thomson's Seasons* has been indispensable, and R. D. Havens's *Influence of Milton in English Poetry* has been important bibliographically. To the Trustees of Columbia University I am indebted for the grant of a Cutting Fellowship which enabled me to pursue research in England and France. To many librarians at the British Museum, the Bodleian, the Guildhall Library, the Bibliothèque Nationale, the New York Public Library, and the libraries of Columbia, Harvard, and Yale Universities, I owe much for helpful coöperation. The suggestions of Professors Jefferson B. Fletcher, Charles S. Baldwin, Frank A. Patterson, Adriaan J. Barnouw, and Emery E. Neff, and of Doctor Henry W. Wells, of the Department of English and Comparative Literature in Columbia University, have been a source of inspiration and valuable aid. Professor Hoxie N. Fairchild has given me suggestions of the highest value. To the memory of Professor Ashley H. Thorndike, whose learning and generosity aided so many, I owe grateful reverence. To Professor Ernest H. Wright I owe most of all. This book has grown from a suggestion found originally in his seminar; its progress has been guided by his kind interest and ready scholarship. My debt to my wife for help and encouragement is greater than I know how to express. There is still another, for whom all thanks uttered here were too late, one who " is not by to know my task is done."

D. L. D.

COLUMBIA UNIVERSITY
IN THE CITY OF NEW YORK
August 1, 1935

GEORGIC TRADITION
IN ENGLISH POETRY

I

THE ARTS OF MEN'S HANDS AND THE WORKS
OF NATURE

Omne tulit punctum qui miscuit utile dulci,
lectorem delectando pariterque monendo.
Horace

A LARGE proportion of the poetry produced in all ages has been
" didactic," if we accept the broadest meaning of that term. Some
intention other than a purely esthetic one, a desire to impart
understanding, " truth," philosophical ideas, principles of thought
and conduct, has been present from the very earliest times. Even
if we limit the term further and apply it only to poetry concerned
with laws of technique and with knowledge of nature, the field is
still vast. The names of Hesiod, Empedocles, Parmenides, Lucretius, Vergil, Horace, Ovid, Gratius, Manilius, are the most
familiar in the centuries before Christ. Alexandrian scholarship
produced poets like Aratus, Nicander, and Eratosthenes, more
notable for learning than for genius. In the first Christian centuries Columella wrote on gardening, Oppian of Cilicia, Oppian
of Apamea, and Nemesianus on various sports, and Palladius on
the cultivation of trees. During the Middle Ages the type did not
disappear; it divorced itself from classical models, on the whole,
and developed along independent lines. During the Renaissance
its classical forms reappeared among neo-Latin poets of the humanistic school and were later practiced in the modern languages of
Europe, especially in Italian, French, and English.

The medieval forms of didactic verse had little influence on the
classical revival of such types. Some of them persisted in England,
however, even into the seventeenth century, just as the classical
models continued in force even after the full tide of the romantic
reaction. It will be sufficient to glance very superficially at certain
classes of such medieval verse. Thomas Wright's *Popular Treatises
on Science, Written during the Middle Ages, in Anglo-Saxon,
Anglo-Norman, and English* [1] includes both verse and prose, notably *Li Livre des creatures* by Philippe de Thaun and fragments
on " popular science " from the early English metrical lives of
saints. John Myre's *Instructions for Parish Priests* in verse, dated
in the twelfth century, was edited by Peacock in 1868.[2] There had

been verse on hunting, hawking, and fishing, favorite sports of the nobility, in France in the thirteenth and fourteenth centuries; but the *Vénerie* of Dame Juliana Berners, part of the *Boke of St. Albans* of 1486,[3] seems to have been the earliest of its kind in England. The Italian Bonafede's *Il Tesoro dei rustici,* an un-Vergilian georgic, is of the fourteenth century; and the anonymous translation, *Palladius on Husbandry,*[4] into Chaucerian rime royal about 1420, also un-Vergilian, seems to be the first occurrence of the georgic in English. John Gardener's *Feate of Gardening*[5] is also of the fifteenth century. Medieval allegory sometimes turned to versification of technical knowledge, as in *The Pastyme of Pleasure* of Stephen Hawes, where Grand Amoure is tutored by seven ladies (the seven arts of the Trivium and Quadrivium) in the Tour of Doctrine. Medieval education employed verse as a means of facilitating learning. One of the most interesting phases of such use is found in the versified treatises on manners which formed part of the schooling of youth in the fifteenth and sixteenth centuries.[6] John Russell's *Boke of Nurture* (*c.* 1460), the *Boke of Kervynge* of Wynkyn de Worde (*c.* 1513), and Hugh Rhodes's *Boke of Nurture* (*c.* 1577), all edited by Furnivall for the Early English Text Society,[7] are examples. There were also Francis Seager's *School of Virtue* (1557), Richard West's continuation of Seager (1619), and others.[8] Alexander Barclay translated from the Latin of Dominike Mancin his *Mirrour of Good Maners* (1570),[9] and the *Ship of Fools* (1509) uses preceptive verse — on the training of children, for example.

Precepts on health were often put into verse. The *Regimen sanitatis Salernitanum,* in rhymed Latin verse, originally addressed to Robert of Normandy, son of William the Conqueror, was often translated.[10] Imitations are said to have been produced by the Universities of Paris and Montpellier. Croke[11] lists eight translations of the poem in England between 1477 and 1617, besides many versions in German, French, Italian, Dutch, Bohemian, and Polish. The verses often attributed to Lydgate as "the diatory made by the monk of Bury" were printed by Caxton in the *Governayle of Helthe* (*c.* 1491).[12] Edmund Gayton's *Art of Longevity* (1659),[13] a late poem of a numerous class, has humor as well as precept; and William Austin's *Anatomy of the Pestilence* (1666)[14] is a picture of the plague of 1665 and of the methods used to combat it.

Thomas Tusser's *Hundreth Pointes of Good Husbandry*

(1557), later expanded to *Five Hundred Pointes,* is a georgic evidently without classical influence, a poem long popular and useful. Tusser was an Elizabethan Hesiod in his common sense and practical purpose. In France, Claude Gauchet's *Plaisir des champs* (1583) presented field sports in a manner appealing to the nobles who practiced them. But already in Italy and France the neo-Latin poets of the humanistic revival had begun to follow the lead of Vergil's *Georgics:* Vida, Fracastoro, Conti, Cardinal Adrian, Scandianese, Jacques-Auguste de Thou. Alamanni, Tansillo, Baldi, and others even wrote vernacular poems in Italy, on the model of the *Georgics,* in the sixteenth century.

But no poet writing in English, except Thomas Moufat, who had been in Italy and had caught Italian influence, wrote on the Vergilian model in the sixteenth century. George Ripley's long-famous *Compound of Alchymy* was printed by Ralph Rabbards in 1591 [15] with "additions of other notable writers." Even Elias Ashmole, of the next century, exemplified the credulity of the early English experimenters in science by collecting in his *Theatrum chemicum Britannicum* (1651) [16] a number of verse treatises on the "hermetic mysteries" by previous experimenters like Ripley, Norton, Raymund Lully, "Pearce the Black Monke," and others.

In the seventeenth century John Dennys' *Secrets of Angling* (1613) shows familiarity with the *Georgics,* and an anonymous author followed Dennys' example in *The Innocent Epicure* (1697). Thomas Barker's *Barker's Delight, or the Art of Angling* (1657) is a prose treatise interspersed with bits of very inferior verse, often didactic but showing no classical influence. Simon Ford's *Piscatio,* Cowley's *Liber plantarum,* and Richard Richardson's *Carmen de cultu hortorum* begin a neo-Latin georgic vein in England. On the Continent the neo-Latin versifiers included Rapin, Quillet, Giannettasio, Dufresnoy, and Savary. But in England the medieval independence of the classical models persisted in works like Baptist Goodall's *Tryall of Travell* (1630); [17] various poems of John Taylor, "the water poet," such as *Praise of Hemp Seed* (1620) and *Drinke and Welcome* (1637); [18] the sections of Phineas Fletcher's *Purple Island* (1633) which versify anatomy; and the *Minerva, or the Art of Weaving* by "R. C." (1677). [19] Philosophical verse like that of Henry More, Sir John Davies, or John Davies of Hereford is of another genre, though *Nosce teipsum* includes elements of the crude physics and physiology of the time; and *Orchestra,* with its ingenious elaboration of metaphors of the dance, reflects concepts of the changes of the elements and of the motions of the planets. Fulke Greville had already included details of physical science in his *Of Human Learning.*

The neo-Latin humanistic tradition of the Continent naturally attracted the attention of English scholars. Even before 1500 Poliziano's *Rusticus* and Pontano's *De hortis Hesperidum, Urania,* and *Meteora,* famous didactic poems, began the tradition continued in the next century by Vida, Fracastoro, and others. The writing of such Vergilian and Lucretian essays continued into the eighteenth century. "Fine Latinity" even produced its devoted followers while the new tendencies of romanticism were taking shape. Even the names of most of these poets are unfamiliar today. In the sixteenth century, poetry of scientific knowledge and practical arts was written in Latin by Vida, Fracastoro, Conti, Valeriano, Scandianese, de Thou, Cardinal Adrian, Sainte-Marthe, Buchanan, da Barga, and others. Their subjects included science, medicine, husbandry, and field sports. In the seventeenth century the same and other themes were put into verse by poets like Quillet, Rapin, Savary, Dufresnoy, Spon, Ducerceau, Giannettassio, Cowley, Richardson, and others. Through the eighteenth century the same subjects reappear, and science and practical arts are supplemented by the fine arts of painting, sculpture, music, and poetry. The tradition continues in poets now so obscure or so profoundly forgotten as Vanière, Brumoy, Polignac, Masselot, Lefebvre, Souciet, Roze, Trante, Stay, Nocetti, Boscovich, Geoffroy, Oudin, Tansillo — the list is long.[20] Oxford and Cambridge were not untouched by this taste for didactic Latinity. The *Musarum Anglicanarum analecta,* first published in 1692, its second volume edited by Joseph Addison, had successive enlarged editions and was continued and elaborated in the *Musae Anglicanae,* edited by Vincent Bourne, which first appeared in 1741. Addison himself contributed short Latin poems, among others, on the barometer and the puppet show. All the poems were short and in no way comparable in scope to those of Continental didactic poets in Latin. Simon Ford's *Piscatio* was included, Robert Grove wrote on the circulation of the blood, Thomas Bisse on the microscope, Henry Stephens on the air pump invented by Boyle, and other men of Oxford and Cambridge on such subjects as Newtonian gravitation and the action of the tides, the Copernican system, the principles of optics, Dr. Hales's vegetable statistics, the Newtonian spectrum, the structure of the human body, Woodward's fossil statistics, the aurora borealis. This interest in the new science, however, produced only Cowley's *Liber plantarum* to rival the scope of Continental poets. The universities of France encouraged "fine Latinity." Among the Jesuits, ability in the composition of Latin verses was the ultimate test of scholarship. Vanière was attached to the college at Toulouse with the title of *Ecrivain*. The humanistic aspiration toward a Latin style of purity and elegance persisted among Jesuit writers to a very late date. Ecclesiasts, medical men, and lawyers were others whose training fitted them for such exercises. Polignac, Habert, and Pinon were ecclesiasts; Spon, Charras, and Quillet were physicians; Dupleix and de Boissat were lawyers.

In England after 1650 there was sufficient interest in a number of these neo-Latin poets to warrant translations of them, side by side with the versions of earlier didactic poets like Lucretius, Vergil, Gratius, Manilius, and the two Oppians. Poems of Rapin, Fracastoro, Quillet, Sainte-Marthe, Vida, and Cowley were turned into English verse, and some of them by a succession of translators.

It is illuminating to turn back to the original impulses in Renaissance Italy which produced both the neo-Latin and vernacular didactic verse of Poliziano, Pontano, and their followers. Pontano, Vida, and Fracastoro are typical. Pontano's astronomical *Meteora* and *Urania* and his georgic, *De hortis Hesperidum,* antedate 1500. Vida's *De bombyce* (c. 1527) tries to invest the culture of the silkworm with poetry, in the manner of Vergil's *Georgic* iv on the bees. Fracastoro's *Syphilis sive morbus gallicus* (1530) is the poem of a man of science, emulator of Vergil and Lucretius. As a poet, he had the acclaim of Italy and the praise of critics like Scaliger. One cause for the revival of such verse was Renaissance Maronolatry, the worship of Vergil, which was the very basis of the critical systems of J. C. Scaliger and Vida, in whose opinion poets needed no other guide than the divine Vergil. Scaliger said, "Nothing was omitted by that celestial poet: nothing is to be added, unless by ignorant fools, nothing to be changed unless by ignorant rascals." [21] Poliziano, the brilliant humanist sought out by Linacre, Grocin, and Reuchlin, left in his *Manto* and *Rusticus* poems full of that ecstasy of praise characteristic of the Renaissance scholars.

But there was also an identification of the poet and the scholar, a confusion of poetry and erudition, which was, in part at least, an inheritance from the Middle Ages. Petrarch regarded poetry and rhetoric as the two chief ends of the new learning. One studied the ancients in order to become an orator or poet. Here at the very threshold is the confusion of the temper of the man of learning with that of the poet. In Italy at the Renaissance most men of learning aspired to poetry and even pedants wrote verses. It was an easy step to the idea that all knowledge is the province of poetry. Petrarch's identification of scholar and poet helped to prepare the way for Fracastoro, Pontano, and Vida, the man of medicine, the astronomer, the teacher of practical arts, in verse.

Theories of criticism also encouraged didactic poetry in Latin and the vernacular. To the Horatian principle that poetry exists for delight and instruction, only Castelvetro took exception, insisting that poetry had but one end, to delight. J. C. Scaliger, Minturno, Fracastoro, Patrizzi, and Tasso all held to a didactic theory of poetry.[22] Castelvetro laid claim to the authority of Aristotle, who thought the *actions* of men the proper object of poetic imitation and denied Empedocles the name of poet. Purely didactic teaching seemed to Castelvetro to be specifically excluded. Scaliger, however, admitted any subject susceptible of poetic ornament. Minturno made pleasure subservient to instruction as an end. Fracastoro and Tasso did likewise. The common ideal among theorists of the Renaissance was eclectic: poetry may deal with any subject so long as it be transmuted with beauties of invention and ornament. The poet is a teacher; the function of poetry is teaching mingled with delight. Poetry may take all knowledge for its province, and no kind of knowledge is without value to the poet. Fracastoro says that poetry may teach all arts and sciences. This association of erudition and poetry was far more acceptable to the age than the more rigid Aristotelianism of Castelvetro.

The predisposition of humanism to eclectic learning is only one reason for this strong assertion of didactic purpose. Another reason lies in that attempt at " a justification of imaginative literature " which Spingarn calls " the fundamental problem of Renaissance criticism." [23] Medieval and Platonic criticisms were to be met and overcome if the new learning was to be justified in its love of imaginative literature. Plato had found poetry wanting in both reality and morality. It is unreal since it is but an imitation, by a poet, of another imitation, in the world of phenomena, of some perfect archetype in the world of ideas. As for morality, Homer is sometimes blasphemous, sometimes impure. And poetry, too, stirs up the baser emotions which ought rather to be controlled. In the Middle Ages such charges were amplified: poetry is fiction and falsification; poetry is inseparable from irreligion and obscenity; instead of the beauty of quietism, poetry fosters spiritual unrest; the only poetry really worthy of respect teaches a religious system opposed to Christianity; poetry does not teach effectively the proper conduct of life; poetry is impractical and enervating, whereas other occupations call one to far more profitable pursuits. These were the contentions of some churchmen, repeated later by Gosson and Prynne in England, and by Bossuet and others in France.

The defenders of poetry in the Middle Ages took refuge, of course, in the allegorical interpretation of literature. The wanderings of Aeneas were an allegory of the travels of the soul. The Bible itself was an elaborate allegory. And Dante claimed a fourfold meaning for his *Divine Comedy:* literal, allegorical, moral or philosophical, and anagogical or mystical. Poetry was not judged by purely esthetic standards, but in the light of ethics and theology. But at the Renaissance, finding in Horace and Aristotle new materials, men set up a new defense, though in literary practice the use of didactic allegory continued. Horace afforded the following ideas: poetry aims at both pleasure and instruction; poetry has aided the progress of mankind as a powerful teacher, early poets having been prophets and wise men, the first teachers of all arts and sciences. To these contentions humanists added the universality and divine origin of poetry and the praises and honors accorded it in all times by the greatest men. In Aristotle these ideas were found: as against the Platonic accusation of unreality, the contention that poetry rises to a still higher reality, a presentation of ultimate essences borne in the poetic imagination, a representation *sub specie aeternitatis* of ideal truth, not of bare phenomena; as against the Platonic objection of immorality, the contention that an idealization of the actions of men is of moral value; as against the idea that poetry does not foster quietism but encourages spiritual unrest, the contention that poetry, particularly dramatic poetry, does excite the emotions, but in such excitation purifies and exalts them. There was also, of course, the appeal, equally important, from the Plato of the *Republic* to the Plato of the *Ion* and the *Phaedrus,* with his doctrine of "inspiration," for whom the poet was an instrument of "reminiscence" revealing Ideas hidden under the outward shows of sense.

These theories are the basis of the Renaissance defense of poetry of the new learning. As to the common confusion of poetry and erudition and the favor in which didactic verse was held, these are derived from the Horatian ideas. Horace's emphasis on instruction as an end and his contention that, from the first, poetry has been the means by which wisdom, knowledge, science, and practical arts have been taught mankind — these were seized upon as cardinal points in the defense of poetry, and their repetition tended to a unanimity of opinion as to the function and province of poetry, from which Castelvetro is the only important dissenter.

Not less important for neo-Latin verse was the attempt among scholars of Italy to take up again the thread of culture at the point where poets of the Silver Age of Latin literature had dropped it. They were trying to be, themselves, in so far as they might, like ancient Romans. They wanted to link the Silver Age with their own time, to unite the threads of Latin tradition, to revive the elements of the culture of antiquity. Vergil was the god of their idolatry, and the forms of didactic poetry suited their love of erudition and their taste for imitation of the ancients. The cultivation of fine Latinity in verse, the esteem of style even over subject matter, which account for so much of the prestige of the *Georgics* in that time, has much in common with "Ciceronianism" in prose. In poets like Vida, Fracastoro, and Pontano didactic poetry was not merely an inculcation of teaching, but an attempt to clothe useful subjects in a beauty which could give them vitality; it was also an exercise in painstaking devotion to expression, in the perfecting of style and form. The cult of style, of meticulous craftsmanship, appealed to writers with more erudition than genius and more feeling for form and style than urgency to expression of ideas. Such poets found in didactic verse a means of presenting their erudition in the guise of poetry, and of devoting themselves to finish of execution. The *Georgics* of Vergil, the most striking instance in Latin literature of triumph of style, of consummate craftsmanship, over difficult subject matter, naturally attracted poets like Vida, Fracastoro, and Pontano, who also sought for flawless artistry. These poets represent at once the spirit of Renaissance Maronolatry, the cult of fine Latinity, the effort at a revival of antiquity, the humanistic confusion of learning and genius, the conception of a didactic function for poetry, and that of its close relationship to all phases of human knowledge.

The prose dialogue of Fracastoro, *Naugerius* (1555),[24] expresses all these elements, formulated in critical theory. Fracastoro is a good example of the Renaissance scholar-poet. A physician, he wrote on medicine, astronomy, natural history, philosophy, and critical theory. Poetry was his avocation; as a man of learning he was also a composer of verses. He says, " The poet as a poet is inspired by no other aim than simply to express himself well about anything that proposes itself to him." But he does not forget that poetry should teach. In defending poets as indeed the greatest of teachers, he begins with the admission that they cannot instill useful *fact* so effectively as historians, philosophers, and other teachers in prose. Nevertheless, he represents his friend Navagero as saying:

Because the poet seeks the noblest and most beautiful elements in each subject, it follows that poetry will display more of those qualities which pertain to wisdom and the other virtues. For the same reason, if the poet imitates the things which belong to the intellect, he will teach more because he omits no beauty which can be attributed to things, while all the others, [*i.e.,* other kinds of teachers] are limited, inasmuch as they seek not all but only some of the beauties. Of which the proof is this: those who wrote the Fall of Troy in unadorned, restrained language compressed a whole history into a small volume; but Homer produced an Iliad. Varro and Cato explained the rules of agriculture in a very few books; but Virgil accomplished the Georgics. Therefore I say that poets teach many more things than anyone else.[25]

They teach more than others, that is, because they show in every subject its beauties and perfections, drawing it not as bare fact but clothed in all the beauties which give it vitality, as Vergil drew the life of the husbandman, connecting it with the highest beauties of nature and of the mind.

Didactic poetry is not in Fracastoro's conception a mere preceptation; it is the clothing of a useful subject in all the colors which give it beauty and life. Against the charge that these added beauties are extrinsic, he represents Navagero as replying:

What perfection and beauty are, only the great artists know. And if you take them away from the subject, assuredly you have somehow taken away life itself. Therefore what the painters and the poets add to things for perfection is not extraneous, if we mean by " thing " not the bare object such as common artificers, or those who are controlled and restricted by some purpose make, but the object perfected and given life. . . . Then, if what is added makes manifest the perfection and excellence of the subject, ought we not to concede for all its great usefulness and desirability? So, to return to our subject, what we first promised to show can be demonstrated, that the poet teaches more than any other writer.[26]

A little later he adds,

Then since the poet writes on every subject and, in the second place is concerned, not so much with the mere object itself, but with all the beauties belonging to it, and teaches them, — teaches in a style so wonderful, so divine, who indeed would not venerate him and look on him as a sort of god? If men wish to know about agriculture, natural science, philosophy, and any other subjects that the poet has written about, they will go to the poet, not those who wish to know the bare and in a way rude facts, but those who desire to see objects, as it were, alive, perfected, and adorned with their appropriate beauties. So it is not . . . that the poet is called in for pleasure alone, as a sort of dessert; nor ought you to think Virgil a rather unnecessary author because he writes of the same subject on which Cato and Varro and others wrote earlier. Not for any such reasons should the poet desist, but he should write, lest the beauties of these same subjects, which are altogether neglected by the others, should lie forever in shadow.[27]

In England in the sixteenth century there arose the same necessity for a defense of poetry which had been felt earlier by the Italian critics. Gosson and Prynne were not isolated objectors but spokesmen of traditional ideas. The medieval and the Platonic objections were met again by Sidney, Puttenham, Harington, Lodge, and Webbe. The defenders of poetry in England took much the same ground as those in Italy. The Horatian lines of argument led to an emphasis on didactic function and a conception of the province of poetry as including all knowledge. The Aristotelian doctrine of imitation of universals might seem to suggest lines of defense independent of these Horatian props, but the Renaissance felt the need of them and employed them without being much troubled by their conflict with the Aristotelian exclusion of didactic poetry.

Puttenham employs the Horatian ideas, and in his *Arte of English Poesie* (Chapter XXI) treats " the forme wherein honest and profitable artes and sciences were treated." [28] These arts and sciences were taught in poems of great value to the countries which produced them: " Such were the philosophicall works of Lucretius Carus among the Romaines, the astronomicall of Aratus and Manilius, one Greeke, th' other Latine, the medicinall of Nicander, and that of Oppianus of hunting and fishes, and many moe that were too long to recite in this place." [29]

Lodge [30] uses similar argument against " shameless Gosson " and shows how the apostle Paul " voutsafeth to overlooke Epimenides;

let the apostle preach at Athens, he disdaineth not of Aratus authoritie."

Sidney [31] follows lines of defense like those of the Italian apologists and, citing such didactic poets as Lucretius, Vergil, Manilius, and Pontano, adds " which, who mislike, the faulte is in their judgments quite out of taste, and not in the sweet foode of sweetly uttered knowledge."

But English poets of the sixteenth century did not follow classical didactic models as poets did in Italy. Francis Meres, in *Palladis Tamia* (1598),[32] finds only Tusser to set over against Hesiod and Vergil.

In the next century Henry Peacham in *The Compleat Gentleman* (1622)[33] is still urging the stock defense of poetry on the ground of its service as a teacher of philosophy, the arts of life, and useful knowledge. Henry Reynolds in *Mythomystes* (c. 1633)[34] attacks modern poets for their inferiority to the ancients as natural philosophers:

The last and greatest disparity, and wherein above all others the greatest defect and maime appeares in our modernes, and especially poets, in respect of the aunciers, is their generall ignorance . . . in all the mysteries and hidden properties of Nature, which as an unconcerning inquisition it appeares not in their writings they have at all troubled their heads with. Poets, I said especially, and indeed only, for we have many prose-men excellent naturall philosophers in these late times, and that observe strictly that closeness of their wise masters, the reverend aunciens: So as now a dayes our philosophers are all our poets, or what our poets should bee, and our poesies growne to bee little better than fardles of such small ware as those marchants the French call pedlars carry up and downe to sell, — whissles, painted rattles, and such like Bartholomew-babyes: for what other are our common uninstructing fabulous rimes than amusements for fooles and children.[35]

Thomas Hobbes is opposed to this attitude. Like Aristotle, he definitely excludes didactic poetry, though he is writing just before the beginnings in England of popular interest in such verse. In his *Answer to Davenant's Preface to Gondibert* (1650), he says:

Those that take for poesy whatever is writ in verse, will . . . reckon Empedocles and Lucretius (natural philosophers) for poets, and the moral precepts of Phocylides, Theognis, and the quatraines of Pybracht and the history of Lucan, and others of that kind amongst poems, bestowing on such writers for honor the name of poets rather than of historians or philosophers. But the subject of a poem is the manners of men, not natural causes, manners presented, not dictated; and manners feigned, as the name of poesy imports, not found in men.[36]

Hobbes even takes issue with Davenant on the inclusion of technical terms in poetry, " terms from any science, as well mechanicall as liberall," a theory which Davenant had taken over from the practice of the *Pléiade* in France and in particular from Ronsard.

But other tendencies were at work; didactic poetry of ancients and humanists was coming into favor, and when Sir William Temple published his essay *Of Poetry* in 1690,[37] the Aristotelian exclusion was again ignored and didactic poetry recognized as a traditional genre.

After 1650 English interest in the classical and neo-Latin didactic poets encouraged many translations and the beginnings of adaptation into original English verse. A complex set of circumstances tended to produce an attitude favorable to such poetry. When one sees how in this period Latin didactic poems of Rapin, Sainte-Marthe, and Quillet in France were translated while Ronsard, Du Bellay, and Marot were untranslated; how Fracastoro and Vida were given English dress while Sannazaro, Metastasio, and Dante were read only in the original; how Gratius, Manilius, and the Oppians had the same honor, not yet accorded Catullus, Tibullus, Lucan, Apollonius Rhodius, Pindar, and the Greek tragic poets — when one considers these facts, definite reasons must be sought for so marked an interest.

One important reason is found in the opinions and example of the foreign scholars and critics most respected in England in this period: the French Rapin, Boissard, de Thou, Boileau; [38] the Dutch Heinsius and Grotius; the adopted Englishmen Vossius and Casaubon; the two cosmopolitans the Scaligers. Criticism and scholarship were more closely associated than is usual today; these men were all continuators of humanistic traditions. They all looked with favor upon didactic poetry. Rapin, de Thou, Boileau, and J. C. Scaliger were themselves didactic poets in Latin or modern languages. The influence of Rapin as a critic in England was based primarily upon his Aristotelian commentary, translated by Thomas Rymer into English in 1674.[39] De Thou had been celebrated as the "most eloquent Latin historian of this age," in the phrase of Edmund Bolton (*Hypercritica*) , since the beginning of the century. Heinsius, particularly as a commentator upon Aristotle's *Poetics,* had been influential since the days of Ben Jonson.

The editions of Aratus by Grotius (1600) and of Manilius by J. J. Scaliger (1579) probably helped to stimulate interest in ancient astronomy. The edition of Manilius included a detailed treatise on this subject. The elder Scaliger had lost little of the prestige which made him the mentor of Sidney and the literary deity of Peacham, for whom he was " the prince of all learning and the judge of judgments, the divine Julius Caesar Scaliger."

How far the currency of these reputations and the favorable opinion of didacticism held by such men influenced Englishmen may be inferred from several publications of Sir Thomas Pope Blount. In 1690 he published his *Censura celebriorum authorum*,[40] a kind of encyclopedia of critical opinion on writers, both ancient and modern, in the classical languages. He included all the important didactic poets. In his catalogue the eulogies quoted on such poets are mainly those of the critics spoken of above.

In his *De re poetica* (1694),[41] which begins with a general discussion of the principles of poetry and concludes with " Characters and Censures " of the greatest poets both ancient and modern, Blount reproduced part of his former selection, translating and summarizing into English. The new work, too, included writers in English. Some of the summaries of Blount may be cited as convenient indications of the esteem in which critics like the Scaligers, Boissard, Rapin, and de Thou held the didactic poets.

Of Buchanan, Joseph Scaliger in *Scaligeriana* had said that " for Latin Verse, [he] excels all the poets in Europe." [42] De Thou (*Ad annum 1582*) " tells us that Buchanan had not his fellow in the age he liv'd, either in respect of his natural wit, or of the excellent talent he had in writing." [43]

Of Fracastoro:

Boissardus in his Icones Virorum Illustrium, stiles Fracastorius a person of the greatest learning; as being a physician, a poet, an astronomer, and the most learned philosopher of that age: In which several sciences, according to Boissardus, he got so great a reputation that he very well deserv'd to be counted equal to any of the ancients. He further saith, that Fracastorius's poems are so much esteem'd of among all the men of learning, that they are compar'd even with Virgil's; and that in respect of elegance, smartness of expression, and purity of style, they are so highly extoll'd that by many Fracastorius is call'd, The Divine Poet.[44]

Blount retails again, after de Thou, how Sannazaro, reading Fracastoro's medical poem, cried out that both he himself and

Pontano were now overthrown. The enthusiastic Julius Scaliger in his *De poetica* has called Fracastoro "the very best poet next Virgil" and has written to him the panegyrical poem *Arae Fracastoriae*.[45] These immoderate praises are of course characteristic of the flattery the humanists were wont to heap upon one another, but there was weight of authority then in such names as Scaliger and Fracastoro.

Oppian (for the Oppianic poems were then thought to be by one author) is one of the most highly praised didactic poets. For him Julius Scaliger had "a most particular esteem," and he honored him with another of his comparisons to Vergil:

he seems to have the very air of Virgil, whom he endeavoured particularly to imitate. . . . I have always thought he gave us the true lively image of that Divine Poet.[46]

Ritterhusius, who edited Oppian, and Isaac Casaubon are almost equally laudatory, the former believing that Oppian's poems "came behind none of the Greek poets; nay, that they were to be preferr'd before the greatest part of them." [47] Upon Oppian the opinion of one Englishman, Sir Thomas Browne in his *Vulgar Errors,* is given. Browne says that he "may be read with great delight and profit," adding, "It is not without some wonder his elegant lines are so neglected; for surely hereby we reject one of the best epick poets." [48] Vida's praises are repeated by Boissard, Rapin, and Julius Scaliger. Hesiod, Lucretius, Aratus, Rapin, and other didactic poets are commented on by the same group of authorities.

The new science also played a part in the growth of this interest in didactic verse, not only because it revived attention to the "sciences" and practical arts of antiquity, but because it stimulated general interest in improvement of modern knowledge in those fields. It is no coincidence that Cowley and Evelyn, among the first to give impetus to didactic poetry, were members of the Royal Society. Evelyn was the earliest translator to publish a version of any considerable part of Lucretius. His friend Christopher Wase translated Gratius. His son, the younger John Evelyn, first translated Rapin's *Horti.* Cowley's *Liber plantarum* was the outgrowth of his botanical studies.

Perhaps the sojourns of men like Evelyn, Wase, and Cowley in France or Italy during the Protectorate stimulated their interest both in science and in didactic verse. Evelyn was in France and

Italy from 1643 to 1647, and in France from 1649 to 1652. He studied surgery at Padua and chemistry at Paris. He met Wase in Paris and brought him back to England. Cowley was in France from 1646 to 1656 and wrote his *Liber plantarum* during his retirement in Kent after 1657.

Cowley and Evelyn had their part too, with Glanvill, Hartlib, and Milton, in the new educational ideas growing out of the new science. Comenius' desire, voiced in England by Hartlib, to teach "things not words," found many echoes in English minds. Milton advocated in his *Tractate of Education* and practiced in his tutoring of his nephews John and Edward Phillips, a combining of classical languages and of practical and scientific knowledge, knowledge of things, through the reading of didactic writers both in verse and prose: Cato, Varro, Aratus, Nicander, Hesiod, Manilius, Lucretius, Vergil.[49] Cowley's *Proposition for the Advancement of Experimental Philosophy* (1661) [50] suggested a "Philosophical College" in which languages and practical instruction should be combined in a similar way. He proposed for study the poets Vergil, Gratius, Nemesianus, Manilius, Nicander, Oppian, besides such writers in prose as Cato, Varro, Pliny, Aristotle, and Theophrastus. Similarly, Evelyn had a plan for a "Philosophic-Mathematic College." [51] The teachers in Cowley's college were to be devoted to four ends: "to examine, weigh, and prove all things of Nature delivered to us by former ages; to recover the lost inventions and . . . drown'd lands of the ancients; to improve all arts which we now have; and to discover others which we yet have not." [52]

In this interest in the natural philosophy and the practical arts of the ancients, an interest apparent in the activities of the Royal Society in its early years, we touch an important element in the revived interest in didactic poetry. Then too, the controversies of "the ancients and the moderns" turned not only to questions of superiority in literature but to respective merits in natural philosophy and even in practical arts. Evelyn, for example, writes to Wotton at length, comparing the husbandry and gardening of ancients and moderns.[53] And there were few indeed whose eagerness for knowledge was embarrassed by too critical a spirit at first. Browne in his *Vulgar Errors* can see few instances of faulty natural history in Oppian or Nicander; and the astrology which is found in Manilius was no bar to his acceptance in days when "virtuosi" still gave it credence.

After the establishment by King's charter of the Royal Society in 1662, it became fashionable among men of position at least to affect an interest in science and experiments. King Charles had conferred the prestige of royal favor and royal example; Pepys recounts that the king had had a laboratory equipped at Whitehall for his own use.[54] A year after the final organization of the society it included a hundred and thirty-one Fellows.[55] Two years later began the regular publication of the *Philosophical Transactions*. Though it included men like Boyle, Newton, Ray, and Willoughby, the Royal Society was not an organization of specialists. It was composed principally of amateurs, noblemen, and men of independent fortune, with some physicians and clergymen. The variety of the subjects of their inquiries is amazing. They were not immersed altogether in pure science; their object was improvement of practical arts and mechanical processes as well as inquiry into natural law. But even this will not define the limits of their interest. The *Transactions* discuss such varied matters as a universal language, the power of imagination, grafting of trees, teaching Latin, methods of catching carp, the education of youth, the possibility of resurrection, raising tobacco, and the philosophy of music.

Such a typical virtuoso as Evelyn appears revealingly in his diary, and especially in his letters.[56] His interests are unbounded; we find him writing on education, with proposals for more correct editions of the classics or for the founding of his Philosophical and Mathematical College; on rural economy, with discussion of transparent apiaries, Spanish horticulture, the husbandry and gardening of ancients and moderns, the cultivation of hops; on physics and natural history, earthquakes and their causes, the eclipse of 1652, the anatomy and " vegetative motion " of trees, subterranean rivers, optics and acoustics, and perpetual motion; mechanical processes and inventions, a new-found method of embalming, glass manufacture, Mercator's mathematical instruments, brick-making, manufacture of sulphur, and drugs used in manufacturing treacle; even on such a theme as otter hunting.

As time passed, the activities of men of the virtuoso type attracted more and more attention. Many things combined to catch the public interest: the favor of the king, the disputes upon ancient and modern learning, the efforts of the society itself at publicity, at spreading knowledge and appreciation of its work. Sprat's history of the society is itself such an effort.[57] The sale of the *Transactions* at bookstalls, the influence of students from Oxford and Cambridge (particularly from Cambridge, where Isaac Barrow, Newton, Whiston, and Cotes vastly stimulated the study of exact sciences), popular lectures by men like Desaguliers, and books like Evelyn's *Silva,* Newton's *Principles,* and Hooke's *Micrographia,* helped to arouse interest.

It was Sprat, the historian of the society, who in 1667 recommended the new knowledge of natural philosophy and practical arts as a means to revitalize poetry.

The wit that is founded on the arts of mens hands is masculine and durable: It consists of images that are generally observ'd, and such visible things which are familiar to mens minds. This therefore I will reckon as the first sort [of " wit " in writing], which is still improvable by the advancement of experiments. And to this I will add the works of nature, which are one of the best and most fruitful soils for the growth of wit. It is apparent that the defect of the antients in natural knowledge did also streiten their fancies: Those few things which they knew, they us'd so much, and appli'd so often, that they even almost wore them away by their using. The sweetness of flowers, and fruits, and herbs they had quite devour'd: They had tir'd out the sun, and moon, and stars with their similitudes, more than they fancy them to be wearied by their daily journeys round the hevens. It is now therefore seasonable for natural knowledge to come forth, and to give us the understanding of new virtues and qualities of things: which may relieve their fellow-creatures, that have long born the burden alone, and have long bin vex'd by the imaginations of poets. This charitable assistance experiments will soon bestow.[58]

One notes here that linking of " the arts of men's hands " and " the works of nature " which represents at once the preoccupations of the new science, the avowed field of labor of the Royal Society, and the traditional subject matter of didactic verse.

The special interest in didactic poetry, indicated by the many translations which began to appear after 1650, was at first due, it would appear, to such influences as these: the prestige of the neo-Latin poetry; the high praise given didactic verse by such critics as Rapin, de Thou, and the Scaligers; interest in the sciences and practical arts of antiquity; new educational theories and practice; and a general interest, stimulated by the Royal Society and the universities, in the improvement of modern knowledge of " the arts of men's hands " and " the works of nature."

When English poets began to write original didactic verse on the classical model, they turned not to the neo-Latin poets nor to the Augustan and post-Augustan imitators, but to Vergil himself. Philips and Gay wrote English georgics. Swift, William King, and Gay wrote humorous adaptations of the georgic form.

Dryden had said that " to copy the best author is a kind of praise, if I perform it as I ought; as a copy of Raffaelle is more to be commended than an original of any indifferent painter." [59] The term " imitation," taken over into criticism from Aristotle, often meant, in the first decades of the eighteenth century, simply the copying of literary models. Bysshe, Constable, Felton, Gildon, Steele, Pope, and others used the term in this restricted sense.[60] In the later seventeenth century, even close adaptations of classical and French texts to English settings and subject matter became valid poetic exercises. Horace and Ovid were favorite models for this kind of ingenious versifying. Oldham's Anglicization of Horace's *Ars poetica,* and Soames's and Dryden's adaptation of Boileau's *Art poétique,* which supplied names of English writers for the French, are early examples. Sheffield's *Essay upon Poetry,* with much more freedom, is yet an adaptation of Horace and Boileau. Etherege and Buckingham have been credited [61] with the first essays in this type of verse, adaptations of satires of Boileau. But Sir Aston Cokain in *Small Poems of Divers Sorts* (1658), earlier than either Etherege or Buckingham, adapts Ovid's *Remedia amoris* to English setting and conditions. This practice of adaptation led the way for certain forms which flourished throughout the eighteenth century: satirical burlesque adaptations, especially of Horace or Ovid, like William King's *Art of Cookery* or James Miller's *Harlequin-Horace;* serious amplifications of Horatian, Ovidian, or Boileauesque precepts, like those of Roscommon, Buckingham, Samuel Wesley, Uvedale, Pope, and Brown; serious adaptations of principles of Horace and Boileau to other arts, as in Harte's *Essay on Painting,* Bramston's *Art of Politicks,* Dodsley's *Art of Preaching,* or Moore's *Art of Preaching;* [62] and adaptations to English setting of the texts of poems of still other types, as in Pope's *Imitations of Horace,* or Johnson's copying of Juvenal in *London* and *The Vanity of Human Wishes.*

There were English Horaces and Ovids, English arts of poetry and arts of love; why not English georgics? As Pope's *Essay on Criticism* represents the Horatian didactic tradition, John Philips' *Cyder* represents the Vergilian. As King and Miller exemplify satirical or burlesque adaptation of Horatian didacticism, Swift's *Description of a City Shower* and Gay's *Trivia* exemplify such adaptation of the *Georgics*.

The followers of Vergil in serious didactic verse were guided also by the English form of Maronolatry. The supremacy of Homer or Vergil was still a disputed point. For men like Evelyn and Cowley, Vergil was " the best of poets," and for men like Dryden and Addison the *Georgics* were " that best poem of the best poet " and " the most complete, elaborate, and finish'd piece of all antiquity." Dryden ranks the *Georgics* above the *Aeneid*. Characteristic of him is his high praise in the dedication to *Annus Mirabilis*, where he is speaking of Vergil's skill in presenting images: " See . . . in his Georgics, which I esteem the divinest part of all his writings, the plague, the country, the battle of bulls, the labour of the bees, and those many other excellent images of nature, most of which are neither great in themselves, nor have any natural ornament to bear them up; but the words wherewith he describes these are so excellent, that it might well be applied to him what was said of Ovid — *Materiam superbat opus*." [63] Dryden's translation of Vergil (1697), with all its faults a masterpiece, stimulated interest and imitation. Addison's essay on the *Georgics*, first published anonymously with Dryden's translation in 1697, evidently had a strong influence also. It was the first statement in English of the principles of Vergilian didactic poetry.

Addison begins by distinguishing between pastoral and georgic verse and between his three kinds of didactic poetry — those concerning " moral duties," " philosophical speculations," and " rules of practice." The georgic, " having the most delightful part of Nature for its province," is superior in possibilities to any other type. The poet must choose those precepts at once most useful and most capable of adornment; his method must be natural and unforced, with easy transitions from theme to theme; he should conceal precept in description; he should make skilled use of " moral reflection " and " pertinent digressions "; he should fall into no familiar diction or " low phrases " but maintain " all the pomp of numbers and dignity of words." As for the episodes of Vergil, those praised by Addison are among those later most imitated: the pleasures of country life, the force of love, the Scythian winter, the murrain among the cattle, the praise of Italy, and the signs of changing weather.

Joseph Trapp, first professor of poetry at Oxford, published his lectures in three volumes, *Praelectiones poeticae* (1711, 1715, 1719) at Oxford. He discusses the theory of poetry in general and the laws of the various genres. He is Horatian in his theory of the function of verse, defining poetry in these words, " *Ars quicquid est, vel mente comprehendi potest, metricis numeris imitans vel illustrans; voluptatis hominum, atque utilitatis gratia.*" [64] The Aristotelian canon, imitation of the *actions* of men, as applied by Vossius in his *De arte poetica,* is denied. The inaugural lecture includes a defense of poetry, on traditional grounds, against charges of impiety, untruthfulness, obscenity, and inferiority to other sources of knowledge. For Trapp, Vergil is the greatest of all poets. In his lecture *De poemate didactico* he is indebted to Addison's essay on the *Georgics.* He defines four kinds of such verse, relating " *ad mores; ad philosophiam naturalem; ad vitae humanae negotia, & oblectamenta; ad ipsam denique poesin, sive artem poeticam.*" [65] Moral duties have been presented by Pythagoras, Theognis, and Phocylides; facts of science by Aratus, Manilius, Lucretius, and episodically by Vergil. Among moderns he mentions only Buchanan and the few short Oxford and Cambridge poems of the *Musarum Anglicanarum analecta.* He believes " experiments " might have furthered this type of verse *" si eadem aetas qui Boylaeum tulit & Newtonum, tulisset etiam Virgilium: & nisi antiquis quanto praestantiores sumus philosophi, tanto deteriores essemus poetae.*" [66] As poets of the business and pleasures of life, he cites Vergil above all, Hesiod, Gratius, Ovid, Oppian, Rapin, and Philips. This kind of verse he believes capable of the highest poetry. He lays down the following principles: the selection of such circumstances as are capable of poetic adornment, the presentation of rules of practice by description and narration as well as by precept, and the use of digressions into noble subjects (history or antiquity, reflection on conditions of human life, natural history, fable and fiction, poetic descriptions). The practice of Vergil is always the highest authority he can cite. The greatest of poets achieved in his *Georgics* his greatest work: " *Ad summam, operum omnium Virgilii perfectissimum poema hoc merito existamatur; quinetiam pro omnium quae hodie extant, & quae unquam forsan extitere, exquisitissimo, elegantissimoque, jure habendum est.*" [67] Horace and Boileau represent his fourth class of didactic poetry. Ovid, Quillet, and Fracastoro are censured for the subjects they employed.

In 1711 Thomas Tickell also delivered a lecture at Oxford on didactic verse, *De poesi didactica,* in which he ranked the genre as "second to epic alone." This lecture seems never to have been printed except in an English translation.[68] Like Trapp, Tickell acknowledged the priority of Addison's essay on the *Georgics.* He made a new classification of didactic verse into poems which treat "of morals, of philosophy, of arts, and a fourth class compounded out of these." Poets like Theognis and Pythagoras, Lucretius and Manilius, Horace, Vida, and Boileau, are inferior to Vergil, the supreme example of his fourth class. The *Georgics* are again "the most perfect work of the greatest bard." Tickell exclaims,

What if, at long last, the poets of Britain should gird themselves up to the grandeur of this art! Then surely someone would sing worthily of every rustic craft throughout these woodlands of ours that are framed by Nature for them. To the bards of Britain are left, as themes almost untouched as yet, the science of seamanship, in which we surpass all other nations in the world, or the science of warfare, in which we are either the greatest defender of mankind, or its greatest destroyer.[69]

The translation of Vergil most read after Dryden's was that of Christopher Pitt and Joseph Warton (1753).[70] Warton translated the *Eclogues* and *Georgics* and supplied essays on epic, pastoral, and didactic poetry. His *Reflections on Didactic Poetry,* an elaborate essay, echoes the principles Addison outlined for georgic verse and gives a partial survey of the poems of this genre. The purpose of such verse is "to render instruction amiable, to soften the severity of science, and to give to virtue and knowledge a captivating and engaging air." He estimates critically Hesiod, Aratus, Oppian, Lucretius, Vergil, Manilius, Ovid, Polignac, Fracastoro, Rapin, Vanière, Philips, Somervile, Akenside, Armstrong, and the Italian georgic poets Alamanni and Ruccellai. He distinguishes the more formal didactic poem from those, like Horace's *Ars poetica,* of an epistolary cast, marked by "a graceful negligence" of style. Among the followers of Horace he praises Vida for his *Poetics,* Boileau, Pope, Buckingham, and Roscommon.

Addison, Tickell, Trapp, and Warton gave critical prestige to the georgic genre, and their example was followed by later critics like Hugh Blair, in his *Lectures on Rhetoric and Belles Lettres;* Goldsmith, in the Newbery *Art of Poetry on a New Plan* (attributed to him) ; John Aikin, in his editions of Somervile, Armstrong, and Dyer; Mrs. Barbauld, in her edition of Akenside; and Nathan Drake, in his *Literary Hours.*

The translations of classical and neo-Latin poets which mark the beginning of the English interest in didactic verse, may be briefly glanced at. Translations from the *Georgics* are numerous, of course, beginning with that of Fraunce or Flemyng in 1589. None before Dryden's had a very wide influence or very great literary value, whether translation of the whole or of parts. It is sufficient here to note the considerable number of such translations down to 1750 as evidence of general interest in the *Georgics*.[71]

Before direct imitation of Vergil's *Georgics* began, the interest in other didactic poets, ancient and modern, was considerable.

Mrs. Lucie Hutchinson apparently was the first to attempt a translation of Lucretius. She presented her manuscript to the Earl of Anglesea in 1675,[72] but her dedicatory preface indicates that the work was written much earlier. " I turned it into English," she says, " in a room where my children practised the several qualities they were taught with their tutors." The translation was probably made at some time in the 1640's or a little later. She was prompted by " youthful curiositie, to understand things I had heard so much discourse of," but in 1675, in more mature years, she abhors " all the atheismes and impieties " in the work. Lucretius has become " this lunaticke "; and to her " 'tis a lamentation and horror . . . that men should be found so presumptuously wicked, to studie and adhere to his and his masters . . . execrable doctrines, reviving the foppish casuall dance of attoms, and denying the soveraigne wisdom of God in the great design of the whole universe and every creature in it." The translation is in heroic couplets, a very rough version, but it seems to be the first attempt at a complete translation of Lucretius into English.

Christopher Wase's *Gratii Falisci Cynegeticon* (1654) is prefaced by commendatory verses by Waller. Gratius, contemporary with Vergil, tried to adorn the technique of the chase as Vergil adorned that of husbandry, with the charms of poetry, connecting his subject with all possible associations of beauty and worth. Wase tries to render the hexameters into an equivalent number of rhymed English pentameters, with crabbed results. The Vergilian elements — the account of the origin and growth of the craft, the eulogy of Rome, the description of the ideal hound (like that of Vergil's ideal dam) , the exotic accounts of hounds of various lands (parallel to Vergil's accounts of harvests of various lands) , the picture of plague, the personifications of the hounds under military metaphors (like Vergil's similar personifications of the bees) —

these are typical of the dominance of Vergil's themes among all who followed him in similar subjects.

John Evelyn's *Essay on the First Book of Lucretius* (1656) is also prefaced with commendatory verses by Waller. It is probable that Evelyn's main interest in Lucretius was an interest in the " science " of the ancients. As a virtuoso he was also interested in Gratius, Rapin, and Columella, and in Cowley's poem on plants.[73] He and his friend Jeremy Taylor had had correspondence upon the appropriateness of his undertaking for " a Christian gentleman," and Evelyn had assured Taylor of his intention to avoid imputations of impiety.[74] His intention was not the propagation of Epicurean philosophy. The translation is not a literary success, but Evelyn evidently later finished the remaining books. They were never published. In a letter to Casaubon in 1674, he speaks of his translation, " which still lies in the dust of my study, where 'tis like to be forever buried." [75] It seems clear that he refers to a completed version.

Alexander Brome, who died in 1666, is said to have intended a translation of *De rerum natura*,[76] but he never printed it, if, indeed, it was executed.

The translation of the *Horti* of the Jesuit Rapin by the younger John Evelyn, third son of the diarist, under the title *Of Gardens* (1673) included all four books of that famous neo-Latin poem. But the work is inferior to the later version of James Gardiner (1706).

Sir Edward Sherburne's *The Sphere of Marcus Manilius* (1675), a version of Book I only, is a product of interest in the learning of the ancients. Chalmers says it " was honoured by the very particular and liberal approbation of the Royal Society." [77] It was sumptuously printed in a folio volume dedicated to Charles II. Sherburne's appendix is " an essay of the original and progress of astronomy " and an outline " of the cosmical system." He wants to supplement Manilius and bring the subject of astronomy up to date, and he weighs the ancient as compared with the modern science in this field.

The translation of Lucretius by Thomas Creech, first printed in 1682, had a long popularity,[78] and was even thought comparable to Dryden's Vergil and Pope's Homer. Pope found the translation faulty because Creech imitated the style of Cowley. But Dryden had praised it, as Joseph Warton did later. Creech's contemporaries gave him ungrudging praise. After Creech there seems to have been but one complete translation before that of Good in 1805. His success led him to edit Lucretius in 1695 and to translate from other poets, Horace, Juvenal, Vergil, and Ovid. There was a constant interest in Lucretius, at least from the Restoration onward, in England, but he never rivaled Vergil as a literary model. Many poets who show Lucretian characteristics really seem to get them at second hand, through Vergil's use of *De rerum natura*.

In 1686 was first published the translation by Nahum Tate of that curious neo-Latin poem by Fracastoro, *Syphilis sive morbus gallicus*. There was behind the poet the tradition of plague description in poetry: Lucretius had described, after Thucydides, the plague at Athens; Vergil in the *Georgics,* emulating Lucretius, had described a murrain among the cattle; Manilius followed these predecessors. Fracastoro was a man of science, a physician, writing in the same genre of didactic poetry. Since its appearance in the previous century, the poem had been one of the most highly praised neo-Latin works.

Fracastoro imitated both Lucretius and Vergil. After the usual theme-statement, dedication, invocation, and protestations as to the difficulty of his subject, he launches into a discussion of the origin of the plague. The sun, the stars, the planets have their influence upon the earth; and he describes forcibly the deluges, droughts, winds, hurricanes, and earthquakes which through these influences devastate the earth, picturing the future unpeopled universe out of which some day new worlds, new seasons, perhaps a second breed of giants, shall arise. What is strange in this new plague? Then in terms of the medical ideas of his time, he describes the signs and symptoms of the disease and methods of cure, interrupting this discourse with episodes like that of a beautiful youth slain by the destroyer, or the address to Saturn, father of the Italian race, for mercy. Rome's empire is now gone, Italy is racked with civil war, her sons are made captives; yet a pride in Renaissance Italy recalls to him glories no former time has known, explorations, discoveries, new stars and new worlds sought out, heroes challenging the greatness of the ancients, a Bembus and a Leo. The poem concludes with a narrative episode, as do the *Georgics*. The work is a *tour de force,* an example of Renaissance confusion of erudition and poetry. Its use of many episodes is Vergilian rather than Lucretian; and in the praises of Italy, the exotic allusions, and the narratives, the author has Vergil in mind. Tate's translation, made

further accessible in Dryden's *Miscellany Poems*,[79] served to increase interest in didactic tradition.

Charles Cotton began a translation of George Buchanan's scientific poem *De sphaera*, publishing *An Essay upon Buchanan's First
Book* in his 1689 volume.[80] There is also an anonymous translation,
of this period, from Buchanan, in manuscript, now in the British
Museum.[81] But the famous Scottish scholar and poet seems not to
have aroused very wide interest.

That work of Cowley's retirement, *Liber plantarum*, was published in 1689 in an English translation by venerating admirers,
" J. O.," Cleve, Tate, and Aphra Behn.[82] Its six books are lacking
in unity. Book I, avowedly unmethodic, gives accounts of various
plants, their appearance, nature, uses, and seasons of flowering and
seeding, the whole combined with simile, mythological allusion,
moral parallel, and episode. The second book fantastically represents plants useful in generation or birth, assembled together at
midnight in the Physic-Garden at Oxford. The plants are speakers,
each defending her own beneficent qualities. There are many exercises of pedantic " wit." The third and fourth books frame their
scientific lore in a narrative wherein Flora calls together all plants,
not earthly ones but the plants of Plato's ideal world, upon the
banks of the Thames, to choose a queen. The Seasons come and
lead on their hosts; again respective claims are offered, and Flora
decides for a commonwealth where office for all is successive and
limited to season. There is an episode in praise of the life of retirement, with echoes of Vergil. In the fifth book Pomona holds a similar court of the trees of the American world and of England. The
sixth book is more nearly in the vein of certain parts of the *Georgics*
than anything preceding. " As Virgil [sings] of Rome and Augustus," says Tate, " so here Cowley of England and his monarch."
He uses Vergil's accounts of portents at the death of Caesar for a
similar account of prodigies at the death of Charles I, and includes
a patriotic panegyric paralleling Vergil's in its beginnings, but
leading to fulsome adulation of Charles II. Cowley's occasional
humor, his exuberance of fancy and fantastic " wit " are new elements in such verse; only rather late in his poem does he fall back
upon the common device of relief, extended episode.

Creech's second *magnum opus*, all five books of Manilius, *A
System of the Ancient Astronomy and Astrology* (1697), carries
on Sir Edward Sherburne's partial presentation of ancient learning in this field. A full explanatory apparatus was added. Only the

first book is strictly astronomical. The remaining books are astrological, showing how the stars rule over mankind and how men may read in them the edicts of fate. Manilius was a Stoic rather than an Epicurean, but he imitated Lucretius. Passages like the outline of the rise of the sciences and arts of war and peace, stimulated by want; that of the plague at Athens; the account of the various modes of matter falling into place according to their mass; the Lucretian polemical manner, as in the examinations of theories of Xenophanes, Aristotle, Epicurus, Heraclitus, Empedocles, and others — such passages contribute to the building up of traditional thematic materials.

The younger Evelyn's translation of Rapin's *Horti* was surpassed by James Gardiner's version in 1706.[33] Rapin wanted to supply that omission of the subject of gardening, of which Vergil speaks regretfully in *Georgic* ii. The system of gardening outlined is that of the geometrical French school of Le Nôtre and others, most familiar in Versailles and Fontainebleau. Rapin writes with the sedulous Maronolatry of neo-Latinism. The four books treat the flower garden, the management of trees, the uses of water (lakes, fountains, canals, and rivulets), and the care of orchards. These themes the poet decks out with cumulative similes, mythology, moral parallels, and episodes. Rapin lavishes upon everything the adornments of his classical learning; the combination of erudition and poetry sometimes has a stiff kind of grace comparable to that of the gardens of Le Nôtre. He elaborates Vergil's praises of toil and of rural joys, the exotic allusions, the patriotic eulogy (applied to France and to Paris), the picture of herds stung with desire, and other themes. There are episodes on the development of the art of gardening; on scientific hypotheses of the origin of rivers; on such estates as St. Cloud, Lyancourt, Fontainebleau; on the metamorphoses of flowers; on narrative themes like that of Alcinous, the gardener, who learns from a divine source the art of ripening fruit by reflected sunlight, as Vergil's Aristaeus learns the art of engendering bees. Elm trees remind Rapin of Vergil's Corycian swain bounding his garden with elms, and of Orpheus under an elm lamenting Eurydice. The ash suggests Achilles' ashen spear; the citron, Alcides and the golden apples of the Hesperides; the bay, Apollo and Daphne. A learned allusiveness suffuses everything. Even the precepts are modeled on Vergil's manner and sometimes on his themes.

In 1710 Nicholas Rowe published anonymously his translations of Quillet's *Callipaediae* (in which Sewell, Cobb, and Diaper assisted) and Sainte-Marthe's *Paedotrophiae*,[84] two curious French neo-Latin poems on subjects of genetic theory and the care of children. Both the Abbé Quillet and Sainte-Marthe, physician to Henry III of France, had wide reputations; both had later English translators. In the same year appeared a second anonymous version of Quillet's poem. Like Fracastoro, the two French poets try to achieve a union of poetry with the erudition of a physician. They present systems of knowledge (mingled with superstition) in relation to all their possible associations of beauty and worth. Quillet dedicates his poem to Cardinal Mazarin and acknowledges the *Georgics* as his model. Again we find the usual apparatus of precept, episode, learned allusion, simile, panegyric, moral reflection, and so on. Praise of France, pictures of the golden age, mythology, a synod of gods on influences of the stars in conception, exotic description of other lands, the theories of the atomists — these and many other episodic themes are woven with too obvious artifice about the didactic thread.

Sainte-Marthe had a European reputation. For Tytler, his translator of 1797, he was still " among the greatest [poets] who have appeared since the classical ages of antiquity." It was necessary for Tytler to modernize the medical knowledge and supply amplifications in prose, but as late as 1797 he still considered his poet a master in a genre of poetry second only to epic verse. Addressed to a king, the poem is written in the tone at once of a courtier and a physician. The theory of " *difficulté vaincue* " could hardly inspire a more ambitious effort than this treatise on rearing children, intended especially, it seems, to benefit a prospective royal heir. The learned allusions, the carefully weighed similes, the medical erudition, the account of man's fall dooming him to toil, hunger, and pain, the melancholy reflections on distracted France and the poet's private griefs, the compliments to the king and to the great Scaliger, the tale of Hercules and Paeony — such materials are fitted into their framework with, at least, more than the usual sense of balance and structure.

William Diaper and John Jones, Oxford men, provided an English Oppian in 1722.[85] Oppian of Cilicia had written his *Halieutica* in Greek in the second century after Christ. The translators were motivated by a desire to present the natural history and the craft technique of ancient times, " the nature of fishes and fishing of the ancients." All phases of ancient life and learning were important.

Scaliger had ranked Oppian above Homer, and he had been one of
the first didactic poets praised by English critics. The work is fascinating in content, though it employs a too-rigid alternation of
exposition and simile or short episode. The first book is on the
natural history of fish; the second concerns the predatory cycle, the
war of hunger between gradations of creatures; the third and fourth
describe methods of fishing with line, reel, net, and trident; and
the fifth is on deep-sea hunting of whales, sharks, and fiercer prey,
and the sponge-diver's adventures. Similes are drawn from nature,
myth, the sports of the arena, or the invention of other poets, as in
the case of the Vergilian picture of the heifer in autumn, maddened by the gadfly. Moral parallels abound; the sleeperfish is a
type of gluttony, the mild barbel of the brave, good man. The episodes are interesting: an address to Jove as the soul permeating all
matter, description of the world under the surface of the sea and of
the spring migrations of shoals to the warm Euxine (like the march
of cranes across the sky), matings and rivalries of creatures of the
sea, the power of Venus in the lower world, the gift of all arts and
sciences by deities, exotic pictures of fishermen of Gaul and Etru-
ria, and narratives like that of the kingly dolphin, once a man. The
translators give a not inadequate conception of Oppian's extraordinary poem, in spite of their stereotyped diction.

In 1723 Vida's georgic, *De bombyce,* was translated anonymously
as *Silkworms.* In 1726 John Rooke included a version of it in a
volume of translations from neo-Latin poets in various genres.[86]
Samuel Pullein's version appeared in 1750.[87] Marcus Vida had
been perhaps the neo-Latin poet of greatest reputation since the
sixteenth century. Pullein acclaims him as " of all moderns the
likest to Virgil, both in elegance and simplicity." *Georgic* iv
on the bees is the model; but after Vergil's persuasive sympathy,
Vida seems rigid and artificial. The sensitive humor, wonder, and
beauty of Vergil's poetic comprehension are not present, though
they are imitated. Like *Georgic* iv up to the story of Aristaeus,
De bombyce is partly entomology and partly craft-technique. The
first book begins with the hatching of the infinitesimal eggs and
carries the story up to the spinning of the golden, green, and amber
threads of the silk-balls. There are many interesting minute pictures. Episodes like the accounts of propitious and unpropitious
stages of the moon and of the development of the arts of dress,
the narratives of the divine gifts of flax-weaving and silk to man,
are less interesting than the entomology of the poem. The second

book concerns plagues among the insects, their transformation to butterflies, their mating season, and then their eggs once more, completing the cycle of generation and death. The processes of the loom are added. A tale, in mythological trappings, of the origin of silk-making among men, concludes the poem.

Tipping Silvester's *Original Poems and Translations* (1733) included translations from the *Musae Anglicanae* of Ford's *Piscatio* and Bisse's *Microscopium*. Neither is extensive, but Ford's humorous tale of the invention of the fisher's art by Apollo, and his Oppianic descriptions of the characteristics of various fish, are variations of didactic themes. *Microscopium* describes the wonders of minute insect and plant life and then turns to the telescope and describes the planets it reveals.

The *Cynegetica* of that second Oppian (of Apamea in Syria) evidently had no translator before John Mawer in 1736. Only the first book seems to have been published, though the "Argument" notes that the translator has completed the second. Mawer's *Oppian's Cynegeticks* is another essay in the life and learning of ancient times. Book I is a preliminary account of what is needful for the chase: the ideal hunter, implements and arms, the best coursers, various breeds and their virtues, the best hounds, proper seasons and weather, the ways of tracing game. Episodes are derivative usually, the influence of Vergil being apparent in the accounts of coursers and hounds from many lands (Armenian, Iberian, Sicilian, Moorish), of the power of spring and of Venus over the animal kingdom, and so on. Mawer's dedication to Sir Robert Walpole includes a discussion of didactic verse, again ranked second to epic poetry in importance. Oppian is compared with Homer and considered in many respects superior. Mawer is probably echoing Scaliger here.

Continued interest in ancient and neo-Latin didactic poetry is evident throughout the eighteenth century. Translations continued and will be noticed in their place.[88] Pope's *Selecta poemata Italorum qui Latine scripserunt,* including didactic verse in Latin by Vida, Fracastoro (both *Morbus gallicus* and the *Alcon* now ascribed to Cruceio), and Poliziano, appeared in 1740. Dr. Johnson is said to have planned a similar collection. The *Georgics*, Ovid's didactic verse, and Horace's, attracted many translators. There was a translation of Lucretius in 1743 and others after 1800, but the authority of Creech's version was of long standing. Hesiod was translated by Thomas Cooke in 1728. Elijah Fenton rendered into

English a passage from Book I of Oppian of Cicilia. Aratus, the Alexandrian, was attempted by Jabez Hughes and others. Columella, of the first century, was translated, evidently by M. C. Curtius, in 1745. The *Praedium rusticum* of the Jesuit Vanière of Toulouse was translated and adapted in part by George Jeffreys, Joshua Dinsdale, Arthur Murphy, John Duncombe, and others. Vida's *De bombyce* was retranslated once; Sainte-Marthe and Quillet reappeared. Didactic poets in modern languages aroused interest also: Delille in France, Tansillo in Italy, Yriarte in Spain, had their translators.

EARLY GEORGIC ESSAYS IN ENGLISH

My native soil
Invites me, and the theme as yet unsung.
Philips

THE *Georgics* of course had been familiar to British poets from very early times. Professor Mustard has traced textual echoes in Gawin Douglas, the romance *Launcelot of the Laik,* Barclay, Spenser, Googe, Daniel, Jonson, Shakespeare, Chapman, Fletcher, Herrick, Vaughan, Cowley, Milton, Dryden, and later poets.[1] But Thomas Moufat, in 1599, seems to have been the author of the first georgic in English which showed definite Vergilian influence, *The Silkwormes.*[2] Moufat says he had been in Italy in 1579.[3] Poems on the same subject had been written there by Vida, Spoleto, and Tesauro. Moufat's poem is connected with the effort made for many years to introduce silk-craft into England.[4] James I later even tried to enforce such a plan by royal edict.[5] The poem tries to call attention, through the persuasions of verse, to this neglected source of benefit. Vida's georgic is the chief model, and again entomology, craft-technique, and episodes compose the plan. The didactic matter often parallels Vida's closely. There is much curious learning in Moufat, often very substantial learning upon minute matters — for example, upon the question whether silkworm or " flie " was first created, or upon the development of the arts of costume among men. On the question of the invention of silk, Moufat draws upon both the elder and the younger Pliny, Ovid, Vida, and the Bible. His muse " listeth not of fictions to entreate," but he is full of the lore of mythology. The Vergilian device of human parallels for his insects, echoed by Vida, appears in Moufat and has some appeal. He has a sense of the wonder and poetry in this world of minutiae. The poem sometimes has a charm of naïve and active fancy, besides its aroma of curious, out-of-the-way learning.

Fourteen years later, in John Dennys' *Secrets of Angling* (1613),[6] there is a marked debt to the georgic tradition. Not only has Dennys used the episodic form and the usual theme statements, moral parallels, descriptions, and extended similes, as well as the zodiacal indications of time, but he uses that stock episodic theme of the didactic tradition, the origin of an art and its gradual development. Perhaps he knew Oppian, for he writes episodically of the habits of sea fish and of certain predatory ones. The physical and temperamental qualities necessary to the art, an old didactic theme used by Oppian and Gratius, appears also. Dennys' style is simple, however, and has nothing of the "magisterial" manner of the Latin didactic poets. His precepts treat in detail equipment, methods of angling for various kinds of catch, the proper days and seasons, and the various haunts of various kinds. Dennys' poem has been praised as one of the gems of seventeenth-century pastoral-ism.[7]

A fresher and livelier poem is the anonymous *Innocent Epicure* (1697). This has been attributed to Tate,[8] despite the preface in which he says he received the poem from its "unknown author with commission to publish or suppress it." In an "Author's Pref-ace to the Second Edition" (1713) there is the express statement that the author sent his verses to Tate, depending upon his judg-ment. There seems little reason to attribute to Tate such elaborate duplicity.

The poem is "after the model of ancient poets upon such argu-ments." Its style is "as elevated as was proper for the matter," a statement which shows how the tradition of Walton and Cotton has tempered the halieutic, or fisherman's georgic, as a type. Like Dennys, the anonymous author has adopted the plan of the classical didactic poem, but has altered the style to a more pastoral simplic-ity. It, too, offers precepts on equipment, methods of angling for various kinds of catch, and proper times for various kinds. The author has the usual extended similes, invocations, and moral par-allels. The idea of divine immanence, later so much amplified, is here in his belief that

> Consistent beauty rules the whole,
> Mov'd by an ardent and continual soul.

The contrast of sophisticated society with the joy of country life is a theme seldom absent from this kind of verse.

Of John Whitney's poem *The Genteel Recreation* (1700), little need be said. It is another halieutic, written in a rattling kind of iambic measure divided into irregular stanzas. It is dedicated to Vergil and treats much the same preceptive matter as does *The In-nocent Epicure,* with similar use of episode. A debt to Walton's *Compleat Angler* is evident on nearly every page. It helps to illus-trate the adaptation of the popular themes of Walton to the classic

didactic form, with a changed and more simple style. Beyond this
it has no importance.

In 1706 there appeared the poem which fixed the English georgic
as a type and determined its form — John Philips' *Cyder*. His
choice of blank verse has a certain importance in English prosody,
marking as it does the revival of non-dramatic blank verse as a
popular poetic medium. If Philips had not been earlier interested
in Miltonic blank verse, one would be tempted to account for its
revival in the fact that the Miltonic line is the closest approximation in English poetry to the Vergilian. Milton's inversions, his
periphrases; his artistry in matters of pause, alliteration, grouping
of sounds, and adapting of sound to sense; and his Latinized vocabulary — all these made him the natural model for one who
wished to adapt such a poem as the *Georgics* into English form.
Keats saw the style of *Paradise Lost* as " a beautiful and grand
curiosity . . . a northern dialect accommodating itself to Greek
and Latin inversions and intonations." Certainly the effort of lesser
men to write in the manner of Milton partly accounts for some of
the most artificial and inflated eighteenth-century versification.

Philips' poem is in two books, treating the selection of a site for
the orchard; proper soils, composts, and irrigating trenches; planting, grafting, and pruning; orchard pests; kinds of fruit; the
building of the mill; uses of the pulp; proper mixtures; and ageing
in wood and in glass. All of this — thoroughly English, thoroughly
of Hertfordshire, indeed — he cast into a quasi-Vergilian style,
adding episodes, descriptions, moral parallels — all the Vergilian
panoply.

In didactic passages, when possible, he sticks close to Vergil's
text, seeming to prefer the pedantic pleasure of ingeniously echoing Vergil in terms of English conditions. Like the *Georgics*, *Cyder*
is cast into the form of direct address; it employs the magisterial
manner; it uses cumulative similes. There are the common theme
statements and recapitulations. It lays claim to originality in the
treatment, first among men, of the theme in hand.

Description is a subordinate element in Philips. He tries to adapt
into English terms the Vergilian passage upon portents of good and
bad weather, but he has observed only a few such indications, certain omens from the moon and from the woodcock's return from
northern lands. He has a passage describing the mountains Pen-
menmaur and Plinlimmon, a picture of a phase of nature little appreciated by writers at that time. In both books there are short de-

scriptions of the seasons of the year, especially of that "best season," autumn. Best of these descriptions is that of the fall of the ancient city of Ariconium, destroyed by earthquake and volcano, an episode which echoes Vergil's lines on the portents of Caesar's death and on the eruption of Aetna. Episodes of a moral sort, besides shorter moral parallels, are common. The necessity of labor, the horrors of war, the life of cities and courts in contrast with the retired life, had been themes of the *Georgics*. The patriotic panegyric is really praise of Hertfordshire. Philips begins, like Vergil, with the contrast of foreign wines with that of his own land. He then follows much the same development as Vergil's, praising the vegetable wealth, the herds and flocks, the metals, the hills, fields, and groves, and the undaunted men of his land.

Exotic episodes occur. As Vergil describes life in Libya and Scythia, Philips shows how in various lands nature compensates for her rigors. He has "excursions of fancy" to Ireland, Belgium, arctic and tropical regions, and America. Other parallels are seen in his picture of the joys of rustics in merry companies after seasons of toil, feasting and dancing; and in his "frugal man . . . rich in one barren acre," a kinsman of Vergil's old Corycian.

Philips is something of a virtuoso: he speculates on the causes of earthquake and volcano, the secrets of nature's processes in grafting, the medicinal uses of plants, the wonders revealed by the microscope.

It is apparent how like in impulse this English georgic often is to the English arts of poetry or arts of love. It is ingenious *pastiche,* often closer to Vergil than the neo-Latin poets were. Philips' pleasure in composing it was partly that of a scholar delighting in ingeniously adapting the themes of an admired original into terms of native conditions. The pleasure he hoped to arouse in readers was partly in the recognition of this ingenuity. *Cyder* is often unreadable today for people who can only regard with wonder the high praise it once had. They do not look for this kind of minor merit lying in ingenuity of adaptation. With this poem really begins the adoption into English verse, as a borrowed form, of the classical didactic poem, and the Anglicization of the *Georgics*.

In 1710, Swift, always contemptuous of country pursuits as materials of poetry, and the sworn foe of eclogue, burlesqued a passage from the *Georgics*. The poem is important only because it suggested Gay's *Trivia*. It is called *A Description of a City Shower* and does with the passages in Vergil on the portents of rain and the autumnal storm what the burlesque city-eclogue tried to do with the pastoral: it parodies them and puts them into incongruous settings. Swift painted the portents of storm among city-dwellers; described the storm itself in terms of scurrying beaus, templars, and " tuck'd-up sempstresses "; and concluded with the violent incongruity of the teeming conduits of a thousand streets and alleys tumbling down to Holborn bridge. The idea in such hands as Gay's might have produced a deft piece of light verse; Swift's bludgeoning vulgarity makes it as grotesque as he could have desired.

An early cynegetic, or hunting georgic, was begun by Thomas Tickell, published in part in the *Guardian* in 1713 (No. 125) and in Tonson's *Miscellanies* of 1714 as *A Fragment on Hunting*. It takes its motto from Gratius and is a piece of unrelieved classical adaptation. The theme statement, the claim to priority in treating the subject, the description of the ideal hound, the account of the effects of the mating season in spring among animals, the slight sketch of Nimrod and the origin of hunting, are all stock conventions and themes of georgic or cynegetic. Tickell calls himself " a venturous rival of the Roman praise," but he abandoned his poem before he had done more than turn a few familiar themes into couplets. Like Gay in *Rural Sports* and like Somervile, Tickell evidently hoped to appeal to the powerful class of the landed gentry in their traditional love of country sports.

When in 1713 John Gay published his *Rural Sports, a Georgic*, he was content to leave most of the conventions of the type to other poets. In the strictest sense the poem is not a georgic, but a combination of the three types of poem of field sports, which were georgic offshoots.[9] It gives precepts on country pursuits and urges the happiness of country life in contrast to that of cities; but in following the road " frequented by the Mantuan swain," it sacrifices the episodic variety as well as the more heightened style of Vergil. It is mainly descriptive; the didactic content is negligible, a convention merely. Gay chose whatever points were capable of descriptive embellishment and presented only those. His intention was to paint alluringly the pleasures of country recreations. In this he succeeded. Perhaps he meant to oppose to Philips' pedantic conception of appropriate georgic treatment a more liberal, less imitative method, one which employed description almost to the exclusion of precept.

He seems otherwise uninfluenced by Philips unless his praise of
the *Georgics* is an echo of the same theme in *Cyder*. Gay's lines are
worth citing as an instance of the delight men found at this time
in the lively pictures of Vergil:

> Here I peruse the Mantuan's Georgic strains,
> And learn the labours of Italian swains;
> In every page I see new landscapes rise,
> And all Hesperia opens to my eyes;
> I wander o'er the various rural toil,
> And know the nature of each different soil;
> This waving field is gilded o'er with corn,
> That spreading trees with blushing fruit adorn:
> Here I survey the purple vintage grow,
> Climb round the poles, and rise in graceful row:
> Now I behold the steed curvet and bound,
> And paw with restless hoof the smoking ground;
> The dewlap'd bull now chafes along the plain
> While burning love ferments in every vein;
> His well-armed front against his rival aims,
> And by the dint of war his mistress claims:
> The careful insect 'midst his works I view,
> Now from the flowers exhaust the fragrant dew;
> With golden treasures load his little thighs,
> And steer his distant journey through the skies;
> Some against hostile drones the hive defend,
> Others with sweets the waxen cells distend,
> Each in the toil his destin'd office bears,
> And in the little bulk a mighty soul appears.

Canto I is devoted to fishing, Canto II to fowling and the chase.
The descriptions of the sports have something of the graphic quality of Somervile later; but Gay's greatest strength lies in his pictures
of nature, very fresh and vivid for their time. " All the grateful
country breathes delight " for him. About half of Canto I is a
series of pictures of morning, noon, evening, and night, all expressing this delight. They include short genre sketches of the labors of
the fields. Gay's lines are neither heavily euphemistic nor lacking
in observation:

> When the ploughman leaves the task of day
> And trudging homeward, whistles on the way;
> When the big-udder'd cows with patience stand,
> Waiting the stroking of the damsel's hand;
> No warbling cheers the woods; the feather'd choir,

To court kind slumbers, to the sprays retire:
When no rude gale disturbs the sleeping trees,
No aspen leaves confess the gentlest breeze;
Engag'd in thought, to Neptune's bounds I stray,
To take my farewell of the parting day;
Far in the deep the Sun his glory hides,
A streak of gold the sea and sky divides:
The purple clouds their amber linings show,
And, edg'd with flame, rolls every wave below:
Here pensive I behold the fading light,
And o'er the distant billow lose my sight.

The fourteen lines following these are interesting evidence that as early as 1713 Gay had felt the influence of physico-theological thought and had learned to seek in nature evidences of the divine. This theme was to become one of the most commonly repeated motifs in eighteenth-century verse.

If didactic had begun already to merge into descriptive poetry, it had an early alliance also with humorous verse — a natural development, due partly to the fact that Horatian and Ovidian didactic poetry had already lent themselves to humorous adaptation in poems like William King's *The Poet Banter'd, or Ovid in a Vizor* (1701), and his Horatian burlesque, *The Art of Cookery* (1708). The mock-heroic also helped to lead to the mock-didactic. Scarron's *Virgile travesti* and Boileau's *Lutrin* set the example for Charles Cotton's *Scarronides, or Virgil Travestie* (1670), John Philips' *Maronides, or Virgil Travesty* (1672–73), and others before Garth's *Dispensary* and Pope's *Rape of the Lock*.

After Swift, the first humorous adapter of the *Georgics* seems to have been the same William King who burlesqued Horace and Ovid. *Apple-Pye* was printed in a miscellany,[10] with his name, in 1713, with the subtitle " in Imitation of Virgil's Georgicks." The poem was later claimed by Leonard Welsted in the *Dissertation* prefixed to his *Poems* (1724). In the edition collected by John Nichols in 1781,[11] the poem is also claimed for Welsted. The lines printed by Nichols vary only slightly from those attributed to King. But the merit of this slight *jeu d'esprit* would not weigh greatly for either King's or Welsted's reputation. King's friendship with Swift, who parodied both *Georgics* and *Eclogues,* may be slight external corroboration of King's claim. The poem begins with an account of the origin of tarts, a parody of that common theme, the origin of arts and sciences, which Vergil uses after Lucretius. It traces the development of the art and turns, in direct address (to "Nelly," the kitchen-maid), to advice for each stage of the making.

A really ingenious adaptation appeared the following year, Gay's *Trivia, or the Art of Walking the Streets of London* (1715). Vergil wrote of the arts of the fields; Gay wrote of the arts of London highways and alleys. *Georgics* themes are clothed in delightful incongruity. Gay was already familiar with the sleight of hand by which classical motifs might be transposed deftly into incongruous keys. *The Shepherd's Week* (1714) had given the eclogue such treatment, presenting real British swains instead of Corydons and Damons. Gay's ability in this sort of transposition is the secret of almost all his most successful work. In his *Beggar's Opera* he puts the artificial operatic form into Newgate very captivatingly; in *Trivia* he brings the *Georgics* into London; in *The Shepherd's Week* he puts the eclogue into the fantastic setting of actuality; in his city eclogues, *The Toilette, The Tea-Table, The Espousal,* and others, he puts the same type into houses of fashion.

The subject of the first book of *Trivia* is "the Implements for Walking the Streets, and Signs of the Weather." Vergil prepared his husbandman in *Georgic* i with an account of implements of his trade, and the lines on the signs of the weather in the *Georgics* were those already parodied by Swift.[12] An episode of exotic references, parallel to the Vergilian excursions of fancy to other lands, is introduced: the perils of the streets of Paris, Belgian cities, Naples, Rome, and the lagoons of Venice. The portents of storm in the city are sketched with greater humor and skill than Swift displays. Like Vergil, Gay adds portents of other changes and counsels upon trustworthy omens. Book I concludes with a mock-mythological account of the origin, by divine gift, of pattens, feminine gear which used to lift ladies above the mire of rainy streets. Vergil's Aristaeus had received by divine gift the art of engendering bees.

Book II begins with conventional recapitulation and theme statement:

> Thus far the muse has trac'd in useful lays,
> The proper implements for wint'ry ways;
> Has taught the walker with judicious eyes,
> To read the various warnings of the skies:
> Now venture, Muse, from home to range the town,
> And for the public safety risk thy own.

Book II has the title " Of Walking the Streets by Day," and Book III " Of Walking the Streets by Night." Gay shows how to thread the maze of London safely and pleasurably, seeing and hearing vividly; and seldom elsewhere may one see so well the press of the noisy roads, the gilded coaches and lackeyed sedan chairs, the sway and bustle of Cheapside or Fleet Street. The *Georgics* gave pictures of the employments of the husbandman in seasons of the year, on particular days, and in various states of weather, a theme borrowed from Hesiod. Gay fits this to employments and aspects of London streets, going through the calendar and showing how the changing year transforms scenes and occupations of men. Winter's perils, its games, " the furies of the football war," coachman and matron the butts of schoolboy pranks, the frozen Thames and its frost fair, are typical scenes. He gives, too, a calendar of street cries, from the treble voices vending flowers and herbs in spring to the harsh calls of hawkers of holly and mistletoe at Christmas. As the poet walks through the Strand, reads proffered handbills as he goes, or peers into moldering volumes on the bookstalls, he contrasts the innocent and happy state of walkers with the delusive grandeurs and " false lustre of a coach and six," adapting Vergil's

> O fortunatos nimium, sua si bona norint,
> agricolas! [13]

Book II has another mock-mythological episode, accounting in broad comedy for the origin of bootblacks and the tools of their trade.

The subject of Book III offered fewer possibilities of humorous parallel. Perhaps the conventional patriotic panegyric and contrasts with other lands are echoed in the lines beginning

> Happy Augusta! law-defended town!
> Here no dark lanterns shade the villain's frown;
> No Spanish jealousies thy lanes infest
> Nor Roman vengeance stabs th' unwary breast.

Gay ends with claims of difficulty overcome, and hope that he has served his countrymen. There are minor echoes of the *Georgics* also, too incidental to be spoken of here. The whole poem is one of the masterpieces of what might be called parody, in the broadest acceptance of that term as not only verbal but thematic adaptation.

Soame Jenyns's burlesque *Art of Dancing* (1729) [14] belongs really rather to the Horace-Vida-Boileau-Pope line of didactic poems (arts of poetry and so on) than to the Vergilian, but it has certain elements from the latter. Pope's *Essay on Criticism* exerted the chief influence on its phraseology. But Gay's *Trivia* perhaps suggested the mock-mythological narrative of the origin of the fan through divine gift to mankind. Gay's charming " Patty," for whom Vulcan made the patten, probably suggested Jenyns's " Fanny," for whom Aeolus first made the fan. Vergil's tale of Aristaeus seems to be the original of both. The poem has, too, the statement of theme, invocation, dedication, cumulative similes, and moral parallels, of the more formal tradition. Mock heroic is side by side with an informality drawn from the Horatian epistolary manner.

III

"THE ENGLISH VIRGIL"

Nor, ye who live
In luxury and ease, in pomp and pride,
Think these lost themes unworthy of your ear;
Such themes as these the rural Maro sung
To wide-imperial Rome, in the full height
Of elegance and taste, by Greece refined.
                                        Thomson

A CRUCIAL event in the history of the vogue of georgic verse, was
the appearance of Thomson's *Seasons* (1726–30). The scope of
Vergil's influence was widened by Thomson's successful adaptation
of his form. The poet of the seasons became " the English Virgil ";[1]
these two poets together became the fountainhead of the European
descriptive-didactic tendency. Many English poets contributed to
it; in France also there was a large group — Saint-Lambert, Bernis,
Delille, Roucher, Rosset, Léonard, Desfontanes, and others;[2] in
Germany there were Kleist, Dusch, Zachariae, Wieland, Brockes,
Hirschfeld, Giseke, Blum, Schiller, and others.[3] Lessing's *Laokoon*
tried finally to prove that descriptive poetry was based on a falla-
cious analogy, a confusion of the provinces of poetry and painting.

John Philips had shown Thomson how Milton's blank verse
might be employed on georgic material, how Vergil's plan might
be adapted, how his themes might be Anglicized. Thomson's slight
debt to Armstrong's *Winter* and Riccaltoun's *Winter's Day* has
been shown by Zippel.[4] Another predecessor who may have influenced him was the William Hinchliffe whose *Seasons,* in about
four hundred lines, appeared in 1718.[5] There are close correspond-
ences between his work and Thomson's. Professor C. A. Moore
notices some of these parallels, concluding that they are " merely
accidental " or due to common sources.[6] But if Thomson knew
Hinchliffe's poem, he could have found in it a suggestion for a
poem on the seasons, drawing upon the *Georgics* for models.

Both poets repeat details of Vergil's picture of the Golden Age
of eternal spring;[7] both seem to echo his description of summer's noonday heat, in which languish nature and mankind.[8] With
the latter passages are connected in both poets lines *not* from the
Georgics, expressing desire for solitary poetic inspiration in the

solemn scenes of nature.[9] These are very similar in imagery. In his *Autumn,* Hinchliffe seems to echo Vergil's

> Libra die somnique pares ubi fecerit horas
> et medium luci atque umbris iam dividit orbem [10]

in these lines:

> Soon as the radiant balance *weighs*
> *In equal scales* the nights and days.[11]

Thomson uses exactly the same phrase, perhaps recalling the same lines of Vergil:

> When the bright Virgin gives the beauteous days,
> And Libra *weighs in equal scales* the year.[12]

Both adapt Vergil's striking figure of the war of the winds, and in similar phrases.[13] Both borrow the picture from the *Aeneid,* of the flood bearing away the fruits of the year while the peasant watches from a near-by hill.[14] Each includes the georgic theme of plague and pestilence,[15] though Hinchliffe's use of it is limited to fourteen lines. They have points in common also which are not Vergilian: tableaus personifying all the seasons; a similar kind of pleasure in the grandeur of winter, its more violent, stormy aspects; prominence given to the gloom of autumn and winter storms; and humanitarian sentiment. In each poet's *Winter* is a description of the formation of ice upon a river — of a clear, starry night and a keen eastern breeze which seizes and fixes the stream, of the shining prospect revealed by the light of morning.[16] These descriptions follow the same outlines and include phrases which seem to be echoes of Vergil's " *Concrescunt subitae currenti in flumine crustae,*" [17] Hinchliffe's " sudden th' arrested waters creep," and Thomson's " in its mid career, arrests the bickering stream." Both poets express a wish for a sheltered retreat where friends, " a chosen few," may help them pass gloomier days joyfully.[18] Sometimes the phraseology has a very striking similarity. Hinchliffe exclaims

> Bear me, O Muse, to Pindus' shades!
> To sacred groves! Pierian glades!
> To grottos crown'd with sylvan pride,
> Under th' Aonian mountain's side! [19]

And Thomson says

> Oh! bear me then to vast embowering shades,
> To twilight groves, and visionary vales,
> To weeping grottoes, and prophetic glooms.[20]

There seems a strong possibility that Thomson knew the 1718
Seasons, and he may have found in them a suggestion for greatly
amplified use of *Georgics* material within a framework of the seasons. Mallet and Ralph in 1728, and Savage in 1729, published
poems combining phenomena of the seasons with georgic conventions. But by 1728 the original *Winter* had been expanded, *Summer*
had had two editions, and *Spring* one. *Autumn* did not appear until
the collected *Seasons* of 1730. But the idea of a " descriptive georgic," if the term is admissible, on the seasons, originated with
Thomson and may possibly have been suggested by Hinchliffe.[21]

There is another type of poem to which Thomson is certainly indebted. Richard Blackmore's *Creation* (1712) is a physico-theological work on evidences of the divine in nature. In its form there is
a large debt to Lucretius, though its intention is directly opposed
to the anti-religious one of *De rerum natura*. Blackmore was followed by others: Richard Collins in *Nature Displayed* (1727),
Henry Baker in *The Universe* (1727), Samuel Edwards in *The
Copernican System* (1728), Robert Gambol in *The Beauties of
the Universe* (1732). The type continued to be used by other poets
of the century. *The Seasons* is related to these poems: a central
theme is that of nature as revelation of the deity. But instead of
developing, like Blackmore, an argument mainly from scientific
evidence, borrowing in form from Lucretius, Thomson wrote a
descriptive poem of nature with the *Georgics* as his model. He was
by instinct too much an artist to follow Blackmore: he presented
nature not to the analytical reason but to the senses and emotions.
Yet his theme of natural revelation is like Blackmore's, though he is
a less orthodox thinker. If we assume in Thomson the attraction
of themes of natural revelation in the period of his early studies
and the suggestion from Hinchliffe of a poem on the seasons,
bound up with themes of the *Georgics*, we have a possible hypothesis as to the origin of *The Seasons* in Thomson's mind. It can be
no more than hypothesis; in any case, natural revelation, the use
of divisions of time in verse of descriptive tendency, and the poetic
influence of Vergil, were elements prevalent in the artistic and intellectual atmosphere of the time when Thomson wrote.

The borrowings of the *Seasons* from the *Georgics* have been
shown by Mustard,[22] Nitchie,[23] Macaulay,[24] and Robertson,[25] and
most thoroughly by Zippel.[26] As long ago as 1823 many of these
had been noted by a writer in *The Yorkshire Magazine*.[27] But not
only are there many cases of paraphrase and expansion of Vergil;

the plan of Thomson and the genre of descriptive verse he popularized are based upon the form of the *Georgics*.

The groundwork of Vergil's poem was didactic: precepts and useful knowledge of nature for the guidance of the husbandman. But his aim was also to glorify the life of husbandmen by associating it with the most worthy ideals — patriotism, the virtues of the early Romans, religion, the beauties of nature, the wholesomeness of a life close to the soil. Hence his extensive use of episode: descriptions of nature, sketches of the occupations and recreations of the country and of a countryman like his Corycian, reflections on the necessity and dignity of labor or on the serene existence of the laborer far from cities and courts, praises of Italy, pictures of country life, and scenes in other lands. The content of the *Georgics* combines didacticism (craft technique), useful knowledge of nature (*e.g.*, the description of zodiacal signs and zones of the heavens, and the entomology of *Georgic* iv), description (of Italian and of exotic scenes), genre sketches (of country labors and recreations), narrative, panegyric (both personal and national), reflections on moral or religious themes, and introductory and transitional devices (theme statements, recapitulations, dedications, etc.). The subject matter of *The Seasons* falls into the same categories. Description is the groundwork of the poem. The episodes include moral and religious reflection, useful knowledge of nature, exotic scenes, genre sketches of peasant employments, narrative, panegyric, didacticism. Many of these episodes and descriptive passages are based directly upon Vergil's, his content being Anglicized and usually amplified. Certain elements, such as narrative and panegyric, are given a quite new tone: Vergil's epic vein was beyond Thomson's powers and unsuited to his purpose; Vergil's lofty tone in personal panegyric was inappropriate for Thomson. The exotic descriptive element is much expanded.

Vergil painted the employments of the husbandman through the year, using the pageantry of the seasons as a background. Thomson described the seasons, using the employments of the farmer incidentally as part of his pageantry. The essential motifs of the *Georgics* reappear in *The Seasons:* the glorification of labor and the life of the husbandman through their associations with patriotism, morality, religion, and the beauties of nature. Incidental themes and conventions of form are borrowed quite as freely. Vergil, of course, is not only Anglicized in Thomson, he is also made a man of the eighteenth century, conversant with the philosophy and popular tastes of the time. But when Shenstone placed a memorial to Thomson in " Virgil's Grove " at the Leasowes, he gave appropriate expression to the common veneration of the adopted Scot as " the English Virgil."

After Thomson, many of his followers included Vergilian elements, both through the independent influence of the *Georgics* and through the effect of the Vergilian elements in *The Seasons*. They echoed many things. Such elements of style as the lofty, dignified tone, the cumulative similes, the " magisterial " manner [28] of preceptation in direct address, are common. Theme statements, invocations, recapitulations of subjects treated, addresses to patrons, are conventional. Claims to difficulty overcome and to priority in treatment of subjects recur. Many use the device of indicating times of year by the station of the sun in the zodiac, Vergil's " natural calendar." " Moral parallels " like his are often used, short analogies between nature and the life of man.[29] Vergil's precepts are frequent models. These cannot be separated entirely from the descriptions of nature or of the occupations and pastimes of the rustics. There is often an element of the genre sketch in the precepts themselves, as well as in the picture of the Corycian swain or of the husbandman's winter relaxations. The precepts most often echoed or amplified were those on the following subjects: in Book i, the methods of preparing soils, crops peculiar to different soils, rotation of crops, improvement of soils, and farmers' implements; in Book ii, methods of cultivating trees, the genius of differing soils fitted for differing purposes, divining the nature of soils, methods and time of planting and pruning, care of vines and trees; in Book iii, the ideal dam for cattle and the ideal foal of noble breed, the care of sire and mares, of sheep and dogs, diseases and their cure; and in Book iv, the preparation of the hive and the care of the bees.

But it was Vergil's episodes which were most often expanded. There are exotic episodes in each book of the *Georgics* but the last: in Book i, on the crops and products of foreign lands; in Book ii, on foreign grapes and wines, and the conquests of tillage in the farthest bounds of the earth; in Book iii, on the shepherds of other lands, Libyan nomads, African herdsmen, and the troglodytic life of Scythian winters. The latter includes a contrast of torrid and arctic regions, which appealed to men's imaginations for centuries. Aside from his precepts, Vergil gave useful knowledge through description. Much of his presentation of the Hesiodic works-and-days theme is of this sort: the employments appropriate to various seasons and weathers, to rainy days, holy days, lucky and unlucky days, evening and sunrise, and winter. His description of the five zones of the heavens and the signs of the zodiac, from Aratus the Alexandrian, belongs here too. The powerful and famous descriptions of autumn storm and flood, and of the portents and changes of weather (signs of storm and bright weather, presages of moon and sun), were amplified over and over after Thomson. Others of his descriptions are less " useful " than picturesque — the charming " return of spring " in *Georgic* ii or the " shepherd's summer day " in *Georgic* iii, sketching the whole day from dawn to evening. One of Vergil's greatest excellences is as a descriptive poet of the animal world. His marvelous accuracy of observation and his vivacity remain unexcelled in this field. Whatever he may have borrowed from Nicander of Colophon, Aristotle, Cato, or others, he made his own. *Georgic* iv, on the bees, is the most extended of these descriptions. But there are also the unforgettable pictures of the foal of noble breed, the ideal dam, the chariot race, the gadfly among the herds, the war horse racing the winds, the adder and the water snake of Calabria, and the plague devastating animals and birds. The episode of the sway of Venus in the lower world (the battle of the bulls, the behavior of lioness, bear, boar, tigress, steed, lynx, wolf, dog, and stag, and the " horse-madness " of mares) was another which fascinated poets and stimulated endless emulation. Even Vergil's minor descriptive episodes, like that of the portents accompanying Caesar's death (flood, earthquake, volcanic eruption, comets, etc.), encouraged amplification.

His reflections or " moral episodes " were as much imitated and expanded as any. The " song of labor " (" *Labor omnia vincit* ") in *Georgic* i, with its account of the Golden Age and Jove's sentence of toil, out of which arose the arts of man's hands and his knowledge of nature, echoed through the English poets of two centuries. His praises of the life of the husbandman (" *O fortunatos nimium,*" etc.) in contrast to the luxury and peril of cities, combined with expressions of similar ideas in Horace, Lucretius, Hesiod, Tibullus, Seneca, and others, appealed to the nostalgic taste of an age in reaction against its own luxury and rationalism. The expression of war-weariness and the prayer for peace at the end of *Georgic* i, was another theme echoed by didactic and descriptive poets.

There were religious episodes: description of the rites of Ceres and Bacchus, and references to the belief in divine immanence and in immortality. In *Georgic* iv Vergil says that some believe the bees share in the divine intelligence, and teach that one God pervades all things, earth, sea, and heaven, men and beasts, which draw life from him and return to him without death.[30] Vergil's panegyrics were both personal (addressed to Maecenas and Augustus) and national. The "patriotic panegyric" of Italy ("*Sed neque Medorum silvae*," etc.) eloquent and full of imperial pride, was often Anglicized and much expanded. The narrative of the divine gift to Aristaeus of the art of engendering bees, a first exercise in epic, was less often directly imitated, though the narrative element often appeared in later poets of the tradition.

Long before the time of John Philips, such Vergilian themes as these had been paraphrased, imitated, amplified, and adapted by post-Augustan poets and by neo-Latin versifiers of the Renaissance. With the popularity of James Thomson, many of them became stock materials of English descriptive and didactic poets.

Thomson's *Winter* went through four editions in its first year (1726), and reappeared in 1728, 1730, and 1734. As separate poems, *Summer* had five editions, *Spring* three, and *Autumn* one. The collected *Seasons* appeared in 1730, and went into three editions in that year. They were reprinted, separate from Thomson's other work, at least forty-seven times before 1800, and were included in twenty-two collected editions before that date — a total of at least seventy-two editions from 1730 to 1800. Four editions in both 1802 and 1803, and five in 1805, show an increase of interest, and forty-four editions in the first twenty years of the nineteenth century indicate the redoubled popularity of those years.[31] The testimony of these figures is supplemented by the constant evidence of Thomsonian literary influence over the same period of time.

The Seasons made use of Vergilian materials in several ways. There are many textual echoes and Vergilian conventions. But more important than these is the way in which Thomson expanded the suggestions he found in the *Georgics*. His style emulates the Vergilian dignity and loftiness, owing much to Milton, in whom he found the closest approximation in English to these qualities. The conventions of theme statement, invocation, and address to patrons, are echoed. He calls attention to the difficulty of his subject and writes of the courtships of the birds, " a theme unknown to fame." The " natural calendar," the indication of time of year by position of the sun in the zodiac, is often employed. Moral parallels abound. Advice is given in the georgic manner on com-

bating insect blights and on fishing for trout. Where Vergil showed
the labors and pastimes of the country through precepts, including only a few descriptions of them, like that of winter relaxations
or of the old Corycian and his garden, Thomson showed these employments in realistic genre sketches, seldom giving precepts.
There is a very varied panorama of such sketches through all the
seasons: plowing, sowing, harrowing, fishing, the shepherd's care
of his sheep, hay-making, sheep-shearing, the peasant's home at
midday, swimming, a shepherd's home-coming at evening and the
dairymaid he loves, corn-reaping, fowling, the chase of the hare,
stag, and fox, the drunken revels of the huntsmen after their day
afield, the village celebrations after harvest, and village recreations
in winter in contrast with those of the city. These are not artificial
or idealized but quite truthful, in contrast to the narrative sketches
of rustic character.

In description Thomson took many hints from Vergil. Where the
latter described autumn storms, Thomson describes those characteristic of each season, together with their peculiar portents. Vergil's famous portents of storm and bright weather are drawn upon,
but Thomson also includes a wealth of original observation. These
set pieces in *The Seasons* were admired, imitated, and expanded by
many later poets. The eloquent picture of returning spring in
Georgic ii was amplified in *The Seasons* into a minutely detailed
picture of the gradual conquest of the season over " sullen winter."
Vergil's short " shepherd's summer day " in *Georgic* iii, tracing the
stages of the day from dawn to night, perhaps suggested the outline
of *Summer,* developed through dawn, morning, noonday, evening,
and night, with many echoes of Vergil's text. Thomson admired
Vergil as a poet of the animal kingdom and tried to rival him.
" The sway of Venus in the lower world " echoes details like the
familiar " battle of the bulls," but it is much longer than Vergil's
passage and paints especially the birds, neglected in the *Georgics*.
Their courtships, mating, nesting, brooding, feeding and care of
their young, are passages full of fresh observation and intimate
knowledge of natural history. No part of *The Seasons* seems to have
been more admired. Thomson began with the lower animals, and
traced the effect of the mating instinct in all orders, including man
and woman. Occasionally a Vergilian picture is reproduced in *The
Seasons:* the lament of the nightingale for her young (*Spring*) , the
gadfly among the herds (*Summer*) , and the behavior of animals
and birds as harbingers of changes of weather; but Thomson is as

often independent, evidently hoping to outdo Vergil, at least in the variety of his pictures. Later poets seem to have admired especially the sketches of the bees among the flowers, the summer insects, the insect blight, the herds and flocks at midday, the horse maddened by summer heat, the bird migrations, the robin's winter visits to the houses of men, the exotic birds and animals of the tropic and arctic zones, and the hare and the sheep in winter.

Among descriptive parts of *The Seasons* exploring themes untouched by Vergil, the following were often amplified by later poets: the descriptive personifications of each season at its coming; the many-colored catalogues of spring leaves, blossoms, and herbs; the wild-flower and garden-flower pictures of *Summer* and the orchard one in *Autumn;* the account of autumnal fogs and of the traveler led astray by marsh-lights and lost; the winter snowstorm and the peasant lost in the snow and frozen to death while his family awaits him; the winter night and the formations of ice and frost that glitter in the morning light.

The exotic episodes of the *Georgics,* especially the contrast of torrid and arctic zones, suggested similar themes to Thomson. In *Summer* there is a long description of the vegetable and animal life, the storms and features of nature, in the tropics. *Winter* has a contrasting picture of arctic animals and hunting, nomadic Scythians, Lapland life, the arctic seas, the pole itself, and the troglodytic life of the northernmost men by the Oby River. Sometimes these lines echo Vergil, but Thomson expanded enormously and found many followers in days when travel literature was enjoying a real vogue. Thomson celebrates the vineyards of other lands. In *Winter* he has an " excursion of fancy " to Switzerland, describing the terror of avalanches and snowslides, and another on the winter sports of various lands.

Thomson's most prominent moral episodes are often expansions of Vergil. The " song of labor " in *Autumn* praises toil as the source of useful arts and of knowledge of nature, but Thomson sees it also as the source of government, cities, and commerce. The praise of the life of the husbandman, in contrast with that of cities and courts, is very Vergilian, though of course much expanded. For the rest, such episodes are often of a humanitarian cast: condemnations of fowling, the chase, and the caging of birds; urgings of vegetarianism; admonitions to the wealthy to be merciful, to consider those less fortunate; and praise of such " philanthropists " as the prison reformers. Or they are glorifications of the social virtues, benevolence, public spirit, and love, so prominent in the ethical system of Shaftesbury, who is the moral philosopher singled out for praise in Thomson's list of the great men of England in *Summer;* praise of " social feeling " as against " unrestrained passion "; celebration of the universal harmony of nature, which inspires a moral harmony in the heart of man; praise of domestic happiness; prayer that England may be granted the public virtues and social feelings which secure her power among nations; invocation of " Philosophic Melancholy " as the expression of sympathetic emotions, the " social offspring of the heart "; and assertion of the universal harmony which unites the moral as well as the physical world, despite the " bounded view " which shows " apparent evil."

The panegyric element, strong in the *Georgics,* recurs in praises of friends and Whig patrons like Lyttelton, Dodington, Cobham, Pitt, and Chesterfield, and in the inevitable " patriotic panegyrics," one for England and one for Scotland. Thomson's additions to Vergil's outlines here are praise of Britain's liberty, prosperity, cities, and far-flung commerce. Thomson is the most prominent early poet of the mercantile glories of eighteenth-century England. Trade is celebrated in various ways: praise of pioneer navigators; of the fleece, basis of English trade; and of the plow which would make Britain " the exhaustless granary of the world." The clash between this belief in material progress and the cult of sentimental primitivism in Thomson has been pointed out by Professor Havens.[32] An ardent nationalist, full of enthusiasm for trade and industry, the poet nevertheless clung to his preoccupation with the dream of a simpler, more primitive existence fostering qualities ennobling to the nature of man.

In *The Seasons* narrative becomes a servant of " social feeling." The love story of Damon and Musidora, mingling sensuousness and sentimentality; the tale of Amelia, struck by lightning and dead in her lover's arms; that of Lavinia, the beautiful peasant maid, and Palemon, the benevolent landholder, are all meant to inspire those sympathies and social virtues which are the essence of the " inward harmony " of ethical philosophers like Shaftesbury and Hutcheson. After Thomson such narrative episodes are common in long poems of the period, tales which run true to well-defined types: lovers separated by death (usually just before their marriage day) or by parental opposition, lovers dying together, lovers faithful through trying tests, examples of " sorrows of seduction," Pamela-like stories of " virtue rewarded," maidens separated from unfortunate or unfaithful lovers and gone mad with grief, friendship episodes, parental-love episodes, domestic-love episodes, and tales of benevolent men of wealth who wed lovely and worthy peasant maids. Such stories are often, as in Thomson, at variance with more realistic treatment of village and country life in the same poem. As the century progressed, they tended to become more realistic.

As the theme of rural occupations in Vergil is that of Hesiod's *Works and Days,* so his curiosity as to the nature of things is Lucretian. Like Vergil, Thomson says that he desires first a knowledge of the secrets of nature; failing that, he will be content with a life in the country close to nature. There is a strong element of science in the *Georgics:* entomology, Alexandrian astronomy and natural history, useful knowledge from writers like Aristotle, Theophrastus, Varro, Aratus, Nicander. In Thomson this element too is expanded. He is the first considerable poet to express in English verse the wide curiosity of the new virtuoso. He discusses, for example, the rainbow and Newton's spectrum, the force of gravitation binding the universe together, the supposed effects of the sun's force under the earth, the wonders of microscopic life, theories of the origin of rivers, the courses of meteors, and the nature of ice and frost. It is not important here that Thomson's scientific ideas are sometimes wrong in the light of present knowledge.[33] Sometimes he errs because he introduces original speculations, but more often because he follows inconclusive theories current in his time.

Besides these elements in *The Seasons,* there were minor ones which later poets often echoed: the Miltonic (*Il Penseroso*) theme of the sheltered rural retreat and winter content in books, reflection, and a few chosen friends; the early praises of English gardening and of estates like Stowe; the " hill-prospect " from Shene; the hymn to the sun, informer and sustainer of the universe, with its allegorical dance of Seasons and Hours about the " Lord of Day "; the several plague pictures (an ancient theme of didactic verse) ; and the Lucretian account of the evils of jealousy.

In general, Thomson's additions to the tradition of the *Georgics* were of the following kinds: when he borrowed, he Anglicized, modernized, and amplified; he encouraged the use of Miltonic blank verse and of themes from Milton; he introduced ethical and theological doctrines of his time; he immensely stimulated objective description of nature and the descriptive genre sketch of country labors and pastimes; he increased the element of " useful knowledge " of science, introducing facts and theories of zoölogy, ornithology, botany, physics, and geology; he enlarged the element of travel interest, knowledge of remote lands; he celebrated the Whiggish enthusiasm for liberty and for the growing trade and commercial glory of England.

It is evident that Thomson owes a large debt to the science, metaphysics, and moral philosophy of his period. His philosophy of nature and his ethics have sometimes been regarded as primarily a reflection of the ideas of Lord Shaftesbury. Mr. H. C. Drennan [34] has recently shown reason for modifying this view, most thoroughly elaborated by Professor C. A. Moore,[35] and for recognizing the importance of scientific rationalism and of such Newtonian writers as Bentley, Samuel Clarke, Derham, and others, in shaping the poet's mind. This is not the place to weigh the merits of the questions at issue. Shaftesbury and the Newtonians would have agreed on some points: the postulates of universal order, harmony, and beauty (though they differed, for example, in emphasis on the *utility* of all natural phenomena or the *beauty* of all phenomena); the revelation of God in nature to reason; the uninterrupted chain of cause and effect which leads to the First Cause. Shaftesbury and the Newtonian writers alike tend to speak of God as if he were immanent in his creation. It is with Shaftesbury's doctrine of a "moral sense" and his idea of esthetic sensibility as a guide to virtue, with his ethical system, in short, that scientific rationalism seems in deepest conflict. No reader of Thomson could doubt the influence Newtonianism exerted; and his singling out of Shaftesbury for praise above all moral philosophers is only one of the marks of the other influence, particularly in ethical ideas. Thomson had read widely in the physico-theological works of his day, and he had an admirable grasp of Newton's scientific contributions; he had followed the controversies of the time on questions involving geology and theology; he had also eagerly explored the ideas of the Earl of Shaftesbury. Our concern, necessarily, is not with Thomson's relative debt to the scientific movement of his time, and to the Shaftesburian ideas, but, rather, with as clear a statement as may be made of his leading ideas as they appear in his poetry.

The Seasons are an important expression of ideas current in the eighteenth century. The whole poem gathers significance from the conception of all nature as revelation of God. For Thomson, revelation *is* natural revelation; supernatural revelation does not concern him. Nature is sometimes spoken of as the objective demonstration of God, sometimes as the body in which is immanent the " Univer-

sal Soul " and " Essential Presence." Thomson's conception of deity
is variable; he can speak of God now as immanent in nature, and
now as separate from it. Yet he obviously wants to avoid, on the
one hand, a complete separation of Creator and creation, and, on
the other, a complete identification of them. God " pervades, ad-
justs, sustains, and agitates " the harmonious whole of nature. Science afforded him a useful analogy. He repeats again and again the
analogy of the sun pervading all life with its vital power, and sustaining the moving worlds of the solar system by gravitational force.
God is " great Sun of beings," " Light Himself ": the physical sun
is addressed as " soul of surrounding worlds " in which " best seen
shines out thy Maker."

Nature composes a universal harmony of benevolent design, all
aspects of which, however harsh (winter, storms, seas, mountains,
the rigors of tropical and arctic lands), have their utility and
grandeur. The limited vision of man sees apparent evils in the
physical world, which would fall into proper relationship in the
divine harmony if the whole could be compassed in our view. This
harmonious nature exerts an influence on the soul of man, his
moral being, inspiring a corresponding inward harmony. Nature
can " harmonize his heart " and " serene his soul," attuning the dis-
cordant passions into the universal love which is the soul of virtue
and into the reverence which is the soul of religion.

Virtue is a moral symmetry analogous to the harmony of the external universe. The passions are elements of chaos, disorder, discord, which are " attuned " by the influence of nature and by the
feelings of universal benevolence, the " active flood of universal
love." This attraction of benevolence is analogous to the attraction
of gravitation in the physical world. It is obvious how he has combined his scientific thought with the Shaftesburian ideas to which
he was drawn by their strong appeal to his esthetic sensibility. Sometimes he speaks (like Shaftesbury and the " sentimentalists ") as if
virtue arose from an esthetic perception of " moral beauty," inward
symmetry, harmony, order; sometimes he speaks (like Bolingbroke
and the rationalists) as if virtue were won through reason and
knowledge, which discipline the instincts into subjection. Hobbes's
analysis of man as wholly selfish is opposed by insistence upon
" social feeling " as the essence of virtue, from which all particular
virtues are derived. Again there occurs an analogy with the sun:
from benevolent feeling, this " kind sun of moral nature," flow
all " the social offspring of the heart." It exerts a " moral gravita-

tion," sustaining and adjusting the world of human relationships. Thomson's humanitarianism, his social enthusiasms, his many appeals to softer feelings, are attempts to cultivate and refine the inner harmony which is virtue itself. Thomson embraces also in his ethics the view according to which " apparent evil " in the moral world will disappear when the mind perceives " the great eternal scheme " which, involving all, composes a perfect whole.

There were, of course, in the *Georgics* elements of some of Thomson's most fundamental positions: the immanence of the divine in nature, curiosity as to nature's secrets, appreciation for remote and rugged aspects of nature, benevolent sympathy for the lower orders of men, sensitive perception of the plaintive voices of inferior creatures. But early Vergilian influences were less important here than the systematic science, philosophy, and theology of his period, in which he had read widely.

In description, Thomson appeals to all senses with accurate notations. But he usually describes nature objectively, and the genus rather than the individual. *The Seasons* is a kind of sketchbook of archetypes — not localized or particular phenomena, but a panorama of ideal types. Thomson's influence tended to fix this style as the norm in descriptive poetry. But objectivity is not the invariable rule. For example, there are passages colored by melancholy contemplation, gloomy or awesome scenes with reflections of a related cast. The " poets of melancholy " often found inspiration in *The Seasons*. The scenes of nature are sometimes colored, too, by philosophical, especially theological, ideas, and by a conception of nature as exerting an influence on the moral being of man. But the objective and generalized norm of descriptive style became the usual mode among his followers. They tried, too, to recapture Thomson's broad and vivid color sense, his sensitivity to motion, sound, and odors, his varied knowledge of nature, his broad, general effects. The descriptive genre sketch of country occupations also became an important feature in poetry, and after 1770 its use was so much amplified that by the time of *Lyrical Ballads* few aspects of country or village life were left undescribed. This reflection of peasant life and sometimes of peasant character contributed to an important aspect of romanticism.

As if by divination, Thomson found in *The Seasons* many of the channels into which thought and taste were turning most strongly. His extraordinary popularity was partly due to the fact that he was so broadly representative. His theology and his ethics were unpo-

lemical enough to escape orthodox censure; more unorthodox
thought than his gained ground even among the clergy during the
century. His humanitarianism and love of practical charity suited
the period of Howard, Wilberforce, and Romilly. His emphasis
on sensibility, sympathy, and the softer passions, appealed deeply
to the century of Richardson, Sterne, Mackenzie, Rousseau, and
Diderot. The lush and sensuous sentiment pervading Thomson's
narratives probably seemed the perfection of sensibility. Gainsborough put Damon and Musidora on canvas, and Theophilus
Clarke produced two paintings based on these episodes.[36] Thomson's scientific interests fell in with the growing vogue for such
knowledge in days when Newton, Franklin, and Buffon were popular heroes, and when men like Goldsmith, Priestley, Voltaire, and
Diderot assumed the rôle of popularizer. A related interest in remote lands and in travel literature, stimulated by the growth of
the empire and by the voyages and publications of men like Dam-
pier, Anson, Byron, Wallis and Carteret, and especially Captain
Cook and Mungo Park, had been expressed early in poetry by
Thomson. Love of nature was stimulated by interest in landscape
gardening and landscape painting; by improved facilities for
travel and touring; by the esthetic theorizers like Burke, Knight,
Gilpin, Price, and Alison; by the growing popular interest in natural science and the connection of science with " natural revelation"; and by other causes. Interest in the country and in agriculture grew with the improvements of Jethro Tull, John Mortimer,
Bishop Fleetwood, Viscount Townshend, Robert Bakewell, Lord
Kames, and Arthur Young. The tendency of Whig trading leaders to turn to the land was another factor in such interest. Thomson's ardent Whiggism, glorying in the English liberty which followed the Bill of Rights and the Act of Succession, and in the
glories of English trade and commerce, was another element of
continued popular appeal.

A period which saw a primitivistic reaction against what was considered a decadent luxury and an excessive rationalism, found in
The Seasons a colorful study of nature, of primary emotions, and
of simple life close to the soil. An age which saw the rise of a middle-
class literary public, found in *The Seasons* one of the most successful
appeals to readers of that class. Thomson's democratic humanitarianism, his idealization of social feelings, his glorification of
trade and agriculture, his praise of work, his urging of established
standards of morality, his religious fervor — opposed to the more

rationalistic note of Pope or Johnson, his informative tone, his thorough Whiggism, his closeness to nature, both as sensuous beauty and as religious revelation, endeared him to generations which saw in him a delightful descriptive poet, an edifying teacher, and a defender of ideals natural to a middle station in life.

IV

THE POETRY OF COUNTRY OCCUPATIONS

Nec sum animi dubius, verbis ea vincere magnum
quam sit et angustis hunc addere rebus honorem.
                                              Vergil

THE HORATIAN critical canon of " delight and instruction " and the
eminently practical temper of Roman literary genius came to have
greater influence in England in the eighteenth century than ever
before or since. Poetry of ethical import, philosophic and satiric,
was written by the first poets of the age. That most Roman of literary motives, the didactic, became the guiding principle of English
verse. We have examined the awakened interest in England in
what Addison called the didactic poetry of " rules of practice " and
" philosophical speculations." We have seen how advance in practical arts and in science, interest in the learning of the ancients,
educational theories and practice, literary criticism and scholarship, had all contributed to the early stages of interest in both classical and neo-Latin didactic verse. Philips, Gay, Tickell, and King
helped to naturalize the genre on English soil. With James Thomson, the Vergilian model ceased to wield its almost exclusive dominance. The old elements of technical and of ethical and religious
teaching were not discarded, but changed. The old element of description of nature was much expanded. After Thomson, poets
wrote preceptive georgics on husbandry or preceptive poems on
country sports; they also wrote descriptive poems on the same subjects. They wrote descriptive panoramas of nature, which also present the occupations of the country. Didactic and descriptive poetry
mingle, until a clear distinction often becomes difficult to draw.
The elasticity of the forms offered by Vergil and Thomson appealed
to writers of the period. These forms were flexible, inclusive, unex-
acting. They might serve as an omnibus for all of a poet's favorite
ideas. What could be better suited to an age inhospitable to the
fusing enthusiasm usually necessary to poetic synthesis? These
forms became favored ones with many in the versatile Europe of
the eighteenth century, adaptable vehicles for everything from
country lore to encyclopedic erudition.

It may be said at the outset that I shall not discuss the old question of the artistic congruity of didactic poetry as a genre. The

eighteenth century accepted it as traditional, and I have already discussed the currents in ideas and taste which brought it into acceptance and esteem. To readers of one period, a form favored in another may seem a *faux genre*. Certainly the effort to follow classical example in didactic poetry led to a great deal of wretched verse. Yet, for the history of taste and literature, what is important in didactic poetry is the fact that it served as a vehicle for new material and carried on and extended a country tradition never really lost from English verse. In good time the form itself disappeared, but what was of permanent value in its history passed on to a new generation of poets employing new forms. The faults of didacticism are very obvious and have often been pointed out, but I shall be more interested in inquiring whether it expressed anything vital in the life of the period which produced it.

We shall be concerned in this chapter with poetry of country occupations and of technical knowledge of nature, which is related to the tradition of the *Georgics* either in subject matter or form. It is understood, of course, that not all such poems are derived from Vergil's *Georgics*, either directly or indirectly, though most of them show the influence of Vergil in some degree. More specifically, the following types of poem will be discussed: (1) preceptive georgics on husbandry and the theory and art of gardening; (2) descriptive poems on husbandry, related to the georgics in subject; (3) preceptive poems on rural sports, especially the cynegetic, the ixeutic, and the halieutic,[1] all traditionally derived from the georgic form; (4) descriptive poems on the same subjects; and (5) didactic poems, like those of Erasmus Darwin, designed to teach a knowledge of nature and related to the georgic class in details of form.[2] Having adopted, as most pertinent to my purpose, a chronological method, I cannot avoid somewhat abrupt transitions of subject.

The poems published between 1726 and 1730, the years in which the *Seasons* were appearing, except for descriptive verse based on parts of the year or the day (as in Mallet, Ralph, Savage), do not show any indebtedness to Thomson. Abraham Markland's *Pteryplegia* (1727)[3] is an informal, loosely wrought ixeutic on fowling. Its plan is digressive, but there is no effort to conform to the style of the classical didactic poems. Sometimes Markland seems to have Gratius or Oppian in mind in his themes, as in the allusions to the necessary qualities of the successful fowler, or in describing the tackle and gear of the sport. His dedication to gentlemen sportsmen lays claim, in the conventional way, to priority in treating his subject. But the poem is in an unpretentious, often conversational manner. His humorous apologies, in the dedication, for omitting the usual invocations, are characteristic of him: " I intended (according to custom) an invocation to Apollo, our great exemplar in this art, who shot Icarus flying . . . but considering, upon second thoughts, how many snites, woodcocks, partridges . . . I had lost upon his occasion, and how often I had been glad of the prophane opportunity of turning my backside on his God-ship; I concluded I had little reason to expect his assistance."

Henry Needler's *Of the Seasons Proper for Angling*,[4] in couplets, gives advice on the subject of its title, but not in the more elevated vein of classical didactic. It has slight genre sketches and its description of spring, summer, and autumn is not without observation.

John Laurence, the writer on husbandry, is assumed to have been the author of a rather pleasant poem, *Paradice Regain'd: or, the Art of Gardening* (1728). He describes his flight to the hills near Windsor to avoid a London pestilence and recounts the pleasures of improving his modest house and grounds. The methods of planting the flowers and trees used, the spacing of trees, the process of grafting, the preparation of the greenhouse, the cultivation of vines and various vegetables, the making of fountains and graveled walks, and, in general, his triumphs of reconstruction, are described. The poem is informal in style and, though amateurish in composition, reflects the author's eagerness pleasingly. It is full of his pleasure in landscape, gardens, flowers, trees, streams and the sounds of water, bees, and birds. If there was indifference toward nature in the poetry of the twenties, Laurence is unaffected by it and to all appearances unaware of it. There are Vergilian parallels. But the tone of the work is informal; it would be difficult to prove that Laurence followed the *Georgics* at all.

In 1729 Moses Browne, long the principal poetic contributor to *The Gentleman's Magazine,* offered a variant from the usual tradition, in his *Angling Sports in Nine Piscatory Eclogues.*[5] In his *Poems on Various Subjects* (1739) Browne expanded and revised the original verses, which introduced didacticism into the eclogue. He also planned, but left unfinished, a didactic poem to be called *Rural Sports.*[6] The persons of the eclogues are fishermen, except in Eclogue VIII, where Browne introduces fowlers for the first time, according to his claim. The eclogues mingle the usual pastoral themes (the love lament, the incantation of a slighted shepherdess, the song contest, etc.) with technical advice, natural history, and description. Browne introduces many signs of weather, in the manner of Vergil, but these portents apply particularly to the exigencies of the fisherman's craft, and seem to be the result of original observation. Sometimes these notations are quite minute, like the observations of the leaves of wincopipes as indications of clear days. Sometimes they are more general:

> Nor wants the angler pre-advis'd to know,
> When certain signs disfavouring hours foreshow;
> Oft-times he views, awarn'd by adverse skies,
> His fly, or gliding cork, with hopeless eyes,
> When the dry east-wind parches up the plain,
> Or the wet south pours down the drenching rain. . . .
> When rotting weeds the thick'ning floods distain
> And to the deeps retires the finny train;
> Seek, Anglers, then no more th' uncertain prize,
> Ensuing rains expect, and wint'ry skies.
> When mulb'ries first their early verdure wear,
> And wormy baits the hungry perch ensnare;
> Securely then the peaceful streams explore,
> Ceas'd are the snows, and frosts offend no more.

Browne's praise of the happiness of the fisherman's lot is much in the vein of " *O fortunatos nimium.*" He versifies technical knowledge of the nature and habits of fish, recalling Oppian's use of such materials, though he does not rival him in scope. This element of natural history extends also to descriptions of the otter, newt, swan, bittern, hern, and cormorant, and also to flowers and land birds. His footnotes cite such authorities as Boyle, Bacon, Derham, Walton, Camden, Pliny, Aristotle, and Du Bartas. As a matter of. fact, a good deal of his didactic matter, like John Whitney's, is Walton versified. Browne deserves attention as an observer of nature, though he is not an accomplished poet. The notations are numerous and exact for their time. The weakness is that these are too much in the catalogue manner. But the appearances and sounds of early evening (the furtive weasel, the cricket, toads, beetles, glowworm, and owl) are pleasingly painted. So too is the sunrise and revival of nature and man in Eclogue II. This suggests Thomson, as do the faint-hearted and illogical touches of humanitarianism. To condemn man's cruelty to the denizens of the stream, in a poem on angling, is something less than consistent; but the English gentry were forced into many strange positions by the conflict of the new humanitarianism with their traditional love of field-sports. Browne's eclogues continued to be reprinted; [7] and this and his other poems possess historical interest as studious records of natural phenomena and country scenes in the early years of the century. He exemplifies, too, the taste for natural history as a subject for verse, which was to grow as the century progressed.

A man writing of country occupations from the point of view of the poor thresher and day laborer and writing with honest realism, was an arresting figure in 1730, when the *Poems on Several Subjects* of Stephen Duck quickly went through seven editions in the year of their appearance. Duck, " the Wiltshire Bard," who was taken up by Queen Caroline and given a place at Kew and a salary of thirty pounds a year, displayed in his *Thresher's Labour* some of the splenetic energy of George Crabbe. Thereafter he took orders, became a clergyman, and imitated Pope, Horace, and the more stilted pastoral writers. Duck had been a poor thresher at Charleton, in Wiltshire. He writes from unfeigned experience, describing the typical year of the farm laborer in the employments of the seasons. Never again did the poet write with the same faithful and detailed realism. The day laborer is far from the tone of " *O fortunatos nimium, sua si bona norint, agricolas,*" as we should expect him to be.

> 'Tis all a gloomy melancholy scene
> Fit only to provoke the muse's spleen.

The dust of threshing, the master's tyrannies, the laborers mowing with the scythe, the threshing in the barns — such are his themes. He calls upon the fortunate to pity the poor laborer. Duck is fond of cumulative similes, sometimes incongruously chosen, but on the whole the style is unassuming and the aim is faithful record. The voice of the lowest class of agricultural society has seldom spoken in verse, but here it is in the accents of an authentic, if rebellious, representative.

The first didactic poem in the Vergilian tradition, after Thomson, to win commanding attention and maintain it over a long period of time was William Somervile's *Chase* (1735). There were three editions in the year of its appearance, one in 1743, two in 1757, others in 1766, 1773, and 1796. It was frequently reprinted in the nineteenth century, notably in editions illustrated by the Bewicks, Stothard, Sartorius, and Hugh Thomson. The poet was a country squire of an ancient family, the friend of Lord Lyttelton,

Jago, and Shenstone. He shared the literary ambitions of his friends, and found in Vergil, Thomson, and Gratius models which enabled him to win a wide reputation. Often he is vigorous enough to have deserved it. *The Chase* is a poem written by a country squire for his brothers of the landed gentry. He calls upon them:

> Ye vigorous youths, by smiling Fortune blest
> With large demesnes, hereditary wealth,
> Heap'd copious by your wise forefathers' care,
> Hear and attend! while I the means reveal
> T' enjoy those pleasures, for the weak too strong,
> Too costly for the poor: To rein the steed
> Swift stretching o'er the plain, to cheer the pack
> Opening in consorts of harmonious joy.

Beginning with the origin of hunting, Somervile traces the development of the sport, gives rules for the training, care, and selection of hounds, and describes the chase of the hare, fox, stag, and otter. But, in the georgic manner, he uses digressions to enliven and elevate his subject. These are modeled after the traditional materials; there is the account of the origin and slow development of the art, the patriotic panegyric, the picture of the perfect hound, the exotic digressions (upon Asiatic and African hunting), the element of personal panegyric (of members of the royal family), the picture of the ravages of plague, the Vergilian nightingale mourning the loss of her young, the " *O fortunatos nimium* " theme applied to huntsmen, the expression of the desire first to know the secrets of nature, but failing that, to enjoy the peace of country life. His precepts are often closely modeled on Vergil or Gratius. For example, Book IV imitates the plan of the third *Georgic*.

The poem is in a blank verse influenced by Thomson's. The poet of the *Seasons* also set Somervile an example in the use of themes of scientific interest such as his account of the stages of the malady among hounds and his speculations on animal instincts. Somervile's somewhat inconsistent touches of humanitarianism seem to echo the tones of Thomson. Like Thomson, he paints a picture of the delights of a winter evening's converse with " the mighty dead " in his books and of talk with a few chosen friends. Descriptive passages such as that on autumn in Book II, have the accent of the *Seasons*. He shares also with Thomson some of the Vergilian themes pointed out, and catches his tone in developing them.

Somervile's chief merit is in his animated descriptions of the hunt. In the poet of *Gawayne and the Green Knight,* in Shakespeare, Pope, Thomson, and others, this theme has been vividly treated, but no poet ever wrote of it with more first-hand knowledge or more enthusiasm than Somervile. These pages are still worth reading. Their reality is often proof against the tumidity of a style too overburdened with an artificial " elevation." Historically the poet of *The Chase* is interesting as one of those writers who kept alive a realistic country tradition. Like the didactic poets generally, he avoided the affectations which were the worst fault of the pastoral tradition in the eclogue. His pictures of animals are often especially graphic; he was not surpassed after Thomson, in this respect, until late in the century, by poets like Cowper and Thomas Gisborne. And there are genre sketches where reality compensates for the turgid diction:

> The clanging horns swell their sweet-winding notes,
> The pack wide-opening load the trembling air
> With various melody; from tree to tree
> The propagated cry redoubling bounds,
> And winged zephyrs waft the floating joy
> Through all the regions near: afflictive birch
> No more the school-boy dreads; his prison broke,
> Scampering he flies, nor heeds his master's call;
> The weary traveller forgets his road
> And climbs th' adjacent hill; the ploughman leaves
> Th' unfinished furrow; nor his bleating flocks
> Are now the shepherd's joy! men, boys, and girls
> Desert th' unpeopled village; and wild crowds
> Spread o'er the plain, by the sweet frenzy seized.

The anonymous *Stag Chase in Windsor Forest* (1739) is an acknowledged derivative of Somervile's popular poem, though in couplets. It has some vividness in the description of the chase. Its episodes celebrate the beauties of Windsor and the praises of various nobles.

A long-popular poem of 1740, William Somervile's *Hobbinol,* is on the theme of rural sports, but it is of course related to the georgic and other forms of country didactic verse only remotely through subject and rural setting. It is a mock-heroic narrative telling the story of the triumphs of young Hobbinol and his Ganderetta in the May games of Evesham, on the borders of Gloucestershire and Worcestershire, and ending with Hobbinol's disgrace when Mopsa appears with his two illegitimate children. There are interesting rural types in the poem, graphic caricatures of real rustics: Hobbinol, the rich farmer's son; Twangdillo, the fiddler; Squire Radamanth; Gorgonius, the butcher; Pusca, the gypsy; and others. The dance, the wrestling match, a fantastic battle of factions among the country folk, both men and women, the cudgel-playing, the dinner under the trees, the smock race in which Ganderetta triumphs, are described in a style which mingles the mock heroic with a reality never lost sight of for long. Realism and the mock heroic of extravagant epic similes, orations of "heroes," and Homeric and Vergilian echoes, are interwoven. Mock-heroic and satirical qualities are found also in Somervile's shorter poem on another sport, *The Bowling Green;* but this, too, has only indirect relationship to the georgic form.

In 1740 two poems were printed as original works which are in reality based on parts of the *Praedium rusticum* of the Jesuit Vanière, one of the most famous of the neo-Latin didactic poets. The anonymous *Dove-Cote,* in couplets, is drawn from Vanière's Book XIII. This, in turn, is an expansion of Vergil's matter, borrowing an approximation of his manner. The third *Georgic* is the primary model. The *Dove-Cote* treats the art of breeding pigeons, with elements of descriptive and narrative relief, in particular the Ovidian story of Columba and Milous, the dove and the kite. Joshua Dinsdale's *Modern Art of Breeding Bees* is drawn from Book XIV of Vanière's work. It is a free adaptation of the first two cantos of that book, in couplets. Written on one of the favorite themes of Vergil, the poem shows indebtedness, of course, to the fourth *Georgic.* Dinsdale chose the parts of Vanière devoted to the habits of the bees, rather than anything nearer to the kind of craft technique his title indicates. Vanière had had in mind the filling out of Vergil's outline and the modernizing of his knowledge of the bees. Vergil's device of human parallelisms, so charmingly carried out, is borrowed by Vanière, and hence by Dinsdale, and gives something of reminiscent pleasure. Dinsdale is an indifferent versifier, but his subject matter has interest and can hold a reader. Vanière was not widely known in England in 1740. These adaptations of his text prove again the presence of a reading public which could be appealed to by treatment of themes of country life in another vein than that of pastoral artifice. These adapters single out two of Vanière's more lively themes, less weighted with the versified erudition of Jesuit didacticism than many others. They temper, too, the tone of stiff and arid formality, the manner of the savant in verse, characteristic of Vanière.

Isaac Hallam's *The Cocker* (1742) is "in Imitation of Virgil's Third Georgic." The gamecock has replaced the horse and the flocks! Another sportsman rallying to the muses! Hallam, though, reaches the nadir. He imitates faithfully: theme statement, invocation, claim to priority in the theme, description of the ideal sire, the sway of Venus in this lower world, the conflicts of rivals, the whole scheme of the third *Georgic* in its preceptive parts — he has done what man may do — and has achieved a prodigy of ineptitude. Some men had apparently come to believe that even remotely to follow the footsteps of Maro would insure against disaster, whereas the truth was that successfully to follow in this path demanded qualities nearer Vergil's own than many men could boast. Hallam sometimes tries to bolster up his style with borrowings from Dryden's translation of the *Georgics*. All is to no avail.

William Somervile reappeared in this year (1742) with his *Field Sports,* a kind of expansion of the element of exotic digression already familiar to his readers in *The Chase*. It is really an addition, of that kind, to his earlier poem.

Considerably above Isaac Hallam we might rank another humble poet, Nicholas James, who published at Truro in the same year, in his *Poems on Several Occasions,* a didactic work in couplets, *Wrestling*. He sketches the rural fair, the strolling peddlers and confectioners, the puppet show, the dance and horse racing, and leads us on to the wrestling ring where squire, priest, doctor, lawyer, and poet, all applaud the country wrestler. Then come his precepts, advice upon training, tactics, and conduct after victory or defeat. He warns the winner against the wanton who seeks his money, the boon companions who lure him to the public house, and the gamester eager for spoil. James knows what he is talking about, a great virtue in a poet, but his rude rhymes are far from the sphere of art, though close to that of authentic realism.

William Hamilton of Bangour, the Scottish poet, intended to write two works in this genre, *The Doves* and *The Flowers;* but in the first he did not get beyond forty lines, and in the second he seems to have finished only about an equal number of introductory lines and an episode of some length for Book I, which he published with the title *The Episode of The Thistle*. These fragments were printed in the Glasgow edition of his poems in 1748. The titles may indicate an intention to follow the lead of Vanière. Hamilton was without the faculty for writing a sustained poem of this kind. *The Doves* never went beyond the statement of theme and a rather graceful dedication. *The Flowers* hardly goes further, if we leave *The Episode* out of account. Both fragments reveal the influence of Thomson in their style, and *The Flowers* echoes his invocation in spring to his love, Amanda, to join him in welcoming the season. *The Episode* includes a panegyric of Scotland and relates a legend of St. Andrew's counsels to the Scots and of the founding of the Order of St. Andrew.

In the first half of the century, Vergilian georgic influence was a constant factor. It appears in John Philips, Swift, Gay, Tickell, King, Thomson, Browne, Somerville, Hamilton of Bangour, and, as we shall see, in Allan Ramsay, Armstrong, and Akenside, as well as in other poets whose names have been forgotten by students of the period. A gradually growing interest is apparent and, after Thomson's time, a trend away from humorous treatment of georgic themes toward a serious effort to utilize them in reflecting English country life.

After 1750 the first poet to write an extensive georgic was Christopher Smart, John Newbery's right-hand man, the tireless Seatonian prize winner and author of the remarkable *Song to David*. *Poems on Several Occasions* (1752) included *The Hop-Garden*, in two books. Smart's native Kent is the setting and the poem reflects the beauties of Kentish places such as Boxley-Hill, the Medway, and the village of Shipbourne (the poet's birthplace). A faintly nostalgic mood permeates the poem, but it does not cause distortion of country life in the direction of idealization. The genre sketches of the hop fields and the recreations of the hop pickers are noteworthy for their realism. The troops of folk coming down to Kent from London for the harvest, the various offices and tasks of the field, are painted faithfully. There is one lively picture of the rude custom among the hop pickers of throwing a youth and maiden together into the hop bin, if they are seen walking out together after sunset.

Smart indicates in footnotes his borrowings from Vergil, notably the description of portents of storm, which he tries to adapt to Kentish conditions in lines like these:

> For as the storm rides on the rising clouds,
> Fly the fleet wild-geese far away, or else
> The heifer towards the zenith rears her head,

And with expanded nostrils snuffs the air;
The swallows too their airy circuits weave,
And screaming skim the brook; and fen-fed frogs
Forth from their hoarse throats their old grutch recite;
Or from her earthly coverlets the ant
Heaves her huge eggs along the narrow way:
Or bends Thaumantia's variegated bow
Athwart the cope of heav'n: or sable crows
Obstreperous of wing, in crouds combine.[8]

Sometimes Vergil's preceptive lines are followed, as in the themes of proper soils and their amelioration. The georgic patriotic panegyric celebrates Kent. Smart tries to catch Vergil's manner in the cumulative similes of the epic tradition, as when his rows of hops are likened to the ranks of a marching host. From Thomson or Philips he probably took the hint for the scientific element in his poem — the description of the aurora borealis or of Hales's invention of the ventilating fan. The genre sketches were probably suggested by Thomson. In a poem for the most part stiff and arid, these pictures of country life are an element of vitality. A love of country scenes and of nature is apparent, too, in the descriptions of Kentish places. These represent the tendency in England to a confusion of genres, introducing elements of the topographical poem, separate in origin, into the georgic. Smart's poem is not an artistic triumph, but it is an interesting document in the growth of taste for nature and for realism of country life. It exemplifies the fact that this growing taste went hand in hand with veneration of Vergil and Thomson, as the favorite literary expressions of it.

Robert Dodsley, the printer ambitious to be a poet, published his georgic, *Agriculture*, in 1753. The fact that Dodsley, who certainly knew the world of books, intended to carry on his project in two further parts, *Commerce* and *Art*, the whole to form an extensive didactic scheme under the general title *Public Virtue*, is evidence of the acceptance this kind of poetry could find and the prestige it could confer. *Agriculture* was praised by such typical figures of the period as Walpole, Shenstone, and Spence. Dodsley imitated a good deal, though by no means slavishly. Vergil and Thomson support his steps. It will be sufficient to indicate a number of his Vergilian themes: the farmer's implements, the happy life of the swain, differing soils and their amelioration, diseases of the flock and their cure, the ideal sire of the flock, the combat of rival animals, types of steed, and the patriotic panegyric. In treating the last of these formulas, Dodsley goes beyond Vergil's outline and Thomson's, celebrating especially the many commercial products of Britain. The poem follows the farmer's " various labours thro' the year," as Bloomfield and Grahame were to do later. A pageant of the seasons appears, each personified with its attendants, in the manner of Thomson. Dodsley, like Thomson, celebrates domestic happiness and love of family. Humanitarianism to animals is here. Science interests him: Dr. Hales's theory of vegetation, the processes of nature's revival, and Jethro Tull's innovations in cultivation, are alike worthy of his muse. There are many detailed genre pictures: farmyard scenes, a repetition of Thomson's sheepwashing and shearing episode, graphic pictures of animals and fowl, farm laborers, dairy scenes, the harvest and the harvest celebration. English commerce is another of his themes; its destinies seem to him to rest on the English flocks. Like Thomson, he rebukes " unfeeling wealth " when the stag hunt tramples the hard-won harvest. There are moral admonitions to frugality, temperance, and industry.

Dodsley is interested in agriculture primarily as " the source of wealth and plenty," rather than, as with Vergil, a source of uncorrupted manners and virtuous living. He addresses landlords and men of wealth turning to the land, rather than the small farmers. The poem owes its existence in part to the agricultural improvements and the new interest in the land, due to men like Jethro Tull and Viscount Townshend. In its enthusiasm for both commerce and agriculture, it is an interesting product of the bourgeois muse, rivaling Dyer's *Fleece* in this respect.

In literary history Dodsley's chief claim to recognition is that, in spite of artistic faults, he is a truthful and enthusiastic poet of country life. He presents a pageant of the rural employments of the year. He is as truthful as Bloomfield, in the full tide of the popularity of rural verse in 1800. Genre sketches, for example, of harvest occupations, shepherds' tasks, the labors of Patty his dairymaid, the house and grounds of the slothful farmer, and the contrasting fields, gardens, and landscapes of a true country gentleman, are far from any affectation. His pleasure in landscape includes both cultivated and uncultivated nature, and he is one of the first poets to contribute to the controversies on landscape gardening, condemning the Dutch taste for straight lines, regularity, and clipped trees, which came to England with William of Orange. He describes

birds and animals with a sharpness untinged by false reticences as
to the dignity of verse.

> See where the farmer, with a master's eye,
> Surveys his little kingdom, and exults
> In sov'reign independence. At a word,
> His feathery subjects in obedience flock
> Around his feeding hand. . . .
> The peacock here expands his eyeful plumes,
> A glittering pageant, to the mid-day sun:
> In the stiff awkwardness of foolish pride,
> The swelling turkey apes his stately step,
> And calls the bristling feathers round his head.
> There the loud herald of the morning struts
> Before his cackling dames, the passive slaves
> Of his promiscuous pleasure. O'er the pond,
> See the grey gander, with his female train,
> Bending their lofty necks; and gabbling ducks,
> Rejoicing on the surface, clap their wings.

In spite of faulty accomplishment, Dodsley deserves a modest
place among writers who reflected country life most truthfully.
Where he borrows, especially from Vergil and Thomson, he is not
slavishly imitative. Truthfulness and enthusiasm shine through the
homely fabric of his style. It is interesting, too, to notice how in the
last pages of his first canto, Dodsley reflects that tendency of his
period to turn from contemplation of the beauty and intricate design of nature, regulated by unchanging law, to praise of deity revealed in its works.

An interesting variant of the georgic form occurs in a number of
poems reflecting colonial settings. The purpose of the authors
seems to have been to attract the attention of Englishmen at home
to colonial matters. The georgic was their natural recourse,
since it was the form traditionally associated with husbandry.
Nathaniel Weekes, with the interests of the empire at heart, appeared with his *Barbados* (1754), an account of the products of
that island and an essay on cultivation of the cane and of tropical
fruits, anticipating Grainger. It is in the Thomsonian blank verse
now established as the usual meter in this genre. It employs stock
devices, adapting old materials to a new setting. The patriotic
panegyric, addressed to Barbados, now takes on tropical colors.
Personal panegyric turns about the island Weekes celebrates.
Amoret and Philander are hero and heroine of a Thomsonian

sentimental tale set in Barbados: she dies because she cannot reveal her love for Philander — a turn which would have pleased Mackenzie. Like Thomson, Weekes delights in meditation, in wandering " creation's boundless space " until he reaches the great Cause of all. There is Thomsonian description of daybreak, Thomsonian praise of sobriety. The traditional genre sketches are given in Barbados colors: a native turtle feast, as a scene of hospitality and pleasure, set against the pictures of labors in the cane fields and the orange and citron groves. The trees, fruits, birds, and fish of the island are described, in an effort to follow the example of georgic poets in reflection of nature and attention to natural history. The poem ends with an appeal to England to protect, encourage, and teach the inhabitants of the island.

We may pause long enough to notice a translation of some importance, George Jeffreys's version of Books I and XIII of Vanière's *Praedium rusticum,* in *Miscellanies* (1754).[9] Jeffreys was a writer of tragedy and a translator. His rendering of Vanière is further evidence of interest in writers reputed to have succeeded in the style of Vergil. It would add nothing to our knowledge of the well-defined traits of the genre to summarize Jeffreys's translation. His concern with Vanière is an interesting phase of the tradition we are following. Vanière was an example of the true *goût jésuite* in poetry, full of reverence for learning and practical knowledge, and convinced of the service verse may render by the decoration of themes of utility. *Praedium rusticum* contains a vast amount of such useful knowledge of nature. The cult of " difficulty vanquished " and the Jesuit revival of Alexandrian taste never produced a more characteristic example than Vanière's. His wide knowledge of nature, displayed, for example, in *The Dove-Cote* of Book XIII, was perhaps due as much to reading as to observation, and Jeffreys's interest in him may have been born of the study rather than of the fields. But his lengthy labor of translation shows the presence of an interest in country life to which he might appeal.

The Scots Magazine for April, 1756,[10] has a review of a poem called *The Complete Marksman,* by Robert Coote, published in 1755. It is obviously an ixeutic, but I have been unable to see it. The magazine gives its readers the benefit of the didactic detail of the poem, but does not indicate whether episodes are used. The poem was reprinted in 1767 without acknowledgment, from the edition of 1755, and without Coote's name on the title-page.[11]

John Dyer in 1757 published *The Fleece,* a georgic which has been widely praised. Wordsworth ranked Dyer high. In a letter to Lady Beaumont (November 20, 1811) he said, "In point of imagination and purity of style, I am not sure that he is not superior to any writer in verse since the time of Milton." Wordsworth praised him also in the postscript to the Duddon sonnets, wrote a sonnet to the "Bard of the Fleece," and praised him again in a letter to Dyce.[12] Akenside held *The Fleece* in high esteem. *The Monthly Review* and *The Critical Review* praised it.[13] Joseph Warton, in his essay on Pope, ranks Dyer high. Scott of Amwell calls *The Fleece* "the noblest of didactic poems." [14] Nathan Drake wrote an elaborate essay *On The Fleece of Dyer,* to dispose of Dr. Johnson's objections to it in *The Lives of the Poets.*[15] Gray thought highly of Dyer and voiced his praise in a letter to Walpole.[16] *The Fleece* was often reprinted after 1757 in editions of Dyer's works and in such collections as those of Anderson, Bell, Johnson, and others.

The poem is written with the purpose of connecting the subject with the glory of Britain. Dyer exalts the fleece and trade in general; he tries to surround his subject with associations of poetry, worth, and grandeur, to give to labor something of the dignity lent it by Vergil, and to trade a glory commensurate with its place as the basis of British prosperity. It is the bourgeois muse again, but Dyer is a better poet than Dodsley. He might have taken his text from that passage in *Summer* where, after speaking of the flocks, Thomson says:

> A simple scene! Yet here Britannia sees
> Her solid grandeur rise: hence she commands
> The exalted stores of every brighter clime,
> The treasures of the sun without his rage:
> Hence, fervent all with culture, toil, and arts,
> Wide glows her land! her dreadful thunder hence
> Rides o'er the waves sublime.

Dyer's outline, like Dodsley's is chronological. He leads the reader from the choice of pastures for flocks, through the care of the sheep, their shearing, the uses of wool and the making of cloth, to the exporting of British fabrics and to an account of their conquests on the Mediterranean, in Russia, the Indies, Africa, the Orient, and the Americas. The chief debt to Vergil is in the first two books. In the didactic parts of the poem, such themes as these follow Vergil's model: the various soils suited to various kinds of flocks (as to various crops, herds, and flocks in Vergil) , citation of such localities, repairing the faults of soils, suiting the breed to soil and climate, the ideal sire of the flocks, diseases and cures, care of the young, and treatment of the flocks in winter. In his episodes there are the patriotic panegyric (like Thomson's and Dodsley's, emphasizing trade and commerce) , the sway of Venus among these lower animals, the battle of the rival rams, the portents of fair and of stormy weather, the exotic digressions (the shepherds of remote lands, as in Vergil) , the happy swain, glorifications of industry, and the rise and progress of the crafts of the shepherd and the weaver. Many of these themes were used by Thomson, amplifying Vergil, and Dyer's work shows both influences. More directly Thomsonian are the emphasis on benevolence and philanthropy, the interest in contemporary scientific speculation, and the frequent genre pictures of peasants and workers. The "excursions of fancy," still another northern-winter piece and torrid-zone picture, show the effects of Thomson's example as well as Dyer's own recognized descriptive ability.

Dyer seems to be the first poet of the century to attempt the difficult task of putting into verse descriptions of industrial processes and manufacturing. In Book III he shows the stages by which cloth is made. Book IV, in what seeks to be an epical celebration of commerce, carries the fleece into all parts of the world. It is not only a phase of husbandry but also the chief British development of the industrial revolution, and British economic supremacy in general, which Dyer tries to bring within the province of poetry. It is as if an American of our day were to attempt to create an epic of the motor age, except that he would have no accepted form ready to his hand. Dyer's real failure lies, of course, in the impossible attempt to accommodate the industrial and agricultural England of the 1750's to a literary form of the age of Augustus Caesar; he lacked the power to mold a new form. Few poems in English express so many aspects of their period, however, and few poets perhaps could have hoped for even so much success as Dyer achieved in so grandiose a plan.

One of Dyer's merits, however, has nothing to do with the scope of his plan. He is a poet of the country who writes of honest realities, though never with the simple eloquence of *Grongar Hill*. His genre sketches of peasants and workers, the whole tone of his representation of country life, are realistic. His love of landscape and his ability to describe it, both reflecting his practice as a painter, remain strong. And there are casual bits of sharp observation which show that Dyer merited praise from Wordsworth. Even his precepts sometimes carry an accent of poetry:

> When many-colour'd evening sinks behind
> The purple woods and hills, and opposite
> Rises, full orb'd, the silver harvest moon,
> To light the unwearied farmer, late afield
> His scatter'd sheaves collecting, then expect
> The artists, bent on speed, from populous Leeds,
> Norwich, or Froome; they traverse every plain
> And every dale where farm or cottage smokes:
> Reject them not; and let the season's price
> Win thy soft treasures: let the bulky wain
> Through dusty roads roll nodding; or the bark
> That silently adown the cerule stream
> Glides with white sails, dispense the downy freight
> To copsy villages on either side,
> And spiry towns, where ready Diligence,
> The grateful burden to receive, awaits,
> Like strong Briareus, with his hundred hands.

The description of scenes of " busy Leeds " has unusual interest. And Dyer's vision, not so dubious then as now, of enlightenment, harmony, and civilization following trade over all the habitable earth, is expressed with vigor.

From Dyer's large plan to a humble poem on angling is a violent transition. Further, too, from the orthodox form is the series of eclogues, partly didactic, in couplets, by Thomas Scott, *The Angler's Eight Dialogues in Verse* (1758). These were later pirated by Thomas Lathy in his *Angler*.[17] Ruddiman gave them further currency in his *Collection of Scarce, Curious, and Valuable Pieces* (1773). Besides traits of didactic forms, preceptive verse and data on the habits of fish, these dialogues include local description (of English rivers), mingling at least three genres, the fisherman's idyll, the didactic, and the loco-descriptive poem. Scott evidently knew the Oppianic *Halieutica*. Such themes as the gear of the angler, the suitable seasons, deep-sea fishing, the fierce discord and predatory cycle of life in the waters of the earth, besides the details of natural history, all suggest Oppian, though Walton is obviously Scott's primary source. The scientific data suggest a growing taste for the naturalist's detail. Scott writes as a realist, with genre sketches of his English countryside pastimes and even incidents such as the punishment of a poacher. There are reminiscences of Thomson: the man led astray by marsh lights on the fen, seasonal phenomena, and perhaps some details of a description of winter storm. The eclogues, in setting, follow the progress of the seasons. Scott shows evidence of an eye for nature, but his poetic talent is slight.

An ambitious successor to Weekes's *Barbados*, James Grainger's *Sugar Cane*, appeared in 1764. The island of St. Christopher is the setting: this is a " West India Georgic." Like Weekes, Grainger wanted to exalt the island he celebrated, as a part of the growing empire. The echoes of georgic conventions are many. Though there must have seemed to be much novelty in the *Sugar Cane* because of its exotic setting, its novelty is in the adaptation of familiar themes to that setting. Even here Grainger may have had the suggestion of Weekes's example. To indicate the method of Grainger's adaptation will suffice. Varieties and uses of soils and differing treatments of differing soils, seasons for planting, combating the enemies of the crops, diseases and cures (of slaves here), are among the didactic themes paralleling Vergil's content and manner. The detailed discussion of the care of slaves introduces new material under the guise of an old convention of the form. There is patriotic panegyric — applied to St. Christopher. " Not Grecian Tempe. . . . Not purple Enna . . . can vie, bless'd isle, with thee " — and so on. The portents of rain become those of tropical storm and hurricane. The Corycian swain becomes Grainger's " good Montano." There are several pictures of pestilence: the " blast " in the cane, a locust swarm. Thomson, too, supplies many hints. There is the story of Junio and Theana — she is struck by lightning and dies in his arms; he too dies. There is Thomson's habit of scientific explanation and speculation. There is the note of humanitarianism — urged concerning both animals and men, especially slaves. Grainger seems even to have used Thomson's lavish colors in the torrid-zone picture in *Summer*, as a basis for such sketches as the tropical calm, the earthquake, the hurricane. There are many genre pictures of native life, of some interest. His allegory of the coming of winter is suggested by Thomson. There is the glorification of commerce and trade. One smiles at the introduction of pagan deities and nymphs into St. Christopher, at the perpetual euphemisms, and at the diction which brings Miltonic adaptation to a nadir. Grainger's taste, too, was bad enough to allow the most violent incongruities.

But he enjoyed some prestige as a result of his poem, and his friend Doctor Johnson aided in a commendatory notice for *The London Chronicle*.[18] As Boswell relates, Johnson gave a more forthright estimate of the work in private conversation.[19] *The Critical Review* gave the poem very high praise.[20] *The Scots Magazine* thought highly enough of the tale of Junio and Theana to reprint it in July, 1764. The element of exotic description recommended the poem to many. There are frequent notations of tropical trees, plants, insects, animals, as well as the pictures of landscapes, tropical calm, fire in the cane, earthquake, waterspouts, tidal wave, and hurricane. Grainger tries to appeal to many tastes: to the love of travel literature and exotic scenery, to taste for natural history, to interest in colonial expansion and in the growth of trade and commerce.

William Stevenson, a friend of Dr. Young, to whom his *Vertumnus* is dedicated, published his *Original Poems* in two volumes in 1765. His Thomsonian *Vertumnus* is his longest poem, but there is also the interesting *Rural Sports* in three parts, *Angling, Fowling*, and *Hare-Hunting*.[21] He writes in the elegaic quatrains of Gray and uses both preceptive and descriptive methods, mainly the latter. Like so many of the gentry devoted to country sports, this poet is at odds with himself as both humanitarian and sportsman. He approves of angling, though he abhors the use of living bait and of nets, and he disapproves of fowling and hare hunting. He, too, urges hunters to seek out the fox, the "arch thief," and punish him. But his description of the hare chase is the most lively part of the whole poem. As a poet, Stevenson is unpretentious here and, like many of his brothers in this genre of verse, has a real delight in scenes of nature. There is nothing comparable to the sometimes notable description in *Vertumnus,* but the same impulse is present.

Grainger's example in the poetry of the West Indies was soon followed by John Singleton in *A General Description of the West Indian Islands* (1767). While largely descriptive, the poem belongs here because it uses georgic conventions in dealing with a primarily didactic theme. Desiring to call attention to the importance of the West Indies, Singleton indicates in a survey of the islands their plants, crops, fruits, vegetation, and other resources. He invokes the muse which inspired "tuneful Grainger, nurs'd in Fancy's arms." There are some interesting pictures: an Indian "barbeque," Indian rural sports, wreckers and pirates near the Virgin Islands, a negro burial. The spout and "animal flowers" are

" philosophically described," with that scientific interest characteristic of the genre. Landscape attracts him, especially striking scenes
like the " vale of sulphur " at Montserrat and the dangerous reefs
at Anegada. Perhaps he recalls Grainger's words:

> Doth the love of Nature charm;
> Its mighty love your chief attention claim?
> Leave Europe; there, through all her coyest ways,
> Her secret mazes, Nature is pursued:
> But here, with savage loneliness, she reigns
> On yonder peak, whence giddy Fancy looks,
> Affrighted on the labouring main below.

But he follows conventional themes: praise of the " happy swain,"
Thomsonian tales like that of Aurelia and Philander, humanitarian
exhortations (like Grainger's, deprecating slavery) , a storm which
recalls Thomson's summer storm in its details. Like Grainger's,
Singleton's verse is too overladen with conventionality and imitation to have much merit.

The popular ixeutic vein reappears in Francis Fawkes's *Par-
tridge-Shooting* (1767) . It is relatively short and is descriptive in
manner. Sometimes this description has the virtue of vividness.
Fawkes shares with other poets of field sports, most of them writers
who lay no claim to more than a very minor place, an enthusiasm
for the country and for the sport they love, which often conveys
pleasure and rewards the reader.

Two poems, one important and one unimportant, may be mentioned in passing. Henry Jones's *Clifton* (1767) and Richard Jago's
Edge-Hill (1767) illustrate the tendency to mix poetic genres when
description and didacticism meet. Both poems describe places. But
Clifton includes advice on the new English style in landscape gardening in a poem otherwise in the vein of Pope's *Windsor Forest*.
And *Edge-Hill* not only includes didactic lines on gardening, the
finding of coal, and the process of mining, but leans very heavily
on the themes of Vergil and Thomson. *Edge-Hill* is important in
the development of the prolific school of local verse, and must be
spoken of later in that connection. Here it is enough to indicate
the overlapping of didactic and local poetry in these two examples
published in the same year. The occurrence of precepts of a georgic
cast was fairly common in both local verse and other descriptive
poetry.

The growing reaction in landscape gardening against the geometrical French manner and in favor of a new and freer English

style is shown in an anonymous poem, *The Rise and Progress of the Present Taste in Planting Parks, Pleasure Grounds, Gardens, &c.* (1767).[22] It is a " poetic epistle " in heroic couplets and has in common with the georgic tradition only the fact that it gives precepts in the technique of gardening. It attempts to trace the following of nature away from restrictions of formal art, beginning from the reign of Henry VIII, showing King William's introduction of a Belgian style at Hampton Court and coming finally to " Capability " Brown's triumphs at Blenheim Castle, Croome, and other estates. It is a valuable document of its period and an interesting anticipation of William Mason's georgic.

It is difficult to classify John Aldington's curious *Poem on the Cruelty of Shooting* (1769). Its aim is humanitarian, an attack upon fowling and the chase. It is an answer to such poems as Somervile's, which glorify " the sylvan war." Yet it describes the shooting of partridge, hare, quail, woodcock, and other game. The scenes of shooting are described, and the seasonal conditions under which different game is shot. Aldington writes blank verse, but if he finds a hexameter or a trimeter line convenient, he uses it, and his sense of meter is lame. He illustrates again the use of Thomson's pictures as originals upon which to elaborate. There is, for example, the picture of the thrush grieving for her mate, shot by the hunter; the traveler led astray by vapors and plunged into a gulf; the account of millions of tiny beings, invisible under the microscope, which exist " on every green ting'd leaf "; and the pictures of the peasant watching the flood carry away his herds, cottage, and implements, and of the wolves preying on man and beast, even on the graves of men.

William Mason, the friend of Gray, published his *English Garden* between 1772 and 1782.[23] This poem has unusual interest for all students of eighteenth-century taste,[24] not only as a poem, but as a statement of the new principles which had come to govern appreciation of beauty of landscape. Briefly, it represents the reaction against the geometrical French manner of Le Nôtre and La Quintinie, seen in its highest development at Versailles. Kent, Southcote, the originator of the *ferme orné,* and Brown,[25] the new apostles of simplicity and nature, are Mason's guides. It would be pleasant, but aside from our purpose, to show how Mason tried to reduce to a system the practice of these men. His principles are " picturesque " in the sense that they derive from landscape painting. His fundamental idea is that gardening should employ a " well chosen

variety of curves " instead of " the symmetry of right lines " which
is the law of architectural beauty. The French and Dutch tastes in
arrangement of grounds followed the latter law and were therefore
erroneous. Poussin and Claude Lorraine followed opposite principles and were true painters of nature. The French poet Saint-
Lambert, in his *Saisons,* had already employed this contrast between architectural and picturesque principles.[26] Mason turns
often to scenes which sanction his principles of simplicity and
curvilinear fluidity. There is much description of nature, cultivated and even uncultivated, in the poem. Mason, like Gray, had
a good deal of minute knowledge. His nearest approaches to poetry,
however, are in lines on " picturesque " landscape:

> [To Time] the praise is due: his gradual touch
> Has moulder'd into beauty many a tower,
> Which, when it frown'd with all its battlements,
> Was only terrible; and many a fane
> Monastic, which, when deck'd with all its spires,
> Served but to feed some pamper'd abbott's pride. . . .
> Happy art thou if thou canst call thine own
> Such scenes as these: where Nature and where Time
> Have work'd congenial; where a scatter'd host
> Of antique oaks darken thy sidelong hills;
> While, rushing through their branches, rifted cliffs
> Dart their white heads, and glitter through the gloom.
> More happy still, if one superior rock
> Bear on its brow the shiver'd fragment huge
> Of some old Norman fortress; happier far,
> Ah, then most happy, if thy vale below
> Wash, with the crystal coolness of its rills,
> Some mouldering abbey's ivy-vested wall.

As a georgic, Mason's poem is relatively original. His blank verse
is of the now-hackneyed Miltonic cast, given wide currency by
Thomson, but it is relatively flowing and free from the usual excessive inversions and Latinisms. Its dominant quality is a fluent
monotony. Mason does not draw on Vergil or Thomson heavily.
There is a narrative episode of Alcander and Nerina, of the sentimental cast made popular by Thomson in poetry with a country
setting — Alcander is an enthusiastic " improver " with the orthodox tastes in landscape. Mason was not felicitous in narrative; his
story is an easy target for ridicule. There are moral and descriptive
bits of episode. An interesting detail at the close of Book III is

Mason's elaboration, in rather crude form, of the idea of moral influence emanating from nature upon the mind of man. He says, for example,

> O let reverence lead to love,
> And both to emulation! Not a rill
> That winds its sparkling current o'er the plain,
> Reflecting to the Sun bright recompense
> For ev'ry beam he lends, but reads thy soul
> A generous lecture. Not a pansy pale,
> That drinks its daily nurture from that rill
> But breathes in fragrant accents to thy soul.

Mason seems to have read *The Rise and Progress of the Present Taste,* the anonymous poem of 1767, for in Book I he traces in a similar way the growth of more natural tendencies. Like the author of that poem, he praises Milton for the description of the Garden of Eden, censures Temple's taste for geometric regularity, and finds in Brown the culmination of English purity of style. On the whole, however, Mason is not very derivative and he does achieve a certain grace and ease. He showed that a georgic could be written successfully without undue dependence on the obvious models which served so many of his predecessors. *The English Garden* enjoyed a wide reputation in its time: it was often reprinted both separately and in the editions of Mason's collected verse.

Nathaniel Tucker's *Bermudian* (1774) is a curious hybrid, including elements of the colonial georgic of the type written by Weekes or Grainger, and of Goldsmithian autobiography from *The Deserted Village*. Tucker seems to be writing after leaving Bermuda, and to be describing it and his early life there through a sentimental haze. The work is poetically valueless.

From the mid-century to 1775, the history of the didactic tradition shows a decidedly increased interest in the type. Established poets and ambitious tyros are equally anxious to make their mark in the genre. Thomson and Vergil continue to exert a joint influence. The scope given to description of nature and to descriptive genre sketches of country occupations by poets like Smart, Dodsley, Weekes, Dyer, Stevenson, Grainger, and Mason, indicates an interest in nature and in country life which is neither slight nor perfunctory.

The didactic impulse did not wane before the end of the century. Rather, it increased. Cowper added the impetus of his example, and Erasmus Darwin was extravagantly praised. The stimulation of popular interest in science was an important factor, since it increased interest in nature. Without this popular interest, the poems of Darwin and his imitators and the extravagant projects of John Evans and William Tighe would never have been undertaken. Since this interest had a closer bearing on the development of descriptive poetry, discussion of it is more pertinent in the next chapter. But some evidences of it may be glanced at here in passing: the growth of public museums such as the British Museum, Tradescant's museum in South Lambeth, and the museum of the Royal Society; [27] the collections of botanical, zoölogical, and geological specimens in the public libraries of the period; the "museums of curiosities" which were so often added attractions at the coffeehouses; the growth of such botanic gardens as those at Kew, Cambridge, and Oxford; the demand for works of scientific popularization, shown by the compilation of partial lists of the publications of the Dodsleys [28] and especially of Newbery; [29] the success of such works of popularization as *Martin's Magazine* (1755–64) [30] and of such popularizers as Dr. John Hill. We shall return in more detail to this subject below.

Perhaps we may group together here three poems of that genre of colonial georgic developed by Weekes, Grainger, and Singleton: the anonymous *Jamaica* (1777), George Heriot's *Descriptive Poem, Written in the West Indies* (1781), and Samuel Whitchurch's *Hispaniola* (1804). *Jamaica* is in three parts and mingles exotic description, practical didacticism, and genre sketches of native employments. There are conventional episodes such as the patriotic panegyric and pleas for humanitarianism — especially in the treatment of slaves. George Heriot's poem is better, at least in conception. It is inscribed to the Royal Society and tries to present in a way calculated to appeal to virtuosi the phenomena of climate, vegetation, and bird, insect, and animal life in the West Indies. But the most colorful exotic creatures — flamingo, parrakeet, pelican, humming bird, certain species of iridescent fish, and many more — are described in a blank verse exact and faithful perhaps, but quite prosaic. Heriot makes a sincere effort to present new imagery and new themes of description and exposition, but cannot rise beyond the dull level of his style. Whitchurch's *Hispaniola* is a picture of Hayti and San Domingo, describing scenes and native life. It is written in a rhymed stanza of six lines, and has little interest beyond its approximation in general plan to the formulas of didactic-descriptive poetry.

John Scott of Amwell, in his *Amoeboean Eclogues* (1782), continued the didactic-eclogue type already used by Moses Browne and Thomas Scott. The second eclogue, *Rural Business: or, the Agriculturalists,* is based on the farmer's occupations in the four seasons of the year. It gives precepts, in dialogue, on improvement of soil, draining, rotation of crops, plants suited to various types of soil, soils proper to pasturage, the labors of the orchard, and the duties of the farmer in winter. The eclogue then continues with advice to the fortunate to aid the poor, and to consider kindly the tired laborer and beast. Praise of Hesiod, Theocritus, and Vergil, poets of the land, concludes the bald performance. Scott tried to compress into a single eclogue matter enough for a dozen such poems. The typical fault of didactic poets is not undue compression but diffuseness.

Scott's first eclogue, *Rural Scenery; or, the Describers,* is descriptive of nature, the two parts forming a panorama of country scenes and occupations. Scott says in his introduction:

Much of the rural imagery which our country affords, has already been introduced in poetry, but many obvious and pleasing appearances seem to have totally escaped notice. To describe these is the business of the following Eclogues.

No poem of the period is better calculated to show the taste for rural verse. Throughout, Scott is content with much the same kind of catalogue method he uses in Eclogue II. Merely to amass his notations of country scenes and labors seems to him enough. It is as if he turned a notebook of observations into couplets. In winter

> These pollard oaks their tawny leaves retain,
> These hardy hornbeams yet unstripped remain;
> The wint'ry groves all else admit the view
> Through naked stems of many a varied hue.

In the spring

> In shady lanes red foxglove bells appear
> And golden spikes the downy mulleins rear.

Such lines are characteristic. Scott was a botanist and a systematic observer. He seems to have believed that exact observation was in itself poetic. Both eclogues have their botanical footnotes. Scott's reputation depended especially on his pleasing local poem *Amwell,* in which his faculty of observation has more scope. He was accepted as a representative poet of his period by editors of collections of British poets, and was included in the series of Anderson,

Park, Chalmers, Pratt, Sanford, and Davenport. Hoole wrote an appreciative account of his life and writings.[31] In some ways, Scott's verse reminds one of that written by Gilbert White of Selborne. Both men are keen observers, they have the same pleasure in nature, but neither approached a style which might have given authenticity to his verse.

So we come to William Cowper, who includes in *The Task* (1785) a gardening georgic, his Book III. But Cowper's debt to the didactic-descriptive tradition does not end with one book of *The Task*. He took from it more than any analysis of direct indebtedness could show. The loose discursiveness which was Cowper's native vein was prepared for, at least in part, by the didactic-descriptive tradition which sanctioned, by ancient and modern example, a type of poem admitting moral, descriptive, narrative, scientific, preceptive, and other matter, grouped about a central theme. In *The Task* Cowper gave free rein to his discursive tendency and justified his freedom in the success of his loose development by association of ideas. *The Task,* like *The Seasons,* is mainly descriptive and will be discussed with poems of that cast. In many ways Cowper is the direct descendant of Thomson. Their ideas, their temperaments, their interests, their abilities, had much in common. But the tendencies Thomson represents had been developed by almost sixty years of exploitation before Cowper's *Task* appeared.

The Garden, Book III of *The Task,* does not enter at once on its didactic theme. For some four hundred lines, autobiography, praises of retirement, and humanitarian sentiment are the subjects. Modeling after conventional usage in the georgic, Cowper then gives advice on pruning trees, cultivating cucumbers, and planting and caring for flowers. There follows another long passage, equally traditional, praising the happy life of the man of the country, contrasted with lives of vanity and misery in London, and an attack on the owners of country estates who spend enormous sums upon "improvements." "Capability" Brown fares worse than he did with Mason, because for Cowper he represents extravagance and the restless spirit of fickle fashion. Cowper's georgic has those merits of ease and vividness which have made *The Task* an enduring and popular poem, a classic of the second order.

The country parson William Greenwood contributed to the verse of field sports his *Poem written during a Shooting Excursion on the Moors* (1787). He leans heavily on Thomson and Somervile. Precepts are varied with episodes on the rise and progress of hunting (Somervile had traced the origin of the chase), personal panegyric, short "excursions of fancy" to the southern seas and polar regions, description of the power of instinct and of the migrations of the birds (elements of natural history), pictures of sunset, and so on. The poet is unpretentious and his spirited manner has some modest merit.

In 1789, from the office of a physician of Lichfield, came one of the most astonishing productions of the age or of any age. Erasmus Darwin's *Loves of the Plants*, Part II of *The Botanic Garden*, appeared in that year, followed in 1791 by Part I, *The Economy of Vegetation*. *The Temple of Nature* appeared in 1803. All three may be spoken of together here. The popular success of these poems is surprising only if we forget the popular interest in natural history, which was reaching its height. Horace Walpole said, " Dr. Darwin has destroyed my admiration for any poetry but his own." Cowper and Hayley thought him a very considerable poet.[32]

In *The Botanic Garden* Darwin shows slight indebtedness to predecessors. He had an inexhaustible inventiveness. He could hardly have originated those extensive didactic plans without the example of the georgic poets, but he owes them little that is fundamental. The liberty of digression to reflection on philanthropy, human slavery, and other topics; the freedom of panegyric of personal friends, scientists, and navigators — these are features of the loose organization common to didactic verse. So are the narratives appealing to "sensibility." Darwin sometimes indicates the technique of processes — the strangulation of branches to produce flower buds, ingrafting, driving insects from trees, the methods of cotton spinning. There are reminiscences of earlier themes, like those in the account of " portents of the storm," in the catalogue of rivers flowing from the Alps, and in the picture of marsh lights leading travelers astray. But the debt is slight.

In poets like Henry Brooke (*Universal Beauty*) and Blackmore (*Creation*) it is impossible to see models for Darwin. His form is unlike theirs; and where they were theologians seeking evidences of divine design, he is a scientific investigator seeking sources of organic properties — sources originating within the organisms themselves.

There were other poets who had written of physical science. Many of these wrote in the physico-theological vein. But Henry Baker, Samuel Boyse, Beville Higgons, Moses Browne, Capel Lofft,

Joseph Wise, and other poets of " natural revelation "[33] had little effect on Darwin. Others, interested in science for its own sake, apparently did not influence him. The expositors of the Newtonian system, men like Desaguliers, Richard Glover, and James Thomson;[34] the poets of " philosophy " in various branches, men like Akenside, Henry Jones, and John Walters,[35] had no important influence on him, except for the possibility that he had Akenside's *Hymn to the Naiads* in mind in his addresses to the nymphs of fire, the gnomes of earth, the nymphs of water, and the sylphs of air, basic elements of the design of *The Economy of Vegetation*. French poets of natural science, the Souciet of *Les Comètes,* the Le Coédic of *Le Monde de Descartes,* and preceding *poésie scientifique,*[36] so far as the present writer knows it, gave little to Darwin. One central idea he may have borrowed from the French. In *L'Agriculture* (1774–82) Rosset had extended the old Vergilian theme of the " sway of Venus in the lower world " to include the vegetable kingdom, making use of the "sexual system of plants." This occurs in Chant IV of the 1774 edition and is amplified again in the Second Partie, Chant I of 1782. His idea later attracted Vincent Campenon, whose *Maison des Champs* also celebrates " *l'hymen des fleurs et leurs chastes amours.*" Campenon wrote too late to influence Darwin, but the central idea of *The Loves of the Plants* may have come from Rosset. A minor detail in Darwin also suggests French influence, his interest in Greek mythology as the glorification of natural forces. Diderot and members of *L'Académie des Inscriptions,* Fréret and Sainte-Croix,[37] had worked on the origins of cults of Greek mythology and on the philosophy of the pagan mysteries. *Du Culte des dieux fétiches* (1760) of de Brosses is a synthesis on this subject. But on the whole, Darwin is a poet of unusual, if idiosyncratic, originality. He took only scattered hints from others. He was of ingenuity all compact — ingenious rather than imaginative. It is this fact which explains the early success of his novel verse and its later total eclipse.

He outdoes all predecessors; none had ever tried to put into verse such minutiae of scientific technicality before: the sexual system of plants; the generation of phosphoric acid in the blood; expansion and condensation of air; the formation of limestone, calcareous spar, white marble, nitre, flint, onyx, and the metals; Lavoisier's discovery that water is not a simple element; the lacteal system; the invention of barometer, air pump, balloon, and steam engine; the stages of plant growth; and the specific uses of many plants in materia medica. His poems are too easily available to require detailed analysis of his poetic form, that heterogeneous mingling of science and personification, varied by elaborated similies from mythology, natural history, plastic art, literature, and miscellaneous erudition. One cannot read *The Botanic Garden* without a kind of admiration for the eccentric, prolific, ingenious mind that produced it. On the old principle of " difficulty overcome," there is much that is impressive. The versification of so much learning, especially in science, the occasionally compact statement of factual knowledge in popular terms, is not to be treated with condescension. But as poetry it is a colossal, often a ludicrous, failure. No doubt Darwin could have gone on forever turning out these artificial couplets, so closely patterned on Pope's, cadence by cadence, phrase by phrase; but his fecundity is without poetic vitality, sterile of life. His temple of nature is a palace of ice, its shimmer merely counterfeiting warmth. His botanic garden is finally a monstrosity in wax, the sapless foliage of mere ingenuity. One wonders how conscious that extraordinary mind was of its own deficiencies. At any rate, he wrote to his friend Watt: " As the Loves of the Plants pays me well, and as I write for pay, not for fame, I intend to publish The Economy of Vegetation in the spring." [38]

In *The Temple of Nature* a rough similarity to Lucretius is obvious in a considerable part of the plan. It traces the life principle from its creation to its complex organization in the body and mind of man. A philosophy of the creation of life, a presentation of the reproductive principle, an account of faculties of sense and mind, are present in both, though they differ as the poles. There are incidental resemblances also, as in the description of the effects of jealousy,[39] or of the effects of the mating urge in the animal kingdom [40] (the latter closer to Vergil than to Lucretius). But on the whole, as in earlier poems, Darwin's idiosyncratic originality is obvious, and his debt is slight. Those interested in Darwin's anticipation of evolutionary theories of his grandson Charles Darwin, will find *The Temple of Nature* his most rewarding poem. Artistically it is open to the same criticisms as the earlier work: prosodic imitativeness and monotony, frigid intellectualism, rococo over-ornamentation, all of them symptoms of that malady of ingenuity perverted by arrested development in taste. It is in *The Temple of Nature*, however, that one finds the best expression in verse of Darwin's religious ideas, a " religion of nature " in the sense that the testimony of the physical universe establishes for him the necessity of a Deity as the " Cause of Causes." Design establishes the presence of mind and meaning in the universe. The powers of organic evolution and the physical processes are impressed upon the universe by the " Great First Cause " existing in nature as the embodiment of " firm, immutable, immortal laws."

Darwin's poetry was attacked in the *Anti-Jacobin* parody, *The Loves of the Triangles,* in 1798. As parody this is excellent, but Darwin attracted the fire of the review primarily because he was a Whig, a correspondent of Rousseau, and a sympathizer with the French Revolution, a sympathy freely expressed in his verse. Ellis, Canning, Gifford, and Frere all seem to have had a hand in the parody.[41] The poem is headed *The Loves of the Triangles. A Mathematical and Philosophical Poem. Inscribed to Dr. Darwin.*[42] It exaggerates ludicrously his use of the imagery of love, his figures of speech drawn from incongruous sources, his pedantry, his versification, his inflated vocabulary, his notes, his mannerisms of style. An " exact versification of Euclid's fifth theorem "; the romance of Rectangle, whose love is requited by three curves, Parabola, Hyperbola, and Ellipsis; the invocation to Cissoids, Conchoids, Pendules, Cycloids, and Hydrostatics, rather than to the Muses; the promise of a future poem, *The Algebraic Garden,* to present " the picturesque imagery of the theory of Fluxions " and in which " the Fluents are described as rolling with an even current between a margin of curves of the higher order, over a pebbly channel inlaid with Differential Calculi " — these are among the engaging conceits of a masterly parody. However exaggerated, it often hits off the worst faults of Darwin's manner. Whether it tended to discourage the writing of didactic verse is another question. There is no evidence that it did.

The voluminous editor, compiler, and critic John Aikin, who advised the descriptive poets to turn to natural history,[43] published a small volume of verse, *Poems* (1791). He did not attempt to follow his own advice in a descriptive poem. But his *Picturesque*[44] attacks a restricted conception of beauty in landscape, and belongs with poems of William Mason and Richard Payne Knight among the approaches to theory of landscape gardening and appreciation of nature, though it is not, like them, a formal georgic. William Gilpin and Uvedale Price differed in their understanding of the term " picturesque." [45] For Gilpin it meant " suitable for painting," and he toured Britain seeking scenes adapted for brush and pencil. For Price the term meant irregularity, sudden variation,

roughness in form, color, and lighting. It was Gilpin's idea which
Aikin attacked.

>   Whatever scene,
>   Gay, rich, sublime, stupendous, wide or wild,
>   Disdains the bounds of canvas, nor supplies
>   Foreground and background, keeping, light and shade,
>   To aid the pencil's power; contracts the brow,
>   And curls the nose of Taste's great arbiter,
>   Too learned far to feel a vulgar joy.

Aikin disagrees with the " prospect-critic " whose " half-shut eye "
sees nature amiss. He seeks more just principles. We should expect
him to come, as he does, to the conclusion that *all* of nature is good,
and to scorn the distinctions of theorists. Aikin's training was literary and his great enthusiasm was Thomson, in whom he found a
universal harmony upheld, and in whom he found a strong belief
in the influence of nature on the soul of man. He exclaims,

>   And is it thus the handmaid Art presumes
>   To rule her mistress? thus could she confine
>   The Maker's hand to suit the copyist's skill?
>   In Nature all is fair — or, if ungrac'd
>   With flowing form and harmony of hues,
>   Yet by the force of some associate charm,
>   Some touch sublime, or contrast's magic power,
>   It awes, expands, delights, or melts the soul.

He adds descriptions which illustrate the attraction of all scenes
whether strictly " picturesque " or not, and, in one of his notes,
decries the false fastidiousness which may lead away " from the
perception of those beauties of a superior order which charm the
simpler lover of the country."

In the *Poetical Works* of Henry Brooke (1792), edited by his
daughter, appears a rather animated poem, *The Fox Chase*,[46] which
belongs to the line of Somervile's offshoots. Brooke was long well
known for his *Universal Beauty*. The present poem is much less
ambitious and seems not to have been highly valued by the poet.
His daughter says it is " first printed in the present edition," though
this is the third collected edition of Brooke's work. It has the merit
of spirited description, both of the chase and of the background of
nature, and lacks the more pretentious rhetoric of Brooke's characteristic manner in verse.

Richard Payne Knight's *Landscape* (1794) illustrates again the
tendency to elaborate schemes in didactic poetry. *The Quarterly*

Review called Knight "arbiter of fashionable vertu." [47] His London house in Soho Square was filled with treasures. His collections of bronzes, coins, gems, drawings by Claude Lorraine, and other works of art, when finally bequeathed to the British Museum, enriched it greatly. He interested himself in improving his estate at Downton, Herefordshire, according to his own plans. His *Landscape* was written in direct opposition to the methods practiced by "Capability" Brown and praised by Mason in *The English Garden*. Uvedale Price and Salvator Rosa are more to Knight's taste. The rugged grandeur and romantic wildness and irregularity advocated by Price and painted by Salvator Rosa, carried Knight beyond the more restricted freedom of Brown and Mason. Brown's regulated curves, balanced clumps, and "banks close shaven" arouse Knight's indignation. He loves gloomy overhanging thickets of intricate woods, ivy-hung ruins and walls mellowed by time, romantic caverns, the quarry overhanging beds of stone, the aged oak, vine-covered elms. His first book concerns the mansion and its approach; the second, effects of light and shade; the third, the use and disposition of trees, vines, and flowers. In his own "improvements" at Downton, Knight had tried to produce the effect of wild and romantic intricacy which Hobbema and Salvator Rosa loved. He believed in the importance of "counterfeit neglect" and defended this conception against the less daring theories of Price and Humphrey Repton.[48] *The Landscape* is full of notations of scenery of the irregular, romantic sort, and Knight had, of course, a large fund of knowledge and observation of nature.

Knight falls back on didactic tradition far more than Mason did. He renounces "ambition's vain delusive joys" and hopes to close his life "amidst books and solitude" in contemplative ease. He traces the rise and progress of art, adapting an old Lucretian theme. He has his conventional patriotic panegyric, celebrating especially the beauties of English nature. There is a picture of the northern lands of "annual night" and "annual day," much in the vein of Thomson, and of the dreary winters of Kamchatka. The beauties of other lands, seen by their painters, by Teniers, van de Velde, and Rembrandt, are celebrated. He closes with a statement of faith in a universal harmony, in which evil is apparent, not real,

> And partial ill, if rightly understood,
> Is oft redundancy of gen'ral good.

Knight tried to do too many things ever to be an accomplished poet, but he was a vigorous personality, and this vigor, at least, is reflected in *The Landscape*. It is a highly interesting document of its time.

Very soon after Knight's poem appeared, there came the anonymous *Sketch, from the Landscape . . . Addressed to R. P. Knight, Esq.* (1794). This was a doggerel satire on Knight's attacks on Brown. It paraphrases, in a style of satirical exaggeration, many of the passages of *The Landscape*. Knight's style is attacked and he is accused of thefts from Mason. In his second edition, 1795, Knight rather needlessly answered this anonymous accuser and others. There are points of similarity with Mason, but it is easy to believe Knight's protests that he had not read *The English Garden* before writing *The Landscape*.

The poems of Mason and Knight were directed especially to the wealthy, and expressed the "picturesque" taste for landscape, rather than any knowledge of country life. In Edinburgh the taste for country realism expressed itself again in the publication of two anonymous poems written earlier, *The Har'st Rig* and *The Farmer's Ha'* (1794). The first is said to have been written in 1786 " by a farmer in the vicinity of Edinburgh," and the second by an Aberdeen student about twenty years earlier. Neither is a georgic on the classical model. Both have mottoes from Thomson and are expansions of his matter — the former, of his picture of harvest, and the latter, of that of "harvest-home" — but they are full of homely realism in rough dialectal rhyme. *The Har'st Rig* tells the story of harvest, from the early preparations for cutting the crop and the arrival of the reapers, to the master's paying off. Gleaners are turned off for bad behavior. A storm interrupts the labors. There is " pease-shearing" in the afternoon. Conversations are set down without any attempt to dress them up. The reapers' " bed-making," all in one great room in a company, and their quarrel with the farmer for more blankets, are set down with the same candid realism. *The Farmer's Ha'* is in the same vein and has the same interest of subject matter, with the same rough, homely colloquialism of style.

Gerald Fitzgerald, an Irish parson, continued the ixeutic type with *The Academick Sportsman, or a Winter's Day* (1797).[49] The sport of the fowler, hunter of snipe and woodcock, is described through the parts of the day. The winter setting reveals another admirer of Thomson. Fitzgerald gives an interesting genre sketch of a meal with a humble peasant family. But the episodes are either very stereotyped or quite incongruous: the happiness of rural life, the inhumanity of inclosures and depopulation, the "sorrows of seduction," Braddock's defeat, and the famous sons of Dublin University. Enough variety within a narrow scope!

Certain translations falling within the last years of the century and the first years of the next, should be glanced at briefly as indications of the interest in didactic poetry. William Roscoe, the Liverpool virtuoso, translated Tansillo's Italian didactic, *La Balia*, as *The Nurse* (1798). Henry William Tytler appeared with another version of Sainte-Marthe's *Paedotrophiae* (1797). Interest in the then-famous French poet Jacques Delille, appears to have been great. There was an anonymous translation of the four books of his *Les Jardins*, as *Delille's Gardens* (1789), followed by Mrs. Montolieu's version with the same title (1798). His *L'Homme des champs; ou les géorgiques françaises* was reviewed at great length, with many translations from his text, in the *Monthly Review*, shortly after its first appearance at Basle in 1800.[50] John Maunde's translation of the poem, *Rural Philosopher; or French Georgics* (1801), appeared with great promptness. Arthur Murphy and John Duncombe made further translations from Vanière.[51] John Belfour, the orientalist, translated Yriarte's Spanish didactic poem in five cantos, *La Música*, as *Music* (1807).[52] These àre but the more ambitious of the translations in the late years of the eighteenth and the early years of the nineteenth century. The versions of Delille are the most important.

Jacques Delille, the translator of the *Georgics* and the *Aeneid* and of Milton's *Paradise Lost*, member of the Academy at thirty-four, was reaching the height of his reputation in the last years of the century. His *Jardins* of 1780 antedates Mason's completed *English Garden* and upholds a similar taste for simplicity and naturalness. The geometrical style seen in Le Nôtre and La Quintinie had been praised by Rapin in his *Horti*, in the anonymous *Les Jardins d'ornemens* (1756), and by Rosset in *L'Agriculture* (1774). Saint-Lambert in his *Saisons* (1769) advocated more freedom, and his notes praise the practice of the English school. Delille admits the appropriateness of Le Nôtre's style for settings of royal magnificence like Versailles or the Tuileries, but praises the freedom and grace of Kent for less pretentious plans. Chant I traces the development of the art of gardening, and gives general advice upon choice of setting and uses of contrasts, motion, and variety; Chant II is on the use of trees and shrubs; Chant III on lawns, rocks, streams, and cascades; Chant IV on paths, vistas, buildings, and statues. How much an Anglophile in matters of taste the poet is, appears from his praises of Parkplace, the Leasowes, Hagley Park, Bowton, Foxly, Chiswick, Blenheim, Pope's garden at Twickenham, Stow, Kew Gardens, and the scenery of Devonshire. Bacon, Pope, Milton, and Spenser are for him early legislators in the arts of landscape. The influence of landscape painting and the tendency to a " picturesque " mode of vision is always present. He even recommends the study of Poussin and Berghem to those who plan gardens. Poussin's use of dancing shepherds and nymphs, in contrast to a near-by tomb engraved *" Et moi, je fus aussi pasteur dans l'Arcadie,"* leads him to recommend even urns, tombs, and cypresses in the midst of his *" riants tableaux."* The alternation of cheerfulness, melancholy, and appeal to the imagination is a cardinal principle. The farmhouse, barns, and implements are not to be hidden, but adorned with taste: *" Et sous l'utilité déguisez l'agrément."* Gardening, descriptive poetry, painting, all are virtually one art for Delille. He even cries, *" La ferme est aux jardins ce qu'aux vers est l'idylle."*

L'Homme des champs of 1800, translated almost immediately after its appearance, taught, in the words of Delille,

l'art de se rendre heureux à la campagne, et de répandre le bonheur autour de soi par tous les moyens possibles; de cultiver la campagne de cette culture que j'ai appelée merveilleuse, et qui s'élève au-dessus de la routine ordinaire; de voir la campagne et les phénomènes de la nature avec des yeux observateurs; enfin de répandre et d'entretenir le goût de ces occupations et de ces plaisirs champêtres en les peignant d'une manière intéressante. Ainsi le sage, l'agriculteur, le naturaliste, le paysagiste, sont les quatre divisions de ce poëme.[53]

There are echoes of Denham, Pope, Goldsmith, Thomson, and Saint-Lambert in *L'Homme des champs,* but Vergil is the chief model. The fourth part, giving advice to descriptive and didactic poets of the country, is virtually a digest of the methods of Thomson and Vergil. He says:

> Mais pourquoi ces conseils tracés si longuement?
> Ah! pour toute leçon j'aurais dû seulement
> Dire: " Lisez Virgile."

Delille is a georgic poet in academic cap and gown — or in the robes of the Academy. By comparison, Dyer or Dodsley is simple and unaffected. Delille had a talent for translation and all his work is virtually that — the sentiments of an elegant littérateur and savant steeped in the poetry and the science of nature. The salons and the Academy were the proper setting for his verses. He read

two selections from *L'Homme des champs* at the reception of
Malesherbes and became "*le lecteur par excellence*" in an age of
public readings. His verse is declamatory. He does not pretend to
reflect the life of the peasants, but flatters the Parisian cult of nature among "*gens du monde*" and the fashionable vogue for the
country and for agriculture. Bertrand characterizes his style aptly
as a "*banalité distinguée*" which gave the illusion of "*grand
art.*" [54] Like Saint-Lambert he was really a sterile poet.

A less pretentious georgic poet was the English parson Luke
Booker. Writing as if he were of the generation of Mallet and
Somervile, he published his georgic in two books, *The Hop Garden*, in 1799. The volume included also *A Sequel to the Hop
Garden*, really a part of the longer poem. Even many of the didactic passages are modeled after Vergil: localities suited to the culture of the crop, management of differing soils, the seasons for
planting, and so on. In the episodes Thomson is drawn on heavily.
There are sentimental narrative episodes like that of Osmund and
Emma, lovers who die together in a night of storm. The descriptions — the spring shower, the rainbow, the singing skylark, the
planter's evening walk, sunrise and the waking of man to his labors, and the feeding of the birds in winter — are often suggested
by originals in *The Seasons*, though Booker is not merely a copyist.
The chief element of originality, however, is in his pictures of
rustics: hop pickers, peasants at the inn, cottagers, artisans at a public festival, and the carol singers at Christmas. He shows the troops
of laborers from remote counties on the way to the hop country,
the hardships of their journey by day and night, their employments
in the fields and their recreations at evening, their return home
crowned with the hop clusters and bearing bags of fruit, the gifts
of the planter. The blind musician and his dog, aged bystanders at
the dances of the hop pickers, the old pensioner and his tales of war,
are honest pictures, also, of peasant types. Such sketches are many
and varied, showing close knowledge of country life.

In his *Phytologia; or the Philosophy of Agriculture and Gardening* (1800), Erasmus Darwin includes some verse, short essays in
the georgic vein, none of them of any worth. There are the *Art
of Pruning Wall-Trees*, the *Art of Pruning Melons and Cucumbers*, *The Cultivation of Brocoli* (translated from a Latin poem
of Edward Tighe), a translation of Vergil's passage on grafting,
and an expansion of his own lines on pruning in *The Botanic
Garden*.[55] These are only tentative essays, as supremely dull as

their titles suggest, occasioning no regret that Darwin did not write a long georgic. He probably had one in mind and fortunately abandoned it.

Introduced to the world by the tireless Capel Lofft, the first poem of Robert Bloomfield, *The Farmer's Boy* (1800), appeared at the turn of the century. Lofft's enthusiasm at his discovery of Bloomfield, a humble shoemaker's apprentice in London, had the sanction of critical opinion. Bloomfield had modest gifts of naturalness, simplicity, and sharp observation. He was not merely another of the " untutored geniuses " discovered by men and women grown tired of more sophisticated Muses in the eighteenth century. *The Farmer's Boy* derives from the georgic tradition. There is didacticism in it, but the occupations of the farm are usually presented descriptively. The intention is not to teach but to portray. The framework is that of the duties of Giles, the farmer's boy, during the four seasons of the year. Plowing, harrowing, sowing, the processes of the dairy, feeding the farm animals, the keeping of sheep, the harvest activity, the farmer's monologue instructing Giles in the care of beasts — such are the themes of the poem. There are episodes, of course, descriptions of scenery, of various birds and their songs, the cows and sheep, the summer insects in the fields, the winter fields and skies, the gradual return of spring. Moral episodes — particularly on humanitarian feeling for animals — are common. There is a good deal in the sentimental strain, such as the picture of Mary Raynor, the crazed maiden of Ixworth-Thorp. But Mary Raynor is Mary Raynor, and not an idealized Aurelia or Amoret. The whole poem is realistic, and its homely imagery and diction have truth and a good deal of vividness.

Bloomfield enjoyed an unusual success. Pushed by Lofft and Nathan Drake, patronized by the Dukes of York and Grafton, praised by Anna Seward, George Dyer, Mrs. Opie, and many others, he had a wide reception. Illustrators like Westall, Weir, Hicks, Birket Foster, and Bewick furnished plates and woodcuts for editions of his poem. Robert Burns, the peasant poet, had helped to revive an interest in uneducated writers of verse. Southey, as late as 1831, wrote an essay on the " uneducated poets." [56] Within three years Bloomfield's poem ran to seven editions. It reached a twelfth edition in 1811 and a fifteenth in 1827. Bloomfield's pictures of the occupations of the farm were his chief claim to attention. In observation of nature he was surpassed by many poets of the time: Thomas Gisborne, Grahame, Hurdis, even Bidlake.[57] But he tries

to make his description of nature both minute and fresh. Here is
Giles, the farmer's boy, lying in the grass and naïvely describing
what he sees:

> The small dust-colour'd beetle climbs with pain
> O'er the smooth plantain-leaf, a spacious plain!
> Thence higher still by countless steps convey'd,
> He gains the summit of a shiv'ring blade,
> And flirts his filmy wings, and looks around,
> Exulting in his distance from the ground.

And looking toward the skies, Giles sees the skylark, which is described in such lines as these:

> Yet oft beneath a cloud she sweeps along,
> Lost for a while, yet pours her varied song:
> He views the spot, and as the cloud moves by,
> Again she stretches up the clear blue sky;
> Her form, her motion, undistinguish'd quite,
> Save when she wheels direct from shade to light.

An amusing contribution to Darwin's campaign of poetic popularization appeared in 1801, Frances Rowden's *Poetical Introduction to the Study of Botany.* The author acknowledges Darwin as
her model but has found his language " frequently too luxuriant
for the simplicity of female education," though she has " endeavoured to imitate the classical distribution and versification of this
elegant writer." Full " preliminary lessons " in prose precede the
verse and outline the Linnaean system. In the verse itself, the
classes of Linnaeus are presented by examples of each, described as
to appearance, uses, habitat, etc. Miss Rowden avoids the fanciful
excursions on the " sexual system," which had pleased the lovers
of Darwin's verse; his botanic bridegrooms are replaced by affec-
tionate attendant brothers. Without Darwin's figurative allusiveness, she often takes refuge in pointing neat moral parallels. She
rivals Darwin in the extent, at least, of her plan.

The year 1802 gave proof again, however, that the faults of
didactic poets were not unnoticed. *The Art of Candle Making.
A Didactic Poem, in Twenty Books* appeared in the *European
Magazine* in December of that year.[58] Twenty books, of course,
there are not; but the hit is a palpable one. " Heranio " writes a
preface, feigning to have found on a bench in Kensington Gardens
the beginning of Book I, the " Arguments " of Books II and III,
and a detached episode. Duty to his country compels him to pub-

lish these with annotations — and he hopes the author will come forward with the remainder of the work. The loose structure permitted by the form, the conventional themes, the diluted Miltonic blank verse, are caricatured. Philips, Smart, and Dyer are mentioned by name, but the satire is confined to no single group of poets. The " Argument " of Book II will indicate the quality of this satire:

This book opens with the Genius of Russia pronouncing a panegyric on Russian Tallow — The great benefits arising from Navigation — Argonautic Expedition — Captain Cooke — Remarks on Expeditions in general — For Commerce — For Religion — For Conquest — A Personification of Expedition — Egypt — Address to the Memory of Bruce — Palmyra — Zenobia — The Nile — Crocodiles — Pyramids — The Plague — Tallow Chandlers not affected with the plague of 1665 — Oxygen — Azote — Description of a Tallow Chandler's Shop — Weights and Scales — Episode of Sextillus and Pruinella — Consumptions cured by the Smell of Tallow — Conclusion.

The anonymous author of this satire is not comparable to the *Anti-Jacobin* parodists, but he sees the real faults of the form he attacks.

But didactic poems continued, little affected by the satire of the *European Magazine*. "Charles Clifford," really W. H. Ireland, published another fishing georgic, *The Angler* (1804). There are descriptive episodes. The author defends angling against the charge of cruelty. There is an " excursion of fancy " to northern lands and a Thomsonian description of winter in Greenland. Ireland writes in stereotyped form and style; his poem needs and deserves little comment.

Two works by the provincial poet David Service, *The Caledonian Herd Boy* (1802) and *Crispin, or the Apprentice Boy* (1804), show the influence of Bloomfield. Both herdboy and apprentice are closely related to Bloomfield's Giles, the farmer's boy. Both of Service's poems are unimportant contributions to the literature of their type.

Ewan Clark's *The Rustic* (1805) is another attempt to outdo Bloomfield. In four cantos, *The Child, The Youth, Manhood, Age and Death,* the poet traces rural life and occupations. The third canto gives technical accounts of the pursuits of the farm in the four seasons of the year. Clark is without a glimmering of real poetry, and his many debts to Thomson and Bloomfield hardly warrant attention.

Joseph Holland's *Appendix to the Season of Spring in the Rural*

Poem " The Farmer's Boy " (1806) may also be passed over with scant comment. As the title indicates, it is a sequel or supplement to Bloomfield's poem; but it is not a short fragment, as might be supposed. It is in three parts, a desultory and digressive combination of description and didacticism.

John Evans, who published three of his four projected books on *The Bees* at Shrewsbury between 1806 and 1813,[59] produced one of the longest poems of its type on record. He protests that he does not hope to rival Maro in the great poet's favorite theme — that of *Georgic* iv.

Far from aspiring to emulate his fame, the author would consider his illustrious model as a venerable legislator in the republic of letters, whose laws were the best that could possibly be devised from the infant state of knowledge in his day. Himself he offers as a much humbler member of the same community, who would propose an explanatory and corrective Act, suited to the enlarged views and altered aspects of the present enlightened period.

The " explanatory and corrective Act " becomes an encyclopedic compilation of verse and notes. Swammerdam, Réaumur, Linnaeus, and many others are drawn upon for scientific fact. Evans also borrows from Darwin, Vergil, Thomson, Vanière, and no doubt others. He is exhaustive and exhausting. Not content with his main subject, he draws into his scheme by main force the related theme of the flowers, and versifies botany in the manner of Erasmus Darwin. In his episodes he is flagrantly careless of unity or proportion. The power of instinct in animals and man's slower progress to the arts of communal living, through reason, are traced. The patriotic panegyric praises England as the home of " Truth and Genius," of noble heroes in arms, of supremacy on the seas. Even the new taste in gardening is not alien to his theme. The profusion of cumulative similes drawn from mythology, history, and legend, which marked Darwin's style, reappears — usually incongruously applied to scientific matter. Exotic digressions permit accounts of the flowers of other lands. The materialist's conception of fortuitous creation arouses Evans to rebuttal. Indeed, the minute evidences of benevolent design in the part of nature under his observation, lead him into a good deal of physico-theology. The homely life of the rustic is compared with that of the man of leisured wealth. There is a constant effort to make use of Vergil's human parallelisms for the bees. But enough! It should be clear that Evans's work is one of the most ambitious and formless of didactic poems. It is really a patchwork of elements, oddments of knowledge and imitative art strangely assembled and pieced together. But the age of Priestley and Darwin, of Buffon and Bewick and Pennant, encouraged this kind of fabrication.

A worthy successor to Evans's treatise in verse appeared in London between 1808 and 1811,[60] William Tighe's *Plants,* four cantos with full annotation and documentation. Tighe tries to originate a new scheme of development. His four cantos are centered around the rose, the oak tree, the vine, and the palm. Each is a symbol: the rose, of love; the oak, of liberty; the vine, of friendship; the palm, of religion. About each he clusters associated ideas and allusions. *The Plants* is a virtuoso's poem. In science Tighe draws upon Parkinson, Meager, Linnaeus, Boërhaave, Sowerby, Réaumur, Ray, Curtis, Derham — the list is long. He has rifled the travelers for exotic touches. The East fascinates him; he is an amateur orientalist. He knows Poussin, Titian, Claude, Raphael. His classical reading is wide. History affords many allusions. He is adept in methods of plant and flower cultivation. A large element in the poem is didactic: methods of cultivating the rose, pruning, grafting, forcing new colors in roses, combating the enemies of the oak, planting it, its uses, climates suited to it — and similar themes applied to the vine and the palm. Most of these didactic themes are time-honored ones. But episodes form a greater part of the poem. The rose suggests its use by the Persian poets, its connection with Venus, its origin from the blood of Adonis, its " progress " from Greece to Italy, Syria, Provence, and so to all Europe, the lack of it in lands of northern ice (a conventional northern-winter piece) and in the heart of the torrid zone (conventional also), the praises of retirement, the contemplation of God in the beauty of his works (the old religious theme of the universal harmony of nature), the rose in *Amadis de Gaul* and other romances, the story of Milto and Cyrus the Persian, and that of Pausias and Glycera, from Pliny. The other books follow the same development by loose association of ideas. There are such familiar themes as the patriotic panegyric (suggested by the oak, of course, and celebrating British heroes, the empire, the supremacy of the seas, British liberties); the praises of commerce and navigation (celebrating Drake and Cooke as Thomson celebrated Willoughby); "excursions of fancy" to Africa and to America; praises of labor mitigating the evils of the earth (Thomsonian and Vergilian); the sentimental tale of Agnes and Albert, Swiss peasants who die together in a French invasion;

humanitarian addresses on slavery and to the conquerors of India. All of this shows much as to the nature of the poem, but it is far from exhaustive. Tighe is fatally diffuse; haphazard association is his method. Often the poem is merely tiresome. At other times the ornate and studied blank verse has a certain stateliness which is at least effective rhetoric. Addressing his groves, the poet says,

> Ye oft shall see
> The fleeting generations, like your leaves,
> Decay and vanish at the touch of time;
> Shew them how vain the transitory hours
> That steal our lives with downy pace away,
> And leave us nothing we can call our own,
> But one poor shroud, and one pacific grave.
> Teach them to look to that celestial fount
> Whence sprang the living soul, and in his works
> Revere the fostering Lord of Nature, who
> In love created all the harmonic maze
> Of worlds, reflection of the eternal mind.

Other poets of the new century cling to the old formulas. John Vincent, in his *Fowling* (1808), acknowledges Somerville as his model, in his preface, but Thomson contributes even more. Following the fowler through the year, Vincent describes the shooting of grouse, partridge, pheasant, wookcock, duck, and snipe. This framework allows much description of nature, often straight out of the pages of *The Seasons*. There are stereotyped subjects: genre sketches, praises of British freedom, humanity to animals, the happy life of the countryman, the pathetic tales of Eugenio and Viola and of Robin and Janet, the latter dying together in a night of storm. Altogether a very conventional exercise to appear in five long books in 1808.

W. H. Ireland, the "Charles-Clifford" of *The Angler*, was another who offered a companion piece to Bloomfield's popular poem, *The Fisher Boy* (1808), signed "H. C., Esq." The following year he published another, *The Sailor Boy*. Ireland is, of course, the fabricator of the Shakespeare papers; his refuge under various pseudonyms is understandable. There is some novelty and plenty of direct knowledge in *The Fisher Boy*, in Ireland's tracing of Ned's labors through the four seasons. This is a kind of narrative halieutic, as Bloomfield's poem was a narrative georgic. Ireland describes the manner of " shooting " and hauling the seine, the mending of nets, the manner of preparing whiting, the catching of lobsters, shrimp, salmon, mackerel, and many other fish, the methods of trolling at sea, and the "barking" of nets. There are notes, also, full of natural history and explanation of methods. His nature description, of which there is a good deal, is not very individual. There are interesting and new pictures of the smugglers of the coast and of the picking of samphire on the cliffs. But on the whole, digressions are on such old themes as humanitarian feeling for animals, the evidences of omniscience in nature, and the praises of British seamen. The mother of the fisher boy is the maniac Jane, seduced in youth and now mad, one of a type grown more numerous since Cowper's "Crazy Kate." [61] In spite of his fresh material, Ireland leaves the impression of being a thoroughly imitative poet.

The young hero of *The Sailor Boy* is aboard a man-of-war. Ireland is concocting another mixture of elements, mingling suggestions from Bloomfield and Falconer. Various maneuvers of a man-of-war, various parts of the ship, the organization of life aboard such a vessel, its operation during an engagement, the hero's studies in astronomy and navigation — all these are sketched in an account of the sailor boy's advance in the navy. There are many episodes, such as the celebration of British naval heroes. But this poem is even less deserving of praise than the previous one. Both show more ingenuity in seeking novel matter than ability to make poetry of it.

The last poet in England in the nineteenth century to publish a very ambitious poem of the strictly georgic kind seems to have been James Grahame. After 1810 the impulse begins definitely to wane. Grahame's *British Georgics* (1809) was, however, his *magnum opus* and certainly one of the most thoroughgoing works of its kind. It adopts the division into months of the year, already familiar in descriptive poetry, and traces rural occupations in order, as they arise.

It is my wish [he says in his preface], to draw the attention of the landed proprietors to that most important class of the community [the peasants], and to persuade them, that the welfare of the country depends in a great measure on preserving the cultivators of the soil in that relative state of respectability, comfort, and consequence, which they have hitherto held, but which the fashionable system of agriculture has an evident tendency to destroy. In this view, though I am no friend to idleness, I am humbly of opinion that innocent recreations ought to be encouraged; that festivals, holidays, customary sports, and every institution which adds an hour of importance, or of harmless enjoyment, to the poor man's heart, ought to be religiously observed.

With these ends in view, Grahame teaches the arts of husbandry, sketches the rural festivals and sports of the year, and tries to surround his theme with associations of worth and dignity. Beginning with January and the mending of fences, the shepherd's duties, and the care of the farm animals, he carries his calendar through the ancient round: plowing, cultivation, improving the soils, sowing, haymaking, care of bees, wheat harvest, reaping of oats and of corn, care of trees, and the employments of returning winter. The festivals of the New Year, of Hallowe'en, harvest home, Hogmanay, and Christmas, divide the months. Grahame has a Scot's veneration for Thomson and often takes suggestions from him or tries to rival his originals. The snowstorm, the farmer lost in the snowy fields, ice arresting the streams, morning disclosing the artistry of frost, the horse and the herd attacked by insects, the hay harvest, signs of spring and summer showers, the depredations of floods, the marsh lights deluding travelers, tropical storms, the plaint of the bird robbed of her nest, the robin visiting the homes of men — such themes as these are close to Thomson's; but Grahame was, in his own right, one of the keenest of observers. His genre sketches, too, are full of observation. As a panorama of country occupations, Grahame's poem is full, detailed, realistic, unsentimentalized. There are new adaptations of old, familiar themes: the happy life of the husbandman, praises of Scotland, pity for the poor at the approach of winter, the evening recreations of the city contrasted with those of the country, and scientific interests. Grahame has his own ideas to preach: parish schools for the peasants, a theory of crop rotation and of irrigation, the threat of trade to the ancient peasantry, warnings against heavy imposts and inclosures, and denunciation of absentee landlords.

This synopsis of Grahame's subject matter really does it an injustice. The general plan is not artificial but natural, apart from the episodes and sometimes mechanical transitions. As in *Birds of Scotland*,[62] the poet is one of the closest observers in English verse. The old exactitude is often found, as in the picture of the handiwork of the frost, or the frequent vivid glimpses of many different birds. He knows their ways and can foretell each turn of weather by their conduct. The ending of Grahame's poem is an interesting reflection of the blending of science and religion which occurs so often in poetry of this period which touches nature; it is a rhapsody on the Deity, revealed in the universe,

           that vast power which launched,
Impels this mighty mass, and guides it round,
True to its annual and diurnal course —
Stupendous miracle! — this mighty mass
Hurled loose, through realms immense of trackless space,
With speed compared to which the viewless ball,
Projected from the cannon's mouth, but creeps
At a snail's pace, yet without shock or pause,
Or deviation infinitely small,
Rolling along, with motion unperceived,
As if it moveless lay on ether's tide.

The efforts of Tighe, Ireland, Vincent, and Grahame to give new treatment to old themes are signs of failing vitality. After 1810, as has been said, there was a sharp decline in this type of verse. Except for poems on rural sports, very few attempts on the old scale, and no important ones, seem to have been printed before 1900.

Charlotte Richardson's *Harvest* (1818) describes the harvest season, the labors of the harvest, and the festival of " harvest-home," varied with narrative episodes. A son returns from years at sea, to give his impoverished parents an old age of ease in place of their wretched labors as gleaners in the fields. Edmund, owner of lands, marries Evelina, a maiden working in his fields, as Thomson's Palemon married Lavinia.

Robert Donald's *National Agriculture* (1822) offered the interesting suggestion of a system of government farms to relieve distress and reduce the poor rates. Donald then gave advice on choice of land, draining, working the soil, crops suited to different soils, and methods of sowing and cultivating. Beyond its interest as a social document, the poem is valueless.

The didactic of fishing was one of the most long-lived types. T. W. Charleton's *Art of Fishing* (1819) carries on the accepted features of the genre. *The Angler* (1819) of Thomas Pike Lathy, the novelist, published under the pseudonym " Piscator," rifles, without acknowledgment, Thomas Scott's *Anglers — Eight Dialogues in Verse* (1758). The anonymous *Lay of the Last Angler* (1867), which includes precepts, may fittingly close the long line of poems of its type.

There were later imitations of Darwin's method in the nineteenth century, though Byron in *English Bards and Scotch Reviewers* (1809) had seen evidence of a decline in the popularity of *The Botanic Garden,* which seemed " some proof of returning taste." Sarah Hoare's *Poem on the Pleasures and Advantages of Botanical Pursuits* (1825) is feeble and could have been but little read; but James Jennings's *Ornithologia, or the Birds* (1828) and his *Pleasures of Ornithology* (1828) are at least highly ambitious in design. Jennings argues in his preface to *Ornithologia* that "more simple measures" and "a more familiar style" than those of Darwin may succeed better in advancing the cause of "Truth and Science." A prose outline of classes, orders, and genera, drawn from Linnaeus, Pennant, and Vigors, is followed by two interminable books, one on British and European birds, and the other on tropical birds. The notes are voluminous and full of technical ornithology. The attempts to suggest, in various lyrical measures, the songs of birds, are amusing poetic vagaries. *The Pleasures of Ornithology* is a kind of epitome of the larger work, with the addition of a plea against cruelty to birds. Jennings actually proposed going on "in a similar way with the remainder of the animal kingdom," suggesting five other works to follow: *Mammalia, Amphibia, Icthyologia, Entomologia,* and *Helminthologia.* It is hardly necessary to add that so absurd a program was never completed.

Field sports died hard. William Watt's *Remarks on Shooting* (1839) was one of the most inclusive poems of its type. This was a second "much enlarged" edition of the poem. Watt enjoyed a good deal of fame among the devotees of his subject. Though he never rises above rhymed prose, he can summon the authentic atmosphere of the field, and is shrewd, companionable, and facile. Alexander Webber's *Shooting* (1841) is in the same informal manner as Watt's poem and covers almost the same ground, "a general description of field sports dependent on the gun."

The American Journal of Philology [63] gives an account of the *Virginia Georgics,* written by Charles Carter Lee, brother of Robert E. Lee, and published in Richmond in 1858. To judge by the quotations given, the poem was very inept, but it is interesting as a late offshoot of the tradition. It was in four books — upwards of three thousand lines. Lee says he wishes to serve his country by aiding in restoring the fertility of her soil, impoverished by neglect, Vergil having served Italy by helping to heal the wounds of a century of conflict. Part I is on the enrichment and restoration of the soil; Parts II and III give details of the culture of the soil, and of the raising of stock; Part IV treats gardens, grounds, and buildings. The episodes are said to be narrative and philosophical.

The georgic survived into the twentieth century in William Courthope's *Hop-Garden* (1908),[64] and Victoria Sackville-West's *The Land* (1926).[65] Miss Sackville-West's poem is admirable. Its setting is the Kentish weald. Vergil and Thomson are no more than remote predecessors, though the poet uses the occupational themes of the one and the division by seasons of the other. Her varied measures are full of the intimate knowledge and love of the fields and of the farmer's way of life, which are necessary to a successful georgic poet. She adds a sense of how the "necessities of seasons match the planetary law," and of how they embody the rhythms of an ancient mode of life little changed in essentials since Homer and Hesiod and the Mantuan.

> I sing the cycle of my country's year,
> I sing the tillage, and the reaping sing,
> Classic monotony, that modes and wars
> Leave undisturbed, unbettered, for their best
> Was born immediate, of expediency.
> The sickle sought no art; the axe, the share
> Draped no superfluous beauty round their steel;
> The scythe desired no music for her stroke,
> Her stroke sufficed in music, as her blade
> Laid low the swathes; the scythesmen swept, nor cared
> What crop had ripened, whether oats in Greece
> Or oats in Kent; the shepherd on the ridge
> Like his Boeotian forebear kept his flocks,
> And still their outlines on our tenderer sky,
> Simple and classic, rear their grave design
> As once at Thebes, as once in Lombardy.[66]

The didactic-descriptive poem in England in the eighteenth and nineteenth centuries never overcame faults inherent in it from the first: looseness of form, imitativeness, and a tendency to wander into any subject which had popular acceptance. When it tried to follow the stylistic manner of Milton, as Philips and Thomson had done, it was often turgid, euphemistic, and circumlocutory. Its observation of man and of nature was usually of an external kind. But this observation was not scanty. The English poets, if we except Darwin and his imitators, Tighe, and Evans, avoided most of the affectations of a Delille or Rosset in France. Alexandrian taste and the *goût jésuite* do not characterize Gay, Thomson, Somervile, Smart, Dodsley, Dyer, Stevenson, Cowper, Booker, Bloomfield, or

Grahame. They aim at truthfulness, rather than at any display of scholarship and learning in tricking out nature and the country with meretricious adornment. Darwin, Tighe, and Jennings most closely approximate the Jesuit taste. But most of the poets dealt with in this chapter, in spite of obvious faults, reflected the growing interest of their time in the scenes and the life of the country. They were not men of the salon, like Cardinal de Bernis, Saint-Lambert, Delille, Léonard, Rosset, and Roucher in France, writing for elegant amateurs and savants with pastoral tastes. Their "Nature" was not that of the Petit Trianon, Claude Lorraine, and Gaspar Poussin. Their villages were not copies of the *hameau* of Marie Antoinette at Versailles. They did not exclude the humble peasant from their countrysides, to people them with fantasies of Arcadian shepherds and shepherdesses. With all their faults, they reflected a genuine English taste for the country, relatively unadulterated by sophisticated pastoralism.

The treatments of gardening, from Laurence to Knight, show a good deal of minute observation and knowledge, though Mason, Jago, and Knight reflect more fully the taste for landscape, for wider panoramas, for the "picturesque," as defined by the "prospect critics."

The poems touching phases of husbandry, the occupations of the country, show a wide variety of sympathetic pictures of peasant life; and their observation of nature, tutored by Vergil and Thomson and supplemented by a taste for natural history, is considerable. The "exotic georgic," as in Weekes, Grainger, or Singleton, shows similar tendencies applied to colonial settings in parts of the empire.

The poems of country sports, from Gay and Somervile onward, are the most numerous single class and the class most free of highly mannered style. They reflect country pastimes, one aspect of rural life, often with sharp realism, and they show a spontaneous enthusiasm for the scenes of the country. Sometimes they show very close observation of animals or of birds.

Such poets as Darwin, Evans, Tighe, and Jennings have vices of style which are extreme. Their interest for students lies in the fact that they appealed to the popular taste for science and the technical study of nature. As we shall see below in Chapter VI, this taste contributed to a sharpened observation of nature in poetry, especially from 1780 onward.

But specifically didactic verse fell into critical disrepute during the nineteenth century. The denial of the old Horatian dogma of delight and instruction is complete in De Quincey's repudiation of didactic poetry as a contradiction in terms, in Coleridge's phrase "pleasure, not truth," in Poe's repetition of the same words, or in G. H. Lewes's "not doctrine, but inspiration." The didactic georgic had certainly survived too long. In a special phase of Roman history Vergil's form had been a natural product of social conditions. These conditions were far from those of eighteenth-century England. The georgic expressed the traditionalism of those who employed it; little wonder, then, that so many of its themes remained traditional ones. The highest poetry, it seems probable, will always conform to the canon of Aristotle, representing the actions of men — the "actions" we call psychological as well as those we call physical — and, as Hobbes insisted, avoiding the methods of dictation and precept. The Horatian sanctions of didactic and descriptive verse led away from the rightful province and method of the highest poetry. Yet, granting the traditionalism and the minor rank of the didactic and descriptive forms, one must notice also their reflection, however imperfect, of a new age in process of formation — an age as yet in leading strings to a remote past but marked by its own characteristic modes of thought and feeling.

V

THE MUSE OF "UTILITY"

If it be a true observation, that for a poet to write happily and well, he must have seen and felt what he describes, and must draw from living models alone; and if modern times, from their luxury and refinement, afford not manners that will bear to be described; it will then follow, that those species of poetry bid fairest to succeed at present, which treat of things not men; which deliver doctrines, not display events. Of this sort is didactic and descriptive poetry. Accordingly the moderns have produced many excellent pieces of this kind.

Joseph Warton

As WE have seen, didactic and descriptive poetry tended to merge and to borrow from each other. The confusion of genres went further. Since the georgic association with country pursuits was not always what poets wanted to exploit, didactic poems on other subjects were written. It is necessary to distinguish between poets who employed the form and manner of Horatian epistle, of Horatian and Juvenalian satire, or of the Ovidian amatory poems, and those who approximated the Vergilian form and tone. This distinction is in some cases hard to draw; there are a few poems so mixed and anomalous that a distinction becomes meaningless. It is perhaps better to disregard them. This chapter will discuss poems of didactic form, whatever the subjects, which show any appreciable indebtedness to preceptive or descriptive poetry in the tradition of Vergil's *Georgics*. The range of subjects is wide, including navigation, education, the professions, and the general conduct of life.

Allan Ramsay's *Health* (1730) represents very well the confusion of genres referred to above. A series of "characters" follows the dedication and statement of theme. These "characters," common to satire and to the Horatian epistolary tone, give the poet a basis for his advice on diet and health. His subject matter anticipates Armstrong, but his style is nearer to that of Green's *Spleen*, sometimes dropping into humorous overstatement or satire. But, unlike Green, he seems to owe a debt to the Vergilian tradition, echoing, perhaps through Thomson, the patriotic panegyric and the exotic digression. Britain's mild and healthful climate is praised and contrasted with the severity of Lapland and the rigors of the tropics — their beasts, pestilences, serpents, and uncultivated soil.

Robert Morris, the architect who "modernized" Bubb Dodington's Brandenburgh House and built Inverary Castle, Wimbledon House, and a number of other mansions, delivered a series of lectures on architecture, from 1730 to 1734, to the Society for the Improvement of Knowledge in Arts and Sciences, which he himself had formed. These were published under the title *Lectures on Architecture* (1734). Morris shows the growing taste for didactic verse, and incidentally for blank verse, by turning occasional passages in his lectures, both descriptive and didactic, into meter. There is nothing of sufficient length and unity to constitute a poem of the type. There are advices on landscape gardening, in which Morris anticipates Mason and in which he inclines to the new English school. Sometimes he presents a scene in verse. Sometimes he puts passages like that in praise of "proportion" into meter. He traces the principle of proportion in the vegetable world, in the animal world, and in the heavenly bodies, and places it highest among artistic values. Morris is not expert in meter, but his desire to borrow some of the graces of poetry for his informative lectures shows the growth of the popularity of didactic verse.

Dr. John Armstrong's meretricious *Oeconomy of Love* (1736) first appeared anonymously. It had a popularity which is a commentary on the easy morals of the century. There seems, however, to have been some feeling against Armstrong's treatment of themes of sex, since he found it advisable to insert this notice in later editions of his poem: " This little juvenile performance was chiefly intended as a parody upon some of the didactick poets; and that it might be still the more ludicrous, the author in some places affected the stately language of Milton." *The Oeconomy of Love* is hardly quotable for ten lines together. From youth to maturity the development of sex is traced. Advice is given to married and unmarried lovers. Armstrong outdoes the Ovid of the *Ars amatoria,* who was one of his models, at least in circumstantiality. There is the old episodic celebration of the universal sway of Love in earth, air, and sea, familiar through Thomson and Vergil back to Lucretius. The machinery of theme statement, invocation, and elevated style is employed.

Thomas Yalden, who won a certain recognition through his " Pindarick " odes, wrote his poem *To Sir Humphrey Mackworth on the Mines* at some time before 1736. His theme statement suggests a plan larger than that which he actually completed:

> What spacious veins enrich the British soil;
> The various ores, and skilful miner's toil;
> How ripening metals lie conceal'd in earth
> And teeming Nature forms the wondrous birth;
> My useful verse, the first, transmits to fame
> In members tun'd, and no unhallow'd flame.[1]

There is the praise of Britain, rich in such stores of wealth, great and fortunate beyond her neighbors; speculation as to the process by which metals are formed by nature; and, in an ingenious piece of narrative, panegyric of Mackworth and of the king. Whether or not Yalden originally intended a plan larger than the one he completed, he owes an obvious debt to the didactic tradition.

Matthew Green's *Spleen* (1737) is sometimes confused with Vergilian didactic verse. In reality it does not belong here; it is in an epistolary style nearer the manner of Horace than of Vergil, and owes nothing definite in plan or detail to the tradition here studied. It includes satire, "characters," and informal precepts. It has the subtitle "An Epistle to Mr. Cuthbert Jackson" and conforms strictly to the epistolary genre. The influence of Prior seems apparent in Green's style.

Doctor Armstrong, in 1744, published what was to be a highly successful poem, *The Art of Preserving Health*. It is a commentary on one characteristic mood of poetic composition in its period. Verse has become an art which may flourish apart from any impulses of feeling. It may be an intellectual exercise, ingenious in imitation and in the development of abstract themes. Here is a physician's subject linked to an incongruous Miltonic, or, rather, Thomsonian style, developing analytical and preceptive principles. And it was successful. It was, in fact, one of the most popular of didactic poems. The British Museum Catalogue lists eleven editions before 1800, besides those in the editions of Armstrong's complete poems. Practically all of the compilers of the many series of English poets included *The Art of Preserving Health*: Anderson, Bell, Roach, Aikin, Park, Davenport, Chalmers, Pratt, and Sanford. The poem was translated into Italian in 1824,[2] and a selection from it into Latin, by Thomas Warton.[3]

When Armstrong departs from a preceptive style, he often falls back on Vergil or Thomson. He adapts georgic themes: the claim to credit for the difficulty of his topic and his priority in it, the theme of "*O fortunatos nimium,*" the picture of plague, the ways of improving soils, the exotic digressions to torrid and arctic zones, and the duties appropriate to seasons of the year (here become an account of the ills of the various seasons) ; but most of these themes have come to him through Thomson. He imitates Thomson's hymn to the sun in *Summer*. There are scientific episodes on the function of the blood in rebuilding tissue, on the processes of metabolism and of growth and decay in the organs. He echoes Thomson's passage on the sources of rivers in the mountains. There are pictures of the chase and of fishing. He is humanitarian, calling on those more fortunate to aid the needy. His descriptions, like that of storm in Book I, are much in the manner of Thomson, as is his delight in the pleasures of melancholy,

> the horrors of the solemn wood
> While the soft evening saddens into night.

Despite his theme and his imitativeness, there was a poet in Armstrong. In his didactic passages he is only stiffly ingenious, but he has episodes which allow more poetic turns of imagery or thought:

> Time shakes the stable tyranny of thrones,
> And tottering empires crush by their own weight.
> This huge rotundity we tread grows old;
> And all those worlds that roll around the Sun,
> The Sun himself, shall die; and ancient Night
> Again involve the desolate abyss:
> 'Till the great Father through the lifeless gloom
> Extend his arm to light another world,
> And bid new planets roll by other laws.
> For through the regions of unbounded space,
> Where unconfin'd Omnipotence has room,
> Being, in various systems, fluctuates still
> Between creation and abhorr'd decay. . . .
> New worlds are still emerging from the deep;
> The old descending, in their turns to rise.

In the same year, 1744, Mark Akenside, another whose verse had " poetical sinews," in Sidney's phrase, published *The Pleasures of Imagination,* which has had a lasting reputation. The partial list of the British Museum Catalogue includes almost forty editions of this poem, besides translations into French (by Baron d'Holbach) in 1752, into German in 1757, and into Italian in 1764. Thomas Warton translated a selection from it into Latin, as he had done in the case of Armstrong's poem.[4] Akenside says he writes in the tradition of Vergil's *Georgics,* and this is true, in a very general sense. He says, in his final book,

Lo! thus far
With bold adventure, to the Mantuan lyre
I sing of Nature's charms.

But his poem is a speculative one, related in its plan to georgic verse
only as it employs digressions from the didactic manner, episodes
of descriptive, moral, scientific, and " exotic " kinds; and related in
style in that it employs a consciously elevated manner and devices
like the cumulative simile borrowed by the classical poets in this
genre from the epic. As for Thomson, what can we attribute to
him? Akenside writes in blank verse, but the lines are less luxuriant,
tighter than Thomson's. Akenside finds his own characteristic manner in description, and scientific fact and speculation are treated
with more restraint. In structure, Akenside is more symmetrical
than Thomson. More outstandingly than Thomson, he is a Shaftesburian thinker; but there is no evidence that he took any of this
from Thomson, as others did. In short, Akenside, with Thomson,
Cowper, and perhaps Darwin, came nearer than any other Englishman of his century to making of the episodic didactic form something quite his own, in spite of the fact that his original hints were
taken from Addison's papers in *The Spectator*.[5]

Dividing his subject into a careful logical structure, Akenside
traces the pleasures of the imagination arising from " greatness,"
" novelty or wonderfulness," and " beauty " in objects, and the
causes for these pleasurable emotions; he constructs a hierarchy of
degrees of beauty in objects and in the mind, finding Truth, Good,
and Beauty a single entity accessible to the mind; he outlines
the " adventitious aids " to pleasure in beauty, such as the perception of harmonious design in the universe; he examines the part
played by the passions and by observations of human life in pleasures of the imagination; he describes the imagination exercised in
artistic creation and outlines its processes; he analyses " taste,"
making it identical with the moral sense and showing its power,
through the love of natural beauty, to lead the soul to converse
with God. Virtue seems to him an esthetic development arising
from an internal harmony like the external harmony of God's universe; virtue and the highest beauty are one; the universe is a perfected whole, which exerts a spiritual influence upon man, and
in which God is immanent and accessible to the soul of man.
The seasons, the sights and sounds of nature, attune the mind to
harmony and to God.

The attentive mind,
By this harmonious action on her powers,
Becomes itself harmonious: wont so oft
In outward things to meditate the charm
Of sacred order, soon she seeks at home
To find a kindred order, to exert
Within herself this elegance of love,
This fair inspir'd delight; her temper'd powers
Refine at length, and every passion wears
A chaster, milder, more attractive mien.
But if to ampler prospects, if to gaze
On Nature's form, where, negligent of all
These lesser graces, she assumes the port
Of that eternal majesty that weigh'd
The world's foundations, if to these the mind
Exalts her daring eye; then mightier far
Will be the change and nobler. . . .
He meant, he made us to behold and love
What he beholds and loves, the general orb
Of life and being; to be great like him,
Beneficent and active. Thus the men
Whom Nature's works can charm, with God himself
Hold converse; grow familiar day by day
With his conceptions, act upon his plan,
And form to his, the relish of their souls.

Akenside's later attempt to revise and enlarge his poem remained unfinished at his death. The posthumous edition of 1772 includes the extensive though fragmentary changes made. Book I expands especially his theological concepts, with many Platonic additions, and Book II is an extension of the ethical ideas he had before outlined. The new Book III remained a fragment, and only a beginning was made on a fourth book. Though it has good lines, the new version did not promise to excel the old in poetic spirit, whatever it might have added in philosophical scope.

That strange mélange, James Kirkpatrick's *Sea-Piece* (1750), illustrates the confusion in genres which sometimes takes baffling forms. It is difficult to classify this amorphous poem in five cantos. The author calls it " a narrative, philosophical and descriptive poem." Since it includes some practical didacticism and certain elements carried over from the georgic tradition, its nature may be indicated here. The framework is that of a voyage from Belfast to South Carolina. But Kirkpatrick's themes ebb and flow and change as variously as the sea he celebrates. Nautical terms are impressed for service as they are later by Falconer. How the mariner uses the quadrant for measuring latitude and the log for measuring velocity, is explained in detail. The organization of life aboard ship is shown. There is much speculation on physical laws: on the causes of water-spouts, the nature and laws of light, the causes of earthquakes, the origin and beneficial effects of mountains, various causes of winds, of calms, and of hurricanes. The poet employs physico-theological argument, defending the idea of benevolent design, urging, for example, the beauty and utility of mountains as a part of the harmonious whole. There is description: the scenes through which the ship passes, a calm at sea, a storm of rain and lightning (with reminiscences of Thomson), the dolphins and flying fish near the Azores, sunset and dawn at sea, and the Bermudas. All these elements of description, exotic scenes, natural science, and nautical realism, are appeals to definite popular tastes. The poem loses all sense of structure. As for the verse, it is spirited but woefully amateurish. Something may be said, however, for Kirkpatrick's realism and truth to the life of the sea.

Another mixture of genres is Thomas Marriott's lengthy poem *Female Conduct* (1759). Marriott is under the impression that he follows Vergil. "Vergil, in his Georgics (which is a poem of the same nature as this, tho' different in subject) " does this or that! Marriott defends his episodes by pleading the example of the *Georgics*, " which is allowed by all true critics to be the most finished poem that ever was written." But this poet has nothing in common with Vergil except the habit of varying precept with episode; he owes something to Horace, something to the vein of petty conduct-propriety in the current periodical essays, much to sheer native verbosity. The poem is one dead level of mediocrity.

Much the same may be said of Richard Shepherd's *Nuptials* (1761), a poem in three books on principles governing happy marriage. It is a hybrid and a monumental bore. Shepherd was a writer of copious theological works. Preceptive verse was the order of the day. What pursuit could be more fit for an ambitious and assiduous clergyman? The work has georgic reminiscences: the sway of Venus in the animal kingdom, the celebration of the peasant's happy lot, the claim to honor for difficulty overcome and priority in treating the theme. Thomson's narratives, or those of his followers, were perhaps the inspiration for the tale of Bellair, seduced and deserted by Lorenzo.

William Falconer also produced a curiously mixed poem, of far higher merit, the long-famous *Shipwreck* (1762).[6] It recalls Kirkpatrick's *Sea-Piece*. Like the earlier poem, it is a narrative, but with better structure and more dramatic effect. There is excessive " sensibility " and inflexibility of style, but Falconer had experienced this tragedy and the outlines of the tale preserve an ineradicable dignity. The style is uneven, but often Falconer tries to write like an epic poet. There are cumulative similes and long harangues by the "chiefs," for example. A quasi-heroic vein of narrative mingles with conventional sentimentalism, with didacticism, and with extended description. For his time, Falconer is a very realistic poet of the sea, which he describes in many aspects. The technical element is large and is supplemented by footnotes. It has been said that the poem "contains within itself the rudiments of navigation "; and again, that it includes " the grammar of [the seaman's] profession." [7] Certainly Falconer puts his vessel into almost every possible emergency and shows what measures are taken to free her. Fortunately, he not only instructs but describes. It is regrettable that he tried to compress all his knowledge, marine and literary, all his impressions of the sea and foreign ports, even his own autobiography (he is the Arion of the poem) into one work. But the didactic tradition, which was a part of his inspiration, more and more tended to disunity. His poem has much pedantry and artificiality; it is hag-ridden by stiffness of diction and sentimentality. But real experience and sincere feeling lie beneath the conventional manner. The poem deserved the long popularity it enjoyed, though critics no longer would apply such expressions as " great " and "scarcely a superior " to it.

James Elphinston's *Education* (1763) is the poem of a Kensington schoolmaster. There are four books on the technique of teaching, including even an account of the best writers in a number of subjects of instruction. This kind of thing is relieved by episodes thought to be natural to the subject: invocations of Wisdom and Duty, a sketch of the ideal schoolmaster, allegorical pictures of the " fane of Morpheus " and the " fane of Labour," accounts of the great historians, lawgivers, philosophers, orators, and poets (the didactic ones from Hesiod to Armstrong and Somervile singled out especially), and accounts of the qualities of mind suited to various professions. The verse is wooden. Elphinston perhaps succeeded in representing himself as a careful schoolmaster, but he proved himself a wretched poet. He is known now merely as a correspondent of

Dr. Johnson or perhaps as the translator of Bossuet, Fénelon, and Racine. Johnson speaks favorably of his eccentric friend as a master for boys destined for trade — which is, to be sure, a species of faint praise.[8]

We must notice briefly James Smith's imitation of the *Trivia* variety of "city georgic," *The Art of Living in London* (1768). Smith acknowledges in an "Advertisement" that he took his hint from *Trivia*, and he tries to recapture Gay's manner. His aim is more serious than Gay's, and there is little of Gay's grace and urbanity. But Smith's advice on the London ordinaries, the perils of the crowded streets, and conduct at Drury Lane and Covent Garden is sometimes racy and always pleasant reading.

The didactic form, lending itself so well to purely expository exercises, found its next ambitious poet in Hugh Downman, a physician of Exeter and a writer of tragedies. Following the lead of Sainte-Marthe's *Paedotrophiae* and Tansillo's *La Balia*, Downman published his *Infancy* between 1774 and 1776.[9] He draws on both these predecessors. In the customary Miltonic blank verse, Downman has cast a systematic treatise on the care of the young. The theme statement which begins Book III indicates that he meant to go even further — to put into verse rules on clothing, exercise, and the diseases of infancy! The three books Downman wrote are in the usual mold; there are episodes, of course, intended to vary and to decorate the useful theme, praises of wedded love, defense of the theme as one celebrated by ancient and modern sages, an account of the rise of science slowly overcoming the darkness of superstition, praise of the didactic poets Vergil, Akenside, Armstrong, Mason, and Beattie, "pure ethereal Bards, who nobly stoop'd to teach Mankind." Downman was treated by critics with respect — for his obvious common sense and sincerity, no doubt — though he was anything but a poet.

Another kind of unpoetic merit may be accorded John Langhorne in his *Country Justice* published between 1774 and 1777.[10] A justice in the county of Somerset, Langhorne turned precepts of his calling into a didactic poem. He gives advice to guide the justice in protection of the poor and in according lenity where humanity may dictate. The poem owes only its general conception and plan of episodic variation to the tradition followed here. It is a strongly humanitarian work, concerned with the many vagrants of the countryside, with the state of the prisons, and with laws setting excessive punishments.

John Gay's *Trivia*, the "city georgic" which was a minor classic of the century, had another imitator in the anonymous author of *The French Metropolis* (1784). Its motto is Dr. Johnson's "I cannot bear a French metropolis." The poem is a Parisian *Trivia;* the poet acknowledges his model in the opening lines. Besides much practical advice, there is a Gayesque narrative episode on the origin of the parasol, a gift from Venus to the nymph Parisole, whom Phoebus loved in vain and punished by turning her beautiful complexion to brown, until Venus heard the prayers of her earthly lover and gave the gift of the parasol. On the whole, a piece of imitation which captures the manner of Gay with some success.

Richard Polwhele, the friend of Cowper, is now forgotten. But in the late years of the eighteenth century, his facile muse and vast energies made him a man of some note as a poet, translator, literary chronicler, theologian, and county historian. In short, he was the kind of literary clergyman who could plan a long didactic poem on oratory as his *magnum opus*. No doubt the encouragement of didactic poets like Cowper, Darwin, and Hayley counted for something, but the younger Pitt, the Countess of Chatham, and others lent their patronage. *The Art of Eloquence* (1785) was followed by *The English Orator* (1787), which included his second and third books. The enormous and fatally fluent poem begins with general advice on oratory, divides the subject into provinces of legal, parliamentary, and pulpit eloquence, and turns to advice on each. The last division (Book IV) was never published. The poem differs from more informal ones, on the Horatian model, which treat the technique of various arts, in the elevated and "magisterial" style employed, cast into Miltonic blank verse, and in the systematic method used. Panegyric and moralizing take on large proportions. There is narrative adapted to didactic purposes. There is the view of trials and of legal methods in other lands — in France, Spain, Turkey, and Italy. There is the account of the rise of the arts of oratory and their progress. The characterizations of various orators, Chatham, Fox, Burke, Pitt, Courtenay, and North, approach nearer to eloquence, at least, than anything else in the long poem. The work is an indication of the taste of its time: as a treatise in verse it rivals that of Erasmus Darwin for sterile artifice.

The themes of Falconer are carried on, with further accounts of the processes of life aboard ship, in Charles Fletcher's *Cockpit* (1797). Fletcher also is a seaman. His poem is mainly descriptive, showing the changes in the sky and the sea and on the vessel's decks, the fish and the birds which cross the ship's track; but processes of navigation appear also. Fletcher writes on themes familiar to him, but, like the other followers of Falconer, he has little skill in verse. He appeals to the current taste for exotic scenes and natural history, and to the audience which Falconer had won for themes of life at sea.

A clever piece of humor and satire appeared in 1796. John Anstey, second son of Christopher Anstey of *Bath-Guide* fame, a barrister of Lincoln's Inn, appeared with *The Pleader's Guide,* published under the pseudonym of "John Surrebutter, Esq." [11] The immediate inspiration for Anstey's satire may have been Polwhele's treatise, especially his third book on "the eloquence of the bar." But legal pedantry and chicanery are main objects of Anstey's satire.

> Of legal fictions, quirks, and glosses,
> Attorney's gains and client's losses,
> Of suits created, lost, and won,
> How to undo, and be undone,
> Whether by common law or civil,
> A man goes sooner to the devil,
> Things which few mortals can disclose
> In verse, or comprehend in prose,
> I sing — do thou, bright Phoebus, deign
> To shine for once in Chanc'ry Lane;
> And, Clio, if your pipe you'll lend
> To Mercury, the lawyer's friend,
> That usher of the golden rod,
> Of gain and eloquence the god,
> Shall lead my steps with guidance sure,
> Safe through the palpable obscure.

The statement of theme strikes the keynote. Anstey celebrates the processes of civil and common law with a great parade of legal terms and with precepts on special pleading. He applies the "happy-swain" theme to legal apprentices in excellent mock-heroic vein. The pedantries of legal jargon are turned to humor, with footnotes supplied, in the best tradition of didacticism. Like other didactic poets, Anstey lays claim to lasting honor for his verses. He explains the great advantages of the multiplication of law offices and of the perplexity of legal proceedings. There are complete instructions for pleading at the bar. Counselors Bore'um and Bother'um, pleading a case of "trespass in assault and battery," are presented, with the speeches in full and the cross-examination of witnesses. There are ingenious threads of parody from Milton, Vergil, and Homer, throughout. The following will illustrate Anstey's manner:

> The truth, and all the truth, discover,
> And add such flourishes moreover,
> Such aggravations and additions,
> Embellishments and repetitions,
> As youthful fancy oft begets
> On some young special pleader's wits,
> Which serve, like notes of commentators,
> Or speeches of confus'd debaters,
> To puzzle e'en by explanation,
> And darken by elucidation,
> For puzz'ling oft becomes your duty,
> And makes obscurity a beauty.

Jane West, who opposed the ideas of Mary Wollstonecraft, followed in the tradition of Tansillo, Sainte-Marthe, and Downman with *The Mother* (1809), a poem in five books. She tries to find her own formulas and, beyond the style and the use of varied types of episode, is underivative at least. Her teachings are eminently proper, pious, and maternal. She tries to find new episodes suited to her matter, in stories of Samuel and David; in praises of such models as Lady Jane Grey, Lady Mary Sidney, and the second Queen Mary; in accounts of the family in savage society, in the patriarchal ages, and in the medieval social scheme. The demands of "sensibility" are satisfied by accounts of the anguish of the mother of a courtesan and a spendthrift son, and by the story of a daughter seduced and driven to madness (there was a fatal attraction in this theme for the wooers of "sensibility"). Perhaps Mrs. West is not quite so inept a writer as all this may make her seem; but she is entirely dull, and her enthusiasm for piety and morals is unleavened by imagination.

The French poem of Joseph Berchoux, *La Gastronomie* (1801), which was *L'Homme à table* to Jacques Delille's *L'Homme des champs,* had a translator and an adapter in early nineteenth-century England. The anonymous *Gastronomy* (1810) and Hans Busk's *Banquet* (1819) were based on Berchoux, the former a translation, the latter a very free adaptation. Berchoux said that Delille had shown the countryman doing everything but eating. He repairs the omission. He summarizes the cookery of the ancients, and then in three more cantos conducts us through first and second courses to dessert. It is a pleasant piece of wit, with perhaps a touch of the

Petronius of Trimalchio's banquet. Busk is greatly superior to his anonymous predecessor. He recasts the poem to suit English manners, and treats it, in general, very cavalierly. For example, to make it truly English, he adds a supplement, *The Tea*. In the episode of Vatel, the royal chef who died to satisfy a *point d'honneur* in his code of catering, Busk outdoes Berchoux, which is not faint praise.

In scope if not in merit, the subject of navigation had its most signal treatment in George Woodley's *Britain's Bulwarks* (1811). Here are eight books and some two hundred pages in which " the various duties of the naval character, from the commander to the cabin-boy, are faithfully detailed through all the changes experienced by the vessel, from the time of her launching to the period of her being laid up in ordinary: embracing the diversified labours of the outfit, cruise, blockade, chace, action, and return to port." There is even a full glossary of naval terms. It is needless to speak of the poem in detail. The episodes are very stereotyped, and the wide scope of the plan is unmatched by the epical abilities which would have been needed for success. Woodley thinks of Falconer as his exemplar, but Falconer is a far superior poet.

Less broad in scope but similar in kind, Thomas Downey's *Pleasures of the Naval Life* appeared in 1813.[12] There are three cantos: one on " general employments of the mariner," another on " naval duty," and the last on " naval chiefs of Britain." There is a good deal of description of the sea, especially in the first canto, where the author carries his vessel from Falmouth to the tropics and back again. But Downey is as unpoetical as Woodley and must fall back on imitation. For example, he cannot avoid including Thomsonian details of northern seas, if only as a contrast to the tropical setting in which, at the moment, his vessel lies. Kirkpatrick, Fletcher, Ireland, Woodley, and Downey — the poets whose themes parallel Falconer's — have always lacked the ability to rival even his partial success.

There are certain other poets difficult to classify. They wrote formal didactic poems, analytical or reflective rather than preceptive, which have at least a semblance of systematic treatment, and which rely on various types of episode for relief. Such were Campbell's *Pleasures of Hope*, Rogers's *Pleasures of Memory*, John Gilbert Cooper's *Power of Harmony*, Thomas Noon Talfourd's *Union and Brotherhood of Mankind*, and many others. But beyond the most general features of systematic treatment, episodic plan, and formal style, they show little similarity to the georgic form. It would be impossible to glance at all the didactic poems of the century which are related to the georgic tenuously, only by reason of their preceptive treatment of various arts or techniques. These were often developments from earlier Horatian adaptations, but some are more difficult to classify. Among them are poems on such topics as social usage: Benjamin Stillingfleet's *Essay on Conversation* (1737), Humphrey Smythies's *Precepts* (1753), Lloyd's *Conversation* (1767), Mrs. Cutts's *Almeria* (1775), and William Cooke's *Conversation* (1796). Another type concerned subjects of professional or artistic practice, as in Thomas Gibbons's *Christian Minister* (1772), Dawson Warren's *Parish Priest* (1800), Jerome Alley's *Judge* (1803), Charles Dibdin's *Harmonic Preceptor* (1804), or the anonymous *Pastoral Care* (1808).

Among these poets who sought new subjects to adapt to the form of didactic verse, few are of permanent significance. Mark Akenside is an exception. He gave one of the most systematic expressions in poetry to a philosophy of nature widely current in his time, as well as to a system of ethical thought out of which grew much of the humanitarianism and " sentimentalism " of his period. The effort to bring the world of nature more fully into poetry is illustrated, on the descriptive side, by passages in Armstrong, Kirkpatrick, and Falconer and his followers. The interest in natural history and all phases of science, an important element in the taste of the century, appears in the same poets. Langhorne gives noteworthy expression to humanitarian sentiment and the impulse to reform. Men like Marriott, Shepherd, Elphinston, Smith, and Polwhele are entirely sterile, and represent no more than a feeble literary creation which is the product of forced growth.

VI

DAYS AND SEASONS

*Puissent mes chants être agréables à l'homme vertueux et
champêtre, et lui rappeler quelque fois ses devoirs et ses plaisirs.*
Saint-Lambert, after Wieland

THE IDEA of a poem or a series of poems on natural divisions of
time, parts of the day or of the year, did not originate with Thomson in *The Seasons*. Morning, noon, evening, spring, summer,
autumn, winter, the months, have been the common property of
poets. As the setting of the mind's existence, they have always con-
ditioned its responses in some degree, and have always supplied
imagery to symbolize changing states of the spirit. But some poets
before Thomson used these divisions of time more nearly as he
was to do. The georgic, with its country setting, usually reflected
the changes of the year. The occurrence of the device in pastoral
eclogue was of some frequency. Spenser's *Shepherd's Calendar* is
based upon the months of the year. So too are Phineas Fletcher's
Piscatorie Eclogs of 1633, imitations of Spenser. In the seventh
book of *The Faerie Queene*, the months march in succession before " great Nature," and each is characterized. Charles Cotton
wrote a series of vivid *Morning, Noon, Evening,* and *Night* quatrains, tracing the progress of a summer day. He has two poems
called *Winter*. Gawin Douglas used the seasons in prologues to his
translations of Vergil. Milton's *L'Allegro* and *Il Penseroso* trace
diurnal changes. *The Shepherd's Week* of Gay, Allan Ramsay's
Gentle Shepherd, and Pope's *Pastorals,* are all based on divisions
of time. Ambrose Phillips has a *Winter Piece from Copenhagen*.
Armstrong's *Winter*, Riccaltoun's *Winter Day*, both of which
Thomson knew and was influenced by, are other examples. William Hinchliffe's *Seasons* (1718) have been spoken of. John Dyer's
Country Walk follows a development through the parts of the
day. Lady Winchilsea's *Nocturnal Reverie*, William Pattison's
Morning Contemplation, and Parnell's *Night Piece on Death* are
among other examples before Thomson. There were also, of
course, among shorter poems, Thomson's earlier *Morning in the
Country* and *Month of May*.

Thomson was not the first to paint changes of the day or the year
with some semblance of systematic plan. But he introduced the

long episodic " descriptive poem " as a fully developed genre, and was recognized in England, France, and Germany as one of the poets who presented " originals " — poems which were the foundations of new schools. Actually *The Seasons* do not represent a completely new genre. The " descriptive poem " (on divisions of time), which flourished down well into the nineteenth century, is a form derived from didactic verse. *The Seasons* are offshoots of the *Georgics*. The episodic Vergilian form is turned to the uses of description, which now becomes the primary theme instead of a secondary one. Thomson's treatment of nature differed from that of important earlier poets in that he painted a systematic series of pictures, each one detailed and complete in itself, like the landscapes of a painter, the whole series representing the typical changes of the English year, ideal representations, true *mutatis mutandis* for any year or for all years. Thomson became one of the models for the poets of his century and the early years of the next. His descriptions and his episodes alike, both in part Vergilian, gave suggestions to a large school of followers. He helped poets to learn two things: appreciation for all aspects of nature, rugged, stern, stormy, or gentle, in Burke's terms " beautiful " or " sublime "; and appreciation for and observation of minute appearances that usually escape the eye.

We now use the term " a poet's eye for Nature " to indicate a quality of special keenness in observation. Few seem to realize that they are reading into this conception a property not always attributed to the poet, a quality perhaps not specifically " poetic " at all, since other men often have a hundredfold more of it than many of the finest poets. The eighteenth century contributed much to the building up of this conception of the poet as a being especially endowed with an eye for nature. The taste for landscape painting, for Salvator Rosa and Claude Lorraine, the spread of landscape gardening, the effect of the " grand tour " (fashionable after the War of the Spanish Succession), the discussion of Burke's qualities of the " sublime " and " beautiful " and of Price's and Gilpin's " picturesque " theories, the spread of the touring habit in England itself as the turnpike system was improved, the writing of detailed accounts of these tours — all of this helped to make Thomson more popular; and Thomson helped men to appreciate the broad, general, varied aspects of nature, whether seen on canvas or in the proportions of reality.

But these broad general effects were only one extreme of the range of vision. There was also the minute, the particular, the attention to " the meanest flower that blows." And even when poets began turning to natural history, to close knowledge of birds, flowers, trees, and animals, as they did especially in the later decades of the eighteenth century in order to satisfy a taste for exactitude and faithfulness to minutiae, Thomson was still their guide. Naturalists like Pennant and Daines Barrington recommended him — and natural history — to the poets. Critics like Joseph Warton, John Aikin, and Mrs. Barbauld did also. A taste for natural history had become fashionable by this time; intellectuals studied botany and ornithology, and poets heeded Aikin's admonitions to " studying in fields and woods." But Thomson was like a long familiar habit of mind for them. They learned to see, partly by seeing through his eyes. *The Seasons* did not begin to lose its prestige until the full triumph of the strictly romantic view of nature, the subjective attitude toward it. When poets read themselves into nature, when the scene is no longer observed for itself, when romantic individualism and nature worship are merged, Thomson begins to seem out of date. He served an extremely useful purpose in helping to teach poets and readers to observe. One must *see* before one can *feel*. The long descriptive poem is now an outmoded genre; but it helped to extend, in every direction, the range of men's observation and therefore the richness of their experience. Like many didactic poems and poems of localities, it shows also an extended range of interest in the lives and pursuits of men of the country. Genre sketches of country life replace the unreality of idyllic pastoral Arcadias and bring realism to the countryside. Humanitarianism is only a contributing factor here; the peasant and laborer are interesting as men shaped by contact with nature, and as men moving among the scenes of the country and forming an integral part of them.

Thomson's view of nature as a revelation of the divine, the concept that underlies and unites the scenes of *The Seasons,* had its influence on other descriptive poets and turned them to similar themes. Thomson's " philosophy of Nature " made a profound impression on readers of his century; it encouraged development in poetry of themes of " natural religion," and so contributed to the growth of a nature worship which was one of the most characteristic phases of romanticism.

In this chapter we shall consider the development of the descriptive poem based on divisions of time and growing out of the tradition of the *Georgics*. The connection of *Seasons* and *Georgics,* and the persistent outlines of each which pervade descriptive verse, have been set down in detail above.[1] It will be necessary, however, to indicate the continuity in subject matter which runs through the genre. I have chosen to follow a chronological order and to discuss the longer works individually, both because many of these poems are not easily available to readers and because, so presented, the growth of tendencies and ideas can be more clearly observed.

David Mallet's *Excursion* (1728), James Ralph's *Night* (1728), and Richard Savage's *Wanderer* (1729) were first published before *Autumn* appeared, the last of the *Seasons*. Mallet and Thomson were fellow Scots and friends. They corresponded while *Seasons* and *Excursion* were in progress. Each gave and received suggestions. Thomson paid Mallet the compliment of imitation, and Mallet borrowed from his friend. As reprinted with " considerable alterations " in 1743,[2] Mallet's poem is still more Thomsonian; and the expanded editions of *Winter* and *Summer* in 1730 and 1744 show further suggestions taken from *The Excursion*.[3] Following the progress of a summer day, *The Excursion* is partly descriptive and partly physico-theological, in the manner of Blackmore's *Creation*. The second canto is largely apologetics, an exposition of the solar system as evidence of the divine in nature. The two parts are not really homogeneous, though the poet tries to connect them as a survey of the earth and the heavens. Mallet is interesting as, with Thomson, one of the first poets to present connected, detailed scenes from nature, and to delight in wild and awesome scenes. Thomson thought much of his friend's poem " charmingly dreary."

Like *Summer* (1727), *The Excursion* is based on the parts of the day. It paints the appearances of morning, the heat of noon, the languishing of nature, the portents of storm, the storm itself and its effects on the earth, the reappearance of the sun, the revival of nature, and the setting of the sun. The *Georgics* are here expanded upon. Night is a period of solemn moral reflection on time, life, and eternity. When morning dawns again, the poet's fancy takes flight to the polar seas and to the torrid zone — a reminiscence of the *Georgics*. Like Thomson, Mallet finds solemnity and grandeur in the bleak North and in the torrid South, with its earthquakes, pestilences, and volcanoes.

Already in Mallet there appear many elements which Thomson encouraged. Storms and the barren regions of the earth have their grandeur. Mallet has caught, through Thomson and the poetry of apologetics, the habit of scientific exposition, not simply in the astronomy and Newtonian physics of the second canto, but in passages in the first, like those on the supposed causes of storm or of earthquakes and volcanic eruptions. In description, he sometimes uses Thomson as a model, but he had himself a certain energy in broad effects.

> The neighbouring Sun shines out in all his strength,
> Noon without night. Attracted by his beam,
> I thither bend my flight, tracing the source
> Where morning springs; whence her innumerous streams
> Flow lucid forth, and roll through trackless ways
> Their white waves o'er the sky. The fountain-orb,
> Dilating as I rise, beyond the ken
> Of mortal eye, to which earth, ocean, air,
> Are but a central point, expands immense,
> A shoreless sea of fluctuating fire,
> That deluges all ether with its tide.
> What power is that which to its circle binds
> The violence of flame! in rapid whirls
> Conflicting, floods with floods, as if to leave
> Their place, and, bursting, overwhelm the world!
> Motion incredible! to which the rage
> Of oceans, when whole winter blows at once
> In hurricane, is peace. But who shall tell
> That radiance beyond measure, on the Sun
> Pour'd out transcendent! those keen-flashing rays
> Thrown round his state and to yon worlds afar
> Supplying days and seasons, life and joy!

The second canto, in some ways superior to the first, surveys the solar system and the fixed stars, as expressions of the Deity immanent in his works. It is strongly Newtonian, showing a grasp of new scientific ideas comparable to Thomson's. The contemplation of nature and natural law, says Mallet, inspires the soul of man

> With virtuous raptures, prompting to forsake
> The sin-born vanities, and low pursuits
> That busy human kind,

and lifts the mind to the great " First Independent Cause " whose presence " fills th' immensity of space " and " the frame of things pervading actuates." Nature in earthly phenomena or in the wide range of space inspires man with moral feeling and spontaneous worship. And this nature, to such a pure intelligence as Newton's,

now set free " from frail mortality," is revealed " in its ideal harmony " of universal perfection, however much we may wonder at
the " unfathom'd wisdom " which visits upon men earthquake,
volcano, tempest, and plague.

James Ralph, the American who accompanied Franklin to England in 1724, published his *Night* in 1728. It really anticipates the
completed *Seasons*, since its four divisions follow the parts of the
year. The Thomsonian influence is plain, and is perhaps tacitly
admitted in the preface of the second edition where, after condemning the triviality of much current verse, Ralph says, " 'Tis consider'd with what applause Mr. Thomson's admirable poems were
generally receiv'd by the favourers of learning and good sense; an
undeniable argument that if the Muse is really the inspirer, the
world, even to a serious author, will not be wholly ungrateful." [4]
Night is an episodic descriptive poem in blank verse. Its method is
a free-hand copying of Thomson and Vergil, supplemented by
original observation. Ralph's method may be indicated by a short
synopsis of his descriptive content. A spring nightfall confronts us,
full of the early flowers, birds, and odors. But winter returns on
the unconfirmed season, scattering blight on flowers and fruits.
Spring returns once more; the halcyon is again on the waves. A
rain replenishes the earth and gives joy to all creatures. Summer
midday heat drives living creatures to shelter and sick nature is at
last revived by the dews of evening and the breezes of night. The
country girls bathe in the streams and are driven to shelter by the
approach of a boat. Autumn brings scenes of the harvest and of
peasants returning from their labors, their festival at night, the
deep silence of midnight, the marsh fires deceiving the wanderer,
and a thunderstorm which topples to earth the stricken oak and the
buildings of men. On the ocean, we see the fury of the storm, the
scene aboard a ship long out of control, and its appalling wreck.
Winter shows the traveler lost and drowned, the glitter of the ice
and frost, the devastations of a landslide, the flood which sweeps
away trees and peasants' cots, the snow covering all in one vast
desolation.

The most effective episodes are the Vergilian and Thomsonian
descriptions of the polar regions and the torrid zone. The vapors,
baneful dews, and pestilences of the South are described, and the
burning suns, tremendous storms, and malignant vapors of Africa,
where seamen are often lured by deceitful calms to shipwreck. In
Book IV the half-yearly winter of Greenland's bleak coast, the

northern lights, the " combats " of clashing icebergs, the enormous whale, the Baltic's terrors, which engulf the sons of Sweden — all these are massed into an effective contrast to the picture of tropical terrors. Ralph has not forgotten America, and praises her, as well as England, in Vergilian patriotic panegyrics. Moral episodes occur, where he laments the horrors of war, sings the pleasures of rural retirement, or calls in almost the very accents of Thomson on the sons of grandeur to pity those less fortunate.

Ralph is usually imitative, but he has zest and energy. The eagerness with which he seizes upon Thomson's nature description, his humanitarianism, his " sensibility," indicates a volatile nature full of enthusiasm. Ralph does not make as much of the ideas of natural revelation of the divine as do Thomson, Mallet, and Savage; there is, however, in Book III an interesting celebration of the wonders of the stars, worlds which reveal the Creator of the universe. The physico-theological ideas of the time are again reflected here.

Richard Savage's *Wanderer* (1729) is a descriptive and reflective poem which illustrates its period revealingly. Its merits and its faults are equally illuminating. It is a curious hybrid of different genres. There is no consistent plan except that of the poet's imaginary wanderings in time and space. The phenomena of the seasons are a descriptive bond of unity. The parts of a winter's day and night bind together the first three cantos. The coming and passing of spring is described early in Canto IV, and a summer's day and night then form the link between the fourth and fifth cantos. The fantastic figure of a philosophical hermit, who discourses on ethical and religious topics, appears and reappears, his last visit forming a climax of supernatural vision in the final canto. Descriptively Savage owes a good deal to Thomson; but, as in the case of Thomson and Mallet, there are debts on each side. Thomson's expansions of *Winter* in 1730 and 1744, the first edition of *Autumn* in 1730, and the final version of *Summer* in 1744, all owe a few suggestions to *The Wanderer*,[5] though Savage owes more to Thomson than Thomson to him. As a descriptive poet, however, Savage is a pioneer, and he deserves attention as an observer, though his artistic taste is not impeccable. His poem is broad and sometimes detailed in observation. He paints landscapes, mountains, bold exotic scenes of arctic wastes, the northern lights, comets, and volcanoes. But he is minute too, noticing effects of light and shade in the fields and in the sky, the shifting shapes of clouds, the minute work of the frost, many trees, herbs, and flowers, and many birds, animals, and insects. His colorful descriptions of sunrise and sunset are striking for their time, and not without a bold dramatic quality. He has more of Thomson's highly developed color sense than any other contemporary poet. He likes the bravura effects of a poet like Ralph, and paints the mountains where " rocks in rough assemblage rush in view " or the wide panorama of the rising winter moon and her light shed gradually over the earth.

> Orient, the queen of night emits her dawn,
> And throws, unseen, her mantle o'er the lawn.
> Up the blue steep, her crimson orb now shines;
> Now on the mountain-top her arm reclines,
> In a red crescent seen; Her zone now gleams,
> Like Venus quivering in reflecting streams. . . .
> Dark fires seem kindled in nocturnal blaze;
> Through ranks of pines, her broken lustre plays,
> Here glares, there brown-projecting shade bestows,
> And, glittering, sports upon the spangled snows.

But his minute observation is also interesting. Notations like these are unusual in 1729, however inadequate their expression:

> The bullfinch whistles soft his flute-like notes.
> The bolder blackbird swells sonorous lays;
> The varying thrush commands the tuneful maze;
> Each a wild length of melody pursues;
> While the soft murmuring, amorous wood-dove coos.
> And, when in spring these melting mixtures flow,
> The cuckoo lends her unison of woe.
> But as smooth seas are furrow'd by a storm;
> As troubles all our tranquil joys deform;
> So, loud through air, unwelcome noises sound,
> And harmony's at once, in discord, drown'd.
> From yon dark cypress, croaks the raven's cry;
> As dissonant the daw, jay, chattering pie:
> The clamorous crows abandon'd carnage seek,
> And the harsh owl shrills out a sharpening shriek.

Like others in this period, Savage reflects ideas of natural revelation and of a divine harmony in nature and the moral world. He sees the divine immanent in nature, " God in all." The hermit counsels the poet, " To know thy God, paint Nature on thy mind," insisting that truth and religion are revealed there through contemplation, free from all " traditionary falsehood."

Savage is little concerned with man in nature. There are a few Thomsonian genre sketches of peasant labors and of country sports, but these are never of much interest. The scientific element reappears often, both as exposition and description. Savage's hermit is a philosopher more garrulous than profound. His favorite topics of discourse are the old georgic theme of the dignity and accomplishments of labor, the calamities of human life, the riot and intemperance of cities and the delights of philosophic retirement, the ungenerosity of the great, the worth of humanity, benevolence, and " public zeal " — the cardinal virtues of the Shaftesburians.

The established school of poetry did not look with favor on these descriptive writers, whatever may have been Pope's personal attitude toward Thomson. The pontiff of English letters several times delivered pronouncements on descriptive verse: " a feast of sauces " was his characterization. The younger Samuel Wesley, however, seems to be the only poet of the time who attempted a satire of the descriptive form. His *The Descriptive. A Miltonick. After the Manner of the Moderns* appeared in 1736.[6] His " Argument " is worth quoting as an illustration of his point of attack:

The invocation: The poem slides insensibly into the midst of things, and presents a flower-piece; then proceeds to the heat of Africa, the fertility of harvest, and the cold usually ensuing: This naturally leads to the stages of man's life; Infancy: A bird's-nest, illustrated from Homer: Youth . . . the next two ages slightly touched, make way for a sketch of the morning: A moral reflection on the uncertainty of human things, by way of transition to night; wherein is introduced an assemblage of allegorical persons, perfectly picturesque, and highly suitable to the nature of this kind of poetry. The conclusion.

Neither the burlesque of the diffuse plan of descriptive poetry nor the parody of the descriptive style stands in need of comment:

> Thee, torrid zone adust, thee who shall praise?
> Except by Sirius or his brother star
> Haply inspir'd. Phoebus' meridian fires
> Intense, extreme, (while the fierce Lion reigns,
> Malignant reigns, morbific, pestilent)
> Heat Afric's furnace into sev'n-fold flame. . . .
> Behold he comes with trembling pace, but sure,
> Whose icy breath the circumambient air
> Chills frore; by rustic foot or carriage prest;
> Unyielding, unobsequious stands the frost,
> Nitrous, incrusted, crispy, crackling, crimp.

The long descriptive poem did not become immediately widespread after 1730. Thomson's influence first affected the poets of shorter lyrical forms, the didactic poets, and even those who celebrated places throughout the kingdom. Very probably his influence also counted strongly on the scientific and philosophical side with poets who wrote the long physico-theological poems of the period, such writers as Moses Browne, Bevill Higgons, Henry Brooke, and, later, William Sotheby. But until the seventies, most descriptive poets seem to have been overawed by the reputation of Thomson. Didactic poetry reached its peak first. The decade of the fifties really established it as an outstanding genre of verse: Smart, Dodsley, Dyer, Thomas Scott, and Weekes were of that decade. It remained firmly intrenched through the rest of the century, enjoyed a new and vigorous lease of life between 1800 and 1810, and declined rapidly thereafter. The descriptive form, however, lagged behind until 1770, and thereafter grew rapidly to a climax especially marked between 1800 and 1810, declining after 1820, though it produced some of its most detailed examples in the thirties and even later.

Shorter lyrical poems are worth an attention here impossible. Throughout the century and into the next, many poets who wrote short poems on phases of nature found inspiration both in *Seasons* and *Georgics*. They borrow their themes and elaborate them. They learn to sketch from nature by adding their own observation, especially to Thomson's outlines and suggestions. They learn to respond as he did to the wide variety of the "beautiful," the "sublime," and the "picturesque." They compose pictures, landscapes, as he did. They write, in short, not long episodic descriptive poems in blank verse or couplets, but fragments of such poems, short descriptions, single scenes or short successions of scenes, in stanzaic and lyrical measures. These are usually "odes" and "elegies" (poems in the elegaic quatrain). Michael Bruce, John Scott, Akenside, Thomas Warton, John Cunningham, William Woty, Cuthbert Shaw, John Logan, Anna Seward, Mrs. Barbauld, and Bowles afford typical examples.[7] A list of such poems, capable of indefinite expansion, would include also such less easily available poems as these: Edward Stephens's *Occasion'd by a Violent Storm* (1759); [8] Francis Leighton's *January, February, March, April, May,* and *November* (1769); [9] the anonymous *Winter, An Elegy* (1770); [10] Richard Valpy's *Seasons* (1772); [11] Samuel Bentley's *Haymaking* (1774); [12] Joseph Wise's *May* (1775); [13] the anonymous *Spring* and *Autumn* (1776) ; [14] Elizabeth Fell's *Spring, Summer, Autumn,* and *Winter* (1777) ; [15] Ewan Clark's *Odes to Spring, Summer, Autumn, and Winter* (1777) ; [16] John Hoy's *Spring, Summer, Autumn, Winter,* and *A Thunderstorm* (1781) ; [17] Robert Alves's *Winter Night* (1782) ; [18] John Henry Colls's *Winter* (1786?) ; [19] John Macgilvray's *Caledonian Spring* and *To May* (1787) ; [20] Hugh Mulligan's *Months* (1788) ; [21] George Sackville Cotter's *Odes to Spring, Summer, Autumn, and Winter* (1788) ; [22] Thomas Skelton Dupuis's *Winter* (1789) ; [23] Peter Newby's *Prospective Contemplations* and *Winter* (1790) ; [24] William Mavor's *Approach of Spring* and *Autumn Morning* (1793) ; [25] Henry Man's *Thunder Storm* (1802) ; [26] William Richardson's *Ode on Winter* and *Morning Walk* (1805) ; [27] George Woodward's *Hours* (1805) ; [28] James Murray Lacey's *Year* and *April Storm* (1809) ; [29] William Hersee's *Harvest Storm* (1810) ; [30] Patrick Brontë's *Winter Night Meditations* (1811) ; [31] Washington Allston's *Sylphs of the Seasons* (1813) ; [32] Patrick Brontë's *Winter* (1813) ; [33] Matthew Hartsonge's *Ode to Desolation* (1815) ; [34] Thomas Crossley's *Winter Night, Spring,* and *Summer* (1828?) ; [35] and William Calder's *Songs of the Seasons* (1838) .[36]

The work of the Wartons in descriptive poetry stands somewhat apart from that of the followers of Thomson. *The Enthusiast* (1740) of Joseph Warton and *The Pleasures of Melancholy* (1747) of his brother Thomas, are poems organized on a reflective rather than a descriptive outline. Thomas Warton's *On the Approach of Summer* (1753) and *The First of April* (1777) are odes, short poems closer to the Thomsonian model of description of appearances of specific times of year; but they do not make use of extended episode. *The Enthusiast, or the Lover of Nature* contrasts all forms of art and " taste corrupt " unfavorably with the charms of un-adulterated nature. It is a strong expression of the primitivistic re-action against artificiality and luxury in human society. Warton's mind even returns with longing to the first stages of the life of man in his primitive freedom, as these stages of society were painted by Lucretius. The poem is exceptional for its notations of birds, ani-mals, insects, the sounds of the seashore, the appearances of the fields, and the phenomena of the sky. Joseph Warton is one of many after Thomson who finds in nature powerful influences on the moral nature of man. These influences all conspire " to raise, to soothe, to harmonize the mind." *The Pleasures of Melancholy* celebrates the " mother of musings, Contemplation sage," but it is

often strikingly exact in description. The love of harsh winter
scenes is more Thomsonian than Miltonic. The description of
scenes of twilight and midnight and of the sounds of night are
close and faithful. The description of a stormy morning and of its
effects on birds and men suggests similar details in both Vergil and
Thomson, though neither is copied.[37] The Arabian traveler in the
midst of the terrors of a tropical night suggests Thomson.[38] So too
does the Siberian exile in the land " where winter ever whirls his
icy car." [39]

Milton was the strongest influence on the poetry of Thomas
Warton. But the odes *On the Approach of Summer* and *The First
of April* also show Thomsonian features and are fairly long poems
on particular seasons. The first lines of the former indicate Warton's double debt to two great descriptive predecessors:

> Hence, iron-sceptered Winter, haste
>   To bleak Siberian waste!
> Haste to thy polar solitude;
>   'Mid cataracts of ice
> Whose torrents dumb are stretch'd in fragments rude
>   From many an airy precipice,
> Where, ever beat by sleety showers.
> Thy gloomy Gothic castle towers;
> Amid whose howling aisles and halls,
> Where no gay sunbeam paints the walls,
> On ebon throne thou lov'st to shroud
> Thy brows in many a murky cloud.[40]

Here Warton's description of the retreat of winter before returning spring, his pictures of various noontide retreats (the scenes of
contemplation) , his account of the revival of nature and man after
the summer storm, his African traveler longing for water in the
midst of the trackless desert, his effort to mark the phenomena most
characteristic of early summer, are all reminiscent of Thomson.
though they emulate rather than imitate him. *The First of April*
paints the gradual return of spring, the earliest growths of flowers,
herbs, and grain, certain birds and insects of the month, the various
hues of green appearing, the fisherman's sport, and the behavior
of animals in early spring. The pleasing quality of Thomas Warton's observation is apparent everywhere in these verses.

The facile William Thompson was once highly esteemed for his
poems *Sickness* and *An Hymn to May*. The first echoes Young,
Spenser, and James Thomson. The latter combines influences of
Spenser, Thomson, and perhaps Vergil. *An Hymn to May* (1740?)

is in Spenserian stanzas. In it, pastoral artifice and archaic language are side by side with occasional realism. We recognize Thomsonian colors in the accounts of the rainbow after the shower, of the bees among the flowers, of the scents of flowers, herbs, orchards, and gardens. The flocks and herds again "renew their loves." The "stately courser" and the birds are moved by the season's influences. There is a "prospect" or landscape from the summit of a hill, a picture composed and painted in detail. Where a fully developed descriptive poem would introduce longer episodes, there are short passages on rural retirement, British liberty, the delights of peace, and the necessity for the wealthy to protect those less fortunate. Pastoral artifice appears in the invocation of shepherds, shepherdesses, dryads, fauns, and satyrs, and in the episode of Venus' court on the country hillside. William Thompson shows the mingling of idyllic affectation and realism in descriptive poetry at this period.

After Wesley's parody in 1736, I am aware of no very detailed episodic poem on divisions of time before the anonymous *Pastorella, A Description of the Seasons,* which appeared in *A Banquet of the Muses* (1746), a miscellany printed for Jacob Bickerstaff.[41] This seems to have grown out of a desire to see *The Seasons* put into heroic couplets. Shortening each one, the author casts the four parts of Thomson's poem into that measure. He adds little of his own, but he omits at will, especially non-descriptive episodes. Everywhere vividness and color are sacrificed for rhyme. It is worth observing, however, what seemed to this adapter the most appealing parts of his original. In *Spring* he shows the revival of nature, the first flowers, and the effects of the season on birds and beasts. He elaborates especially the courtships, matings, and nest-building of the birds. There are the genre pictures of plowing, seeding, and harrowing, and of peasants at evening telling tales, singing, and dancing. *Summer* follows Thomson's changes of a single day, up to the thunderstorm of afternoon, elaborated in detail. There is a picture of growing vegetable gardens and a catalogue of products, like the catalogues of wild flowers and garden flowers in *Spring*. Genre pictures of haymaking and fishing are paraphrased. The new *Autumn* is mainly genre pictures: reaping the corn, the harvest-home festival, hunting, gathering nuts. *Winter* combines details from several of Thomson's parts. The more striking seasonal changes are put into rhyme; and there are pictures of skaters, hare hunters, and fowlers, and of a merry company celebrating the success of the chase. A part of this is from Thomson's *Autumn*. *Pastorella* shows the writer's enthusiasm for parts of *The Seasons* which are most realistic and vivid. The new *Winter* includes some lines taken from Ambrose Phillips's poem on that season, written at Copenhagen in 1709 and addressed to the Earl of Dorset.[42]

It is interesting to note, in passing, the first partially descriptive poem published in the American colonies which suggests the influence of Thomson, *Philosophic Solitude* (1747), by William Livingston, later a delegate to the first Continental Congress, one of the framers of the Constitution, and a governor of New Jersey. The work is really a retirement poem, only in part descriptive. It includes descriptions of parts of the day, sketches the beauties of the countryside, and praises the happy life of the man of retirement, remote from cities and courts. Besides his description of the day, Livingston's "hymn to the sun," his praises of conjugal love, and his account of the delights of reading sages, philosophers, and poets, seem to follow the lead of Thomson. The poem has little originality in such passages or in its episodes on the "beauty and harmony" of creation as proof of God's existence, and on the vanity of riches and grandeur; but it seems to be an early reflection of the desire to adapt ideas of *The Seasons* in American verse. It was apparently not until considerably later that American poets began to recast Thomson into verses on the American seasons and months and country scenes: this tendency appears in the anonymous poet of *Winter Display'd* (1784), and in such men as Samuel Low (*Poems*, 1800), John McKinnon (*Descriptive Poems*, 1802), and John Hayes (*Rural Poems*, 1807).[43]

The anonymous poem *The Landscape* (1746) is a description of the coming of spring, written in elegaic quatrains, and echoing *The Seasons* in painting the return of the flowers and birds. Its nature description, its melancholy contemplations of ruins, and its fanciful pictures of the dances of fairies at night and of fairy circles in the grass at morning, are all reflections of earlier poets. Only in its groping toward realism of description has the poem any interest. The same may be said of *The Seasons* of Moses Mendes, written in 1751 and reprinted in the miscellanies of Richardson and Urquhart, and of Pearch.[44] Mendes was a wealthy stockbroker who wrote ballad opera and "musical entertainments," and who was often visited by Thomson at his estate, Mitcham. His *Seasons* is a contracted descriptive poem in the Spenserian stanza, of which he was fond. Like other "Spenserians," he has a good deal of archaic affectation. Beginning with praises of Thomson, *Spring* pictures the effects of that season on the birds and barnyard fowl, the coming of the flowers, the play of the doves, the effects of spring on mankind, and the festival of May Day. *Summer* shows the languishing of fields, flowers, animals, and men under the ardent sun, the "noontide retreat," the labors of the hayfield, a summer night, and peasants dancing. *Autumn* sketches the harvest, "harvest-home" festival, the ripened fruits, the chase and fowling, and rural content in retirement. *Winter* brings the freezing of the streams, the changed state of animals and men, the peasant's labors mending hedge and draining — and his winter-evening pleasure in merry companies. There is little in Mendes for which he could not have found at least the suggestion in Thomson. But a genuine taste for nature and pleasure in observing the life of the country are present.

An autumn piece illustrating the spread of a taste for landscape description and for genre sketches is George Roberts's *Prospect, or Rural Sports* (1754). The poet climbs to a hilltop and surveys the scene before him, the autumn fields at dawn and the beginning of man's activity as the reapers and gleaners go to the fields. The hay and corn harvest, partridge shooting, and fox-hunting are described. Roberts writes a poem combining elements of local, descriptive, and didactic verse. His realism exists side by side with a piece of idyllic idealization of the sort common to the eclogue — an episode in which Phillomella and her shepherd exchange vows of love.

John Scott of Amwell was a poet whose themes were of country life and whose effort was toward realism; his eclogues, elegies, odes, and epistles all express this feeling for truth. The *Elegies, Descriptive and Moral* (1760), four in number, on the four seasons, form a very slight descriptive poem, but one of some interest. Scott's indications of scenes of nature are hardly more than jottings; the same may be said of his pictures of country tasks. But they are sketched from life. There are phrases and themes that betray Thomson's influence; but, however crude as a poet, Scott had, at least, independent observation and knew the country. The moral element of the poem is of a jejune kind, but it is interesting to notice that Scott is another who looks to nature for the proof of a divine creative intelligence, apparent in the minutest flower, pebble, or insect. Scott's verse has qualities of honesty and simplicity, whether in the *Amoeboean Eclogues* already spoken of, in his *Moral Eclogues,* his *Elegies,* or a brief epistle like his *Winter Amusements in the Country.*

But independent treatment gained ground slowly. The anonymous poem *On the Winter Solstice* (1765), written in rhymed stanzas of irregular line lengths, indicates the character of its Thomsonism in its invocation to the poet of the seasons,

> Instructive bard! whose sylvan tale,
> With Doric charm, and fancy bright
> Inspires my trembling wings to trace thy nobler flight.

Realism is present in winter landscapes and in pictures of country amusements: the rural feast and dance, the village matron telling tales of ghosts and witches, and the fowling episode. The Vergilian "excursion of fancy" appears in a "northern-winter piece" and a "tropic picture." The Vergilian-Thomsonian "patriotic panegyric" then follows — Albion is free of the excesses of both extremes; she has her groves and fields, the Thames, beautiful hills and promontories, great oaks, kindly seasons, and a hardy race free of tyranny and born to rule the seas.

A poet of nature who deserves attention is William Stevenson, a friend of Dr. Young. *Vertumnus: or the Progress of Spring*,[45] in six books (1765), is an extensive series of pictures of the season and its occupations and sports. Stevenson acknowledges both Thomson and Vergil as his masters. His numerous sketches of country employments are less detailed than those of many later poets. His closer approaches to peasants, as in his narratives of rustic lovers, have a good deal of artificiality. These lovers speak in a vein of lush sentiment, and even reason on the laws of love. But there are realistic sketches, though not detailed ones, of the plowman, the angler, hunters, peasants dancing at evening in the villages, the gardener training and caring for his flowers, and the young men of the village at quoits, running and leaping, swimming, weight throwing, bowling, and archery. But Stevenson's most sincere delight is in nature, and though his debt is obvious, he is more than merely imitative. He is like many of the English descriptive poets in his delight in birds. The marvelous economy of the bees, the subject of the fourth *Georgic*, is another favorite. The greenhouse, the orchard, and the vegetable garden are of course pictures suggested by Thomson. One of the interesting passages is the account of sounds that break the stillness of evening in spring:

> The pool in gentle undulations shook
> By the swift lapse of some near-falling brook;
> The milk-maid, as she bears her fragrant load,
> Singing aloud to cheer the dreary road;

The beetle's drony pinions, slowly stirr'd,
The frequent hoots of Night's ill-omen'd bird;
The shepherd's horn with lusty cheek full-blown;
The gentle finger'd haut-boy's milder tone;
The break successive, and deep hollow roar,
Of billows lashing some contiguous shore;
The ceaseless hum of insects, hov'ring round,
And flocks penn'd up with sleepy tinkling sound;
The partridge shrill, in some adjoining park
Seeking her mate scarce obvious in the dark;
The swallow, twitt'ring from her mud-built nest,
As if to soothe her callow young to rest;
Or noisy martlets, in phantastic play,
And keen pursuit, winging their airy way.

The digressions range from narrative to moral exposition and follow conventional lines; for example, the effects of spring on the minds of various conditions of men, and the flight of fancy to the torrid zone, with contrasting praises of Britain's plenty, virtue, peace, freedom, religion, science, art, and commerce. Stevenson's preference for country to city is obviously sincere, though his praise of the peasant is extravagantly colored by romantic primitivism:

> Blush, ye that boast a garter or a star;
> Behold a peasant, more ennobled far.

The religious element is very strong in Stevenson. He is orthodox in his views, denying the claim of deists that reason suffices for man's contact with God. " Reason assisted " by faith brings man to knowledge of his Maker. Stevenson's use of natural revelation differs little from that of less orthodox poets, though he does not believe in the sufficiency of such revelation. The idea of divine immanence is clearly present, and the closely related idea of an influence on the moral nature of man appears also. Each object of contemplation proclaims its divine origin:

> Here, to ennoble, and instruct mankind
> In knowledge boundless as the godlike mind,
> Each with sublime solicitude essays
> To celebrate what soars above all praise.

The same poet included, in his 1765 collection, *The Progress of Evening*,[46] a descriptive poem on a smaller scale, and such more fragmentary descriptions as *A Sketch of Noon* and *Ode on Spring*. *The Progress of Evening* has new genre sketches of country pur-

suits and new pictures of nature. Sometimes it has this kind of
vividness:

> Martlets now quit their airy circling range,
> Increasing still their clamour as they fly;
> The lone bat, flitting with incessant change,
> On leathern pinion wings the darksome sky.
>
> The wheeling hornet no one course confines,
> On heedless here, now there, dull drone, he holds;
> In lucid spangles, lo, the glow-worm shines,
> As o'er the blade he drags his spiral folds.

It is not lack of observation in such verse that spoils its effect; it
is conventionalized diction. But Stevenson deserves attention as a
poet preoccupied with nature and the country, striving to paint
faithfully.

Francis Noel Mundy's *Winter,* in elegiac quatrains, was begun in
1757 but evidently remained unpublished until 1768.[47] Like
Thompson's *Hymn to May,* it is a short descriptive poem without
much elaboration of episode, but it is more realistic in tone. Realism goes hand in hand with influence from *The Seasons.* "Stern
Winter's" coming with his stormy train, the silence of the birds,
the robin finding its way to the haunts of men, the bewildered
traveler in the dazzling snow fearing death, the peasant's content-
ment in his sheltered hut in winter evenings, are subjects from
Thomson. Mundy has merely tried to sketch from the originals
of the acknowledged master.

Christian apologetics, description, exhortation, and narrative
are combined in James Foot's extensive *Penseroso, or the Pensive
Philosopher in his Solitudes* (1771), in six books. Foot wants " to
recommend piety, the social virtues, and a love of liberty " through
the reflections of his solitary sage, and he takes "occasion to em-
bellish the poem with pastoral description and relieve the reader by
presenting him with a pleasing view of natural appearances." The
seasons of the year furnish a background for the poem. It would be
strange if we did not find Foot's descriptions echoing Thomson's.
He adds observation of his own, some of it worth attention.

> The ruffian blasts
> From Heav'n's high hall discharg'd, where late they lay
> Confin'd indignant, now through fields of air
> Rush furious forth in such excursions rude
> As shake the growing forest, 'til each walk

With wither'd leaves is strown. The mountains heave,
And dismal sigh the hollow rock-hewn caves,
As if a troubled spirit of the air,
Inchantment drear, was thence to distant lands
Loud on a tempest borne. The ocean lifts
Its waves, and scarce the forelands tow'ring height,
Though firmly ribb'd with everlasting rocks,
The dashing surge endures; and eagle fowls,
Sea-gazers, seek the cliffs, where, scoop'd, is formed
Their solitary haunt; where, seated now,
They deem themselves secure, and hear unmov'd,
The tumult of the working seas below.
Lo! other birds, for shelter, to the woods
Fly screaming, whilst the ever-lonely owl
Waves in her ivy-house; the cattle reach
The neighboring sylvan fence, or sheltering stall,
Lodg'd safe beneath the storm; and swains in cots
Securely rest; but at the flapping doors,
The rural damsels start, and hear, in winds,
Through whistling crevices, or think they hear,
The approach of ghosts unlaid. Their flying down
The thistles shed around, and bladed grass
Sings in the wind swift-flitting o'er the lea.

Foot seems to follow Thomson's manner in scientific exposition also, with conjectures as to the causes of bird migrations, comets, the distribution of the stars in space, and other phenomena. The long descriptions of plague, earthquake, and flood often seem to echo details from *The Seasons*. There is a " patriotic panegyric " of Britain in the familiar Vergilian vein. The praises of retirement which recur are indistinguishably Vergilian or Horatian, but Foot does not forget, as Crabbe was to remind men later, that poverty, sickness, and oppression grind down the peasants. The moralizing content of *Penseroso* is the largest element. The sage reflects upon the sources of happiness, none trustworthy but virtue, the absurdity of Epicurean belief in chance creation, the pathway through contemplation of nature to contemplation of God, the terrors and delights of the day of judgment, the growth of true religion out of idolatry, the attributes of God, and the qualities of a good civil government — exemplified in the main in that of Britain. Though an orthodox believer, Foot illustrates the tendency to develop ideas of natural revelation. He speaks of nature sometimes as separate from " the great mind which form'd [its] vast design "; sometimes he speaks of God as immanent in creation. The moral influence exerted by nature is an idea to which he returns at intervals:

> The sight of nature is the sight of God,
> And this fair sight to virtue leads, and Heav'n.
> Then be it mine to scan great Nature's works,
> The grand designs of rectitude supreme,
> That virtue may direct my steps to Heav'n.

Up to 1770 many who wrote description chose the " sublime," rather than the " beautiful " — wild and rugged aspects of winter and stormy scenes, for example, rather than more restrained effects of repose, delicacy, or gradual variation. Samuel Law shows this tendency in *A Domestic Winter Piece* (1772) , a poem " exhibiting a full view of the author's dwelling place in the winter season." The falling of the snow, a traveler lost and frozen among the drifts, a frosty night succeeded by a morning which displays a world locked in ice, the wandering sheep on the wide plains of snow, the sudden thaw followed by floods, storms of hail, rain, sleet, and wind, are all described with a real pleasure in what Thomson called " charmingly dreary " scenes. The transition of the season through serene, calm days and starry nights to the gradual approach of spring, gives the poet less real delight. Law too falls back upon the art of the master of descriptive verse, though he protests in his preface that he avoids imitation of Thomson. It is interesting to notice that he apologizes for his use of couplets, believing blank verse the proper medium for description.

But in the following year John Huddlestone Wynne turned Thomson again into couplets in *The Four Seasons* (1773) . A friend of Goldsmith, Wynne was one of the historical writers flourishing in this period, and an editor of the *Lady's Magazine*. His advertisement says:

Thomson's Seasons being written in a sort of verse which is not equally read or relished by every one, it was judged that something of the same kind in rhyme might be executed with some novelty and a prospect of success, and be productive of some moral entertainment to the readers; especially such of the fair sex as might be inclined to partake of a rational amusement, and whose leisure might not allow them to peruse a larger work.

Rededicating the parts to Lady Almeria Carpenter, the Duchess of Northumberland, Lady Charlotte Finch, and Lady Betty Mackenzie, Wynne rewrites, adding little of his own and leaving out at will. Writing for feminine readers, he makes much of the mating season of the birds in *Spring*, but he leaves out the pictures of the brute kingdom in that season, the effects of love on man and woman, the picture of the extravagances and sorrows of ill-advised love, and the Lucretian account of the scourge of jealousy. Thomson's narrative episodes are usually left out, perhaps because the tone of some of them was felt to be too forthright or, in the case of Amelia, struck by lightning, too awesome. Few of the pictures describing nature are entirely omitted. Many are shortened, and all of them are made less sharp in outline, less exact and colorful. Wynne's praises of retirement anticipate Cowper when he insists

> But those who haunt the sweet retreats of life,
> Far from the court's deceit, the city's strife,
> Must seek the blessing with a social train.
> So shall their joys still undisturb'd remain.

He adds, too, to the "patriotic panegyric," praises of his native Ireland. Thomson's genre sketches of country occupations are not usually added to, but in *Autumn* Wynne adds a picture of artless rustic lovers, celebrating the charm and modesty of country girls. His episodes include the popular "excursions of fancy" to torrid and arctic zones, much of Thomson's humanitarian sentiment, and his appeal to "sensibility" and praises of God immanent in nature, who "pervades, supports, and rules this beauteous all." Wynne's rewriting of Thomson reminds us that Lord Lyttleton planned to do the same thing, omitting what was unorthodox and what failed to satisfy his Lordship's exacting notions of elegance and dignity.[48]

Edmund Rack is another in this decade who turned Thomson into rhyme. He was a prominent figure at Bath, and one of the group of poetasters grouped about Lady Miller of Batheaston, whose "poetical amusements" at her villa are well known. His *Poems on Several Subjects* (1775) include *To Spring; Spring, a Pastoral; Winter;* and *A Thunderstorm;* all of them except the first, which is in blank verse, are Thomson in rhyme. *Spring* adopts the device of casting imagery from *The Seasons* into a pastoral dialogue between Damon and Melalcas. *Winter* is a series of pictures, only slightly varied by original details, from Thomson: the "icy chains" binding the streams, the herds seeking shelter, the flocks seeking food in vain on the snow-covered fields, the robin visiting the haunts of men, the artistry of the frost, thaw and flood, and the revival of spring. Humanitarian appeals to the "opulent and great " to reflect on the ills of poverty, are from *The Seasons* too. Rack is also another of the many poets of natural revelation and physico-theology of the period.

The anonymous *Night* (1776) ,[49] a descriptive, narrative, and reflective poem, may be cited as a further example of adaptation, in its passages on nature. The poet longs for the pen of Thomson, that he may adequately picture the appearances of night, and he follows his original as a model from which he tries to depart in lines of original observation.

A moralist whose works had some currency for a time, George Wright, found a new formula for Thomsonism. His *Rural Christian,* a long work, appeared in a second and enlarged edition in 1776, and reached a fifth edition in 1816. His later *Retired Pleasures* (1787) was also a good deal read. The method was that of description moralized. *The Rural Christian* is in four books upon morning, noon, evening, and night of a summer day. His couplets adapt Thomson and add moralistic glosses. Narrative episodes vary the scheme. The framework may be indicated by a summary: the dawn of summer morning, portents of storm, thunderstorm, flood, nature's revival, the rainbow, the " noon-day retreat," summer flowers stricken by the sun, bathing in the country streams, a " prospect " from Richmond Hill, summer evening, sunset, and starlit night. But every stage of the day, every phenomenon of nature, has its moral tag. The flood has a moral counterpart in the sweeping away at once and forever of " vain hopes " in the storms of distress and failure. The rainbow is like the promise of new life which the believer enjoys. Darkness is an emblem of the soul's despair, the moon a symbol of faith shining far off for the faithful. The episodes of Altamont and Theron contrast the life and death of the libertine and the believer. The pathetic account of Zephalinda follows the description of the withering of summer flowers, and illustrates the transience of beauty.

Wright was, of course, a thoroughly orthodox man; it is interesting to notice his divergences from Thomson. These appear most clearly in his annotated edition of Thomson's *Seasons,* which he first published, evidently, in 1770. His notes comment on the religious doctrines of Thomson. The ideas of " natural revelation " he approves heartily, citing passages from Addison, Young, and Pope to the same purpose. But he finds it necessary to insist on doctrines of redemption from sin by the atonement of Christ and the supernatural revelation of God in " his word." He insists, as does Cowper, that God alone " can enlighten the mind by his spirit, and teach us the knowledge of his wondrous works."

Such was the situation in descriptive poetry, one of stagnation and unoriginal adaptation, when John Aikin published his *Essay on the Application of Natural History to Poetry* (1777). Thomas Pennant, his Warrington friend, the eminent naturalist, had already recommended science to the poets, in the preface to his famous *British Zoölogy*,[50] first published in 1766. While urging theologians (for the sake of Christian apologetics), painters and sculptors, country gentlemen, and those anxious for a " correct taste " in any of the arts, to study natural history, Pennant put an especial injunction upon the poets.

Descriptive poetry is still more indebted to natural knowledge than either painting or sculpture: the poet has the whole creation for his range; nor can his art exist without borrowing metaphors, allusions, or descriptions from the face of nature, which is the only fund of great ideas. The depths of seas, the internal caverns of the earth, and the planetary system are out of the painter's reach; but can supply the poet with the sublimest conceptions: nor is the knowledge of animals and vegetables less requisite, while his creative pen adds life and motion to every object.[51]

Pennant was high authority. In the *Zoölogy* itself his " descriptions " of birds, animals, and fish often include quotations from the poets, from Vergil, Ovid, Horace, Gratius, Oppian, Lucan, Ausonius, Spenser, Milton, and Thomson. Thomson is especially praised: " The great beauty of that celebrated poet," he says, " consists in his elegant and just descriptions of the oeconomy of animals; and the happy use he hath made of natural knowledge in descriptive poetry, shines through almost every page of his Seasons." [52] Daines Barrington is another naturalist, one of the associates of Pennant, who has especial praises for Thomson.[53] These men of science, in praising Thomson for his close fidelity to nature, were adding their voices to those of literary critics like John Scott (*Critical Essays*), Joseph Warton (*Essay on the Writings and Genius of Pope*), and John More (*Strictures on Thomson's Seasons*), who had praised him for the same qualities. A little later than Pennant and Barrington, Robert Heron, who published a number of works on science and topography, edited *The Seasons* (1789) with a " Critical Essay " in which he praised Thomson as exemplifying " the union of the naturalist with the poet."

There had been increasing popular attention to science in England. The partial list furnished by Welsh of books printed by John Newbery between 1740 and 1802,[54] the hand list furnished by Straus of Robert Dodsley's publications from 1735 to 1764,[55] and even earlier titles issued by Curll between 1706 and 1746,[56] show this mounting interest. Newbery was especially active in producing such informative books. Among his books for the young, for example, which were one of his special activities, natural history is popular, and becomes increasingly so. If we had similar lists for the Tonsons, for Lintot, for the presses of Richardson, Andrew Millar, and others, they would probably show similar evidence of widening curiosity and of demand for popularizations of natural philosophy. Popularizers flourished: men like " Sir " John Hill; [57] Benjamin Martin, of *Martin's Magazine* (1755–64) and innumerable works on science for " youth of both sexes "; Benjamin Stillingfleet, with his translations of Swedish naturalists; J. C. Lettsom, with his *Naturalist's and Traveller's Companion, Containing Instructions for Discovering and Preserving Objects of Natural History* (1772) , suitable for those now touring Britain to see native scenery; the Goldsmith of *A History of the Earth, and Animated Nature.* Intellectual ladies like Elizabeth Carter, Mrs. Delany, or Anna Seward dabbled in science. Elizabeth Carter's translations of Algarotti's *Newtonianismo per le dame* is only one of the evidences of her scientific interest. Mrs. Delany made " paper mosaics " of flowers, very exact reproductions praised by even Erasmus Darwin. She became famous for these, and Madame d'Arblay says she finished nearly a thousand specimens before her eyesight failed.[58] Anna Seward disclaimed real command of natural history, but she corrected zoölogical errors of Helen Maria Williams's verses,[59] and she made one of the Lichfield enthusiasts about Dr. Darwin. This Lichfield circle, in the sixties and seventies, besides ornaments like the unparalleled Mr. Day of Bear-Hill, author of *Sandford and Merton,* included such botanical votaries as Sir Brooke Boothby, Mr. Saville, and Richard Edgeworth, F.R.S. Matthew Boulton, F. R. S. is described as devoted to " mechanic philosophy," the Rev. Mr. Mitchell as " skilled in astronomic science "; and there was of course Watt " the improver of the steam engine." [60] Dr. Darwin's " Lunar Society " of Lichfield and Birmingham included among its members nine fellows of the Royal Society, the most notable being Joseph Priestley and James Watt.[61] But Dr. Darwin was disappointed at being unable to enlist the frivolous youth of Lichfield in the botanical society he established there. Daines Barrington, John Stuart — third Earl of Bute, the prime minister and an indefatigable enthusiast — and the Duchess Dowager of Portland, who contributed a number of species to Pennant's *British Zoölogy,* are examples of devotion, particularly to botany and zoölogy, in the higher ranks.

Of course an interest in science had not disappeared among literary people since the days of Cowley, Dryden, Evelyn, Creech, and Margaret Cavendish, the Duchess of Newcastle. John Hughes's *Ecstasy* and Glover's poem on Newton, Yalden's poem to Watson " on his ephemeris of celestial motions " and his *Insect,* Young's interest in astronomy in *Night Thoughts,* and Akenside's *Hymn to Science,* are other examples, among many, of persistent interest in science.[62] There were didactic poems devoted to science and to physico-theology, the tracing of evidences of design in nature;[63] and we know how, after Thomson, scientific fact and speculation, as well as elements of physico-theology, became stock motifs in descriptive and didactic writing. Interest in science, both for its own sake and for its fascination and polemical value as " natural revelation," grew among the poets from the earliest years of the century. Men like Moses Browne, Somervile, Dodsley, Dyer, Weekes, Grainger, and others, were at least amateurs of phases of science. John Laurence, Scott of Amwell, and Erasmus Darwin, had technical training. Gray was a very thorough student of natural history.[64] Shenstone liked to color patterns of flowers, and his insatiable love for mottoes is responsible for the poems *To a Lady, with Some Coloured Patterns of Flowers,* written in 1736, and *Written in a Flower Book of My Own Colouring, Designed for Lady Plymouth,* verses of 1753–54. John Langhorne turned botany into fables in *The Fables of Flora* (1771). Hannah Cowley wrote verses on *Chemistry.* Mrs. Barbauld's verses include *To Mrs. P . . . . with Drawings of Birds and Insects* and *To a Lady, with Some Painted Flowers.* Her brother, John Aikin, was the perfect example of the *littérateur* and amateur in science. Dr. Darwin, of course, combined these interests, with tremendous creative zeal in both. Interest in gardening or agriculture led many, perhaps Shenstone, Jago, and Mason among them, to a knowledge of plants, trees, flowers. Crabbe was an enthusiastic and accomplished student of natural history. The impulse given by Buffon and by the example of the scientific enthusiasm which ran high in the world of fashion at Paris, contributed to English interest. " Natural history," Horace Walpole wrote in 1770, " is in fashion." [65] This interest was to grow, and we must continue the subject later. Let us return for the present to Pennant and Aikin.

There is no evidence that these men realized that in urging poets to turn to natural history, they were virtually repeating the advice of Sprat, given in his *History of the Royal Society* in 1667.[66] Aikin's essay seems to have been inspired by Pennant's preface, which in turn was perhaps partly suggested by the oration of Linnaeus urging travel and study in one's own country.[67] Aikin was not a very prominent figure in 1777, though his *Essays on Song Writing,* his collection of English songs, and his translations from Seneca had appeared. But he was to become a voluminous editor and the leading spirit for a time of the *Athenaeum.* He was to edit Milton, Spenser, Dryden, Pope, Goldsmith, Thomson, and others, besides producing such compilations as his *General Biography* in ten volumes and his *Select Works of the British Poets, with Biographical and Critical Prefaces.* He was also active as a popularizer of natural history. The advice given in his *Essay on the Application of Natural History to Poetry* is repeated later in his *Essay on the Plan and Character of Thomson's Seasons* (1778), which was reprinted as a preface in many of the multiplying editions of Thomson.[68]

Aikin begins by deploring the enfeeblement of poetry through the neglect of close observation. If a " picturesque circumstance " is invented by one author, every succeeding one introduces it, perhaps " improves, amplifies, and in some respects varies the idea, and in so doing may exhibit considerable taste and ingenuity," but he forfeits the merit of originality. Shakespeare's " shard-born beetle with his drowsy hums," from *Macbeth,* suggests well-known lines in *Lycidas,* Gray's *Elegy,* and Collins's *Ode to Evening.* " Scarcity of original observations of nature," " the properties of things mistaken," and " faint, obscure and ill-characterized " descriptions, are among the faults of the poets. The Book of Job, Lucan, Manilius, Pope, Congreve, and Young, are condemned for instances of faulty observation. His recommendation to the poets is " the accurate and scientific study of nature." Descriptive poetry stands in special need of this. Aikin is primarily interested in recommending study of the animal kingdom, a fact which reflects his relationship to Pennant; but he does not limit his advice to this department of natural history. Vergil is the first poet cited as an example of the possibilities of close knowledge of nature. Many of

Homer's similes show the closest observation. Milton's description of the bower of Eve, parts of his account of creation, and the exact pictures in *L'Allegro* and *Il Penséroso,* are given high praise. But Thomson's *Seasons* surpass all of these and are supreme examples of the worth of " studying in fields and woods." Thomson is the creator of an important poetic genre and will repay study and imitation.

Aikin dislikes fables. They cannot introduce "minute or uncommon details." But a poem like Jago's *Swallows* offers " the model of a new combination of moral precept with natural description, greatly superior, in many respects, to fable." Jago's poem is on bird migrations and " providential instinct," drawing the conclusion that reliance on the same Providence is reasonable, in man's flight into an unknown future, away from the storms of human life. This type of poem, using nature for purposes of moral analogy, it might be said incidentally, became so widespread in the nineteenth century that we now think of *The Chambered Nautilus,* for example, as based upon a very stereotyped formula.

Aikin's main concern, however, is with descriptive poetry of a more sustained kind. There are many picturesque details in the natural history of birds, insects, animals, and fish, which the poets have never appropriated. Pennant's *British Zoölogy,* along with nature itself, is recommended as a source for " a second Thomson." Novelty can be added also by description of parts of the world where all objects are new. " Such, to the inhabitant of a temperate climate, are the polar and tropical parts of the globe." Vergil and Thomson have set the example in this kind of description, but the travelers have furnished new sources of imagery of which the poets should avail themselves. So the essay concludes. But Aikin returned to the subject to give similar advice in the *Essay on the Plan and Character of Thomson's Seasons* (1778), frequently reprinted as a preface to editions of Thomson.

Such advice was not unheeded. Anna Seward says that Darwin's botanical poems were partly suggested by Dr. Aikin's advocacy of natural history in verse.[69] As we have seen, didactic poets like Luke Booker, John Evans, James Grahame, and William Tighe worked in the spirit of these suggestions. In that prolific genre of poetry devoted to places, there was a similar tendency. John Gisborne is a kind of Derbyshire Gilbert White in verse. Luke Booker, Joseph Budworth, John Leyden, Fortesque Hitchins, Noel Carrington, William Hamilton Drummond, John McKinley,

David Landsborough, and others [70] use botany, ornithology, geology, and other branches of science in their local verse. In descriptive poems on divisions of time, close observation was sought, by a succession of poets, through the discipline of " studying in fields and woods." Hurdis, Cotter, Grahame, the Gisbornes, William Cole, and others continued in carrying out the implications of the advice in the *Essay on the Application of Natural History to Poetry*.

The chief literary figure in the field of natural history in the late eighteenth century is of course Gilbert White of Selborne, who has been called " the father of British popular naturalists." One of John Aikin's many services to literature was his publication of White's papers in 1795 after the naturalist's death; he also edited White's *Works in Natural History* (1802). White's *Natural History and Antiquities of Selborne* (1789) and his useful *Naturalist's Calendar* (1795), published by John Aikin, seem to have exerted considerable influence on descriptive poets. White often quotes notations of natural history by the poets — Lucretius, Oppian, Shakespeare, Milton, Philips, Thomson (" a nice observer of natural occurrences "), and especially Vergil. He was himself a descriptive poet, though Martin's claim for him [71] of " a high position in our national poetry " is absurd. His *Naturalist's Summer Evening Walk* and the few lines beginning " Say, what impels amidst surrounding snow " were the only verses included in his *Selborne*. *The Naturalist's Calendar* included a few lines " on the peculiar still, dry, warm weather sometimes occurring in winter months." Later editors, of 1813 and 1877, culled other poems from his manuscripts, verse written in the sixties and later, showing the effects of the descriptive school. Of these, *Selborne Hanger, A Winter Piece, On the Rainbow, A Harvest Scene,* and *Invitation to Selborne* [72] show White's delicacy of observation. But only the *Naturalist's Summer Evening Walk* could have exerted much influence, and this runs to only forty-four lines, a mere fragment. It is addressed to Thomas Pennant, White's correspondent and his friend, as he was Aikin's. Its sharp observation is that of a delightful ornithologist and entomologist; its expression is not that of an accomplished poet. He often walks out at evening

> To hear the drowsy dorr come brushing by
> With buzzing wing, or the shrill cricket cry;
> To see the feeding bat glance through the wood;
> To catch the distant falling of the flood;

While o'er the cliff th' awaken'd churn-owl hung
Through the still gloom protracts his chattering song;
While high in air, and poised upon his wings,
Unseen, the soft enamour'd woodlark sings.[73]

But White is often a truer poet in his prose than in his verse.
He is an outdoor naturalist who creates the most graphic pictures.
Ornithology is his great enthusiasm, and the letters to Daines Barrington on martlets, owls, swallows, sand martins, and swifts, on
the various flights of birds, and on their many cries and songs expressing their passions and wants, are prose poems of a high order.
Both the letters to Pennant and those to Barrington have constant
sharp notations that capture life and motion, color, sound, odor,
and texture, and often with a masterly command of simple, precise
metaphor. His detailed *Naturalist's Calendar,* the outgrowth of the
invaluable method of keeping calendars of observations, which
Barrington seems to have introduced,[74] and the calendars of appearances of birds and their times of singing (in the *Selborne*) were
excellent guides for amateur students. He says too that he intended
a popular prose *Natural History of the Twelve Months of the Year*
but was forestalled in this undertaking by Aikin's *Calendar of
Nature* (1784).

White's philosophical premises are those of a man of his period.
The evidences of benevolent design and harmony in the universe
enthrall him. The world is an open book of natural revelation. He
sees living creatures as an interdependent " chain of beings " in
a universal harmonious order. The power of God in nature seems
again to be conceived of as an immanent presence. He speaks of

The God of Seasons, whose pervading power
Controls the sun, or sheds the fleecy shower.[75]

In the year after the appearance of Aikin's essay, John Scott of
Amwell published his *Moral Eclogues* (1778), which are a curious
blend of new and old elements. Scott was an accurate, even a scientific observer, but he could not break away from old forms. *Theron;
or, the Praise of Rural Life* is set in spring; *Palemon; or, Benevolence* in summer at morning; *Armyn; or, the Discontented* in summer at afternoon; *Lycoron; or, the Unhappy* in autumn at evening.
Aikin might have been pleased with the accuracy of Scott's notations, but these are in the form of short, plain catalogues of the
plants, flowers, and trees of the seasons. There is no question of his
delight in nature or of his closeness of observation. Several eclogues

present his shepherds looking out across a " picturesque " landscape which is " composed " in the manner of a landscape painter,
the boundaries being indicated, and foreground, middle distance,
and background sketched. In all four Scott's botanical knowledge is
evident. But his shepherds are quite unreal beings who discourse
upon "unperverted Nature's golden reign," " Benevolence the
fair," " Reason's sway," and the necessity that " Reason Love's pursuit approve." Scott had observation and enthusiasm. He had
independently followed out Thomsonian hints in sketching phenomena of parts of the year. His observation was enriched by technical knowledge. But he seldom ventured beyond the method of
catalogue and only in his local poem *Amwell* allowed anything like
sufficient scope to his faculty for description.

Immediate adoption of the advice of Aikin and Pennant is
hardly to be expected. Benjamin West's *Spring Day* and *Morn*
(1780) [76] are as sedulously imitative of Thomson as Rack's verses.
The *Hymn to the Sun* (1782) translated by " O. B." from the Abbé
de Reyrac's " poetic prose " adaptation of Thomson, and Thomas
Warwick's translation from Saint-Lambert's *Spring* (1784), [77] are
apparently the first evidences of awareness in England of the French
school of Thomsonian and Vergilian descriptive and didactic poets,
which by this time included Desnoyers, Bernis, Pezay, Saint-
Lambert, Dorat, Rosset, Roucher, Desfontanes, Delille, Léonard,
and others.[78]

The appearance of George Crabbe's *Village* in 1783 was significant. In form it is most closely allied to the fertile species of local
poetry to which *Edge-Hill* and *Clifton* belong. Many other villages
had been the subject of rhyme before Aldeburgh, but poets had
never chosen to depict the seamy side alone. Crabbe's work does
not belong to the form which is the subject of this chapter, but it
has some importance in the history of that subject. Together with
his work of the early nineteenth century, it presented the most
striking example in verse of the treatment of small-village life in
sternest realism. Both Crabbe and Burns strengthened the tendency, already well established, to realistic truth in reflecting country life. It was not the Thomsonian genre, of course, which Crabbe's
Village attacked. The sentimental idealization of *The Deserted
Village* was the inspiration of the poem, but the specific attack
is against the false pastoralism of the eclogue. The " mechanic
echoes of the Mantuan song," the straying from truth " where
Virgil, not where Fancy, leads the way," were phrases applied to

the imitation of the *Eclogues*. The primary importance of George
Crabbe is his contribution, hardly excelled by any other English
poet, to an honest realism in painting country life. His influence
was not fully exerted until much later than 1873, not until the
appearance in 1807, 1810, 1812, and 1819 of his longer works.

The prolific poet, novelist, biographer, and playwright Samuel
Pratt, a familiar figure on the literary scene in the seventies and
eighties, tried his hand at descriptive verse. *Landscapes in Verse,
Taken in Spring* (1785) is a mélange of description, narrative,
genre sketches, and moralization. Theodorus is lamenting the ab-
sence of Cleone, his love, in spring. "Passion's pale haunts," forest
glooms, a hermit's cell, caverned rocks, a shepherd's hut, a "deep
bushy dell," and other scenes in the current "picturesque" taste,
attract him. The season of spring has colored the landscapes, and
Fancy allows him to see himself and Cleone looking by morning
from a hilltop at the cliffs, mountains, meadows, river, fir grove,
and orchard of a synthetic scene he conjures up. In imagination he
and Cleone share the humble hospitality of two cottagers, who
tell them of thirty years of "virtuous life of wedded love." He tells
Cleone the story of Agenor and Fanny, two lovers who on the eve
of their marriage are separated by death: in a thunderstorm she
imagines him struck by lightning, and, dazed with grief, falls into
a stream and drowns. Agenor becomes crazed with grief over his
loss. This episode ended, Pratt returns to his imaginary spring
landscapes and to moralization upon the powers of poetry over
human passions — with an ode of consolation sung by "the train
Parnassean" to the disconsolate lover Theodorus. Pratt's "elegant
versification" might have given pleasure to James Mackenzie or
to Thomas Day, but this enthusiast is one in whose presence it is
difficult to repress a smile. Descriptively his poem belongs in the
"picturesque" school and adds little to the tendency toward exactitude of observation.

Cowper's *Task* (1785) added great impetus to descriptive
poetry. It is a combination of elements: description of landscapes
and of the seasons and parts of the day, genre sketches of country
occupations and rural character, moral didacticism, didacticism
of country pursuits, personal panegyric, satire, patriotic reflection,
theology, and autobiography. It owes something to topographical
verse, something to the "moral essay," ultimately Horatian, composed of satire, "characters," and ethical counsel, written by Pope
and his followers. But Vergil, Thomson, and the English didactic-

descriptive school are the real ancestors of Cowper in *The Task*. Book I is based upon several country walks in summer and upon two " prospects," one of the river Ouse from an unnamed hill. Book II is a moral essay, preceptive, satirical, varied with " characters " and an allegory of the decay of discipline in the universities. Book III, after a continuation of the manner of the previous book for some three hundred lines, becomes a georgic on gardening. Book IV, *The Winter Evening,* after pictures of country life in that season, turns to the decay of rural innocence and simple country manners. Book V, *The Winter-Morning Walk,* continues the descriptive strain, turning finally to discussion of civil liberty and spiritual liberty through divine " grace." Book VI, *The Winter Walk at Noon,* is again descriptive until the poet turns to the subject of humanitarian treatment of animals, and then to a prophecy of the millenium and a defense of the man who chooses a life of retirement.

There are generalized landscapes in *The Task* which would appeal to the current taste for the " picturesque ": the " prospect " of the Ouse and the surrounding countryside and that of the fields and woods seen from the " proud alcove " of " Benevolus " (John Throckmorton), the picture of " the common, overgrown with fern " and " rough with prickly gorse," the contrast of the meadows seen at evening and at morning after a night of snow, and the effects of the frost seen at a waterfall. But Cowper is more remarkable for sharp, detailed observation. His exactitude is of the kind Pennant and Aiken hoped to inspire. Cowper achieved it through sympathy with nature and country manners and through the intimacy of an untheorizing lover of rural things. The effects Cowper achieved in passages like those describing the varieties of rural sounds; the sheep pouring out of the fold over the hillside; the trees of his woodland, each sharply distinguished from the others; the greenhouse flowers; the animals, barnyard fowl, and birds in winter; the robin, stockdove, and squirrel; the flowers that return with spring, each one painted with exact, sure strokes — such effects are of the kind the two theorists hoped to bring about. Cowper is as exact as Thomas Hardy and, indeed, often reminds us of him more than of anyone else, in the quality of his observation. The sounds of the village bells, affected by the lull and rise of the winds,[79] and the " livelier green " of meadow grass betraying the course of tiny streams,[80] are examples of the Hardyan kind of poignant exactitude.

Cowper's genre sketches of rural occupations are more full than any as yet produced by descriptive poetry after Thomson, and they have the authenticity of all this poet's observation. The loaded wain and its boorish driver moving from the hay field; the gypsy camp in the woods; the thresher; the wagoner and his horse on the snowy road; the detailed picture of the family and the possessions of the poor cottagers; the accounts of the gardener's processes; the country thief prowling at night; the cobbler, joiner, tailor, and baker, " all learned, and all drunk," in the country inn; the modern farmer's daughter; the manner in which the farmer cuts the fodder from his stack in order to keep it balanced; the woodman and his dog; the housewife feeding the barnyard flocks — English poetry has never surpassed the reality of such sketches.

These landscapes, minute sketches from nature, and genre pictures are, of course, in the didactic-descriptive tradition. Sometimes they parallel Thomson or Vergil, without any evidence of conscious borrowing. Besides the third book, which includes a conventional georgic already discussed, there are other elements from the same tradition. Cowper's contrasts of city and country, his belief in the happiness of retirement, his respect for honest industry, his desire to hasten a return to simple country manners and virtues, are old materials given the sincerity of honest conviction. He has the good sense to prefer society to solitude in his retirement, and, like others before him, sees that the " happy swain " is not always happy but often the prey of poverty, intemperance, neglect, and oppression from superior ranks. Autobiography, so prominent in *The Task*, has been frequent in local verse after Goldsmith's *Deserted Village*. Cowper deplores the science which clings to secondary causes and neglects divine illumination, but scientific interest is apparent in the account of the necessity of " ceaseless action " and " revolvency " in the economy of nature, or in the questioning as to the " vital energy " which comes and goes with spring and winter.[81] Cowper's humanitarian sentiment in relation to animals and unfortunate men has been a constant element also. There is one pathetic tale, less extended and less sentimentalized than Thomsonian narratives, the story of " Crazy Kate," an actual figure, driven insane by the drowning of her lover at sea. The other tale, of a horse which revenged itself on a cruel master by throwing him over a precipice, is another true story of the countryside, not at all in Thomson's manner. It is unnecessary to recount all of the ways in which Cowper parallels Thomson.

Celebrations of quiet domestic happiness, attacks upon hunting, personal panegyrics, praises of labor and condemnations of sloth-fulness, the love of rural amusements as more sane and natural than those of the city, delight in contemplating the "human tempest" dimly seen and heard in the peace of retirement, con-demnations of intemperance, certain details of their several barn-yard sketches or of their pictures of winter, are parallels of a close or remote kind. Both are zealous in the cause of rural reform, Cowper attacking absentee landlords and the venality of rural par-sons and magistrates. The "patriotic panegyric" of the didactic-descriptive school becomes in Cowper the mingled praise and blame of London and England and the enthusiasm for English liberty — contrasted with foreign tyrannies.[82] There is another northern-winter and tropic-zone contrast in *The Task*,[83] and the vivid description of the Sicilian earthquake is one of the many ac-counts of the prodigies of nature in tropical lands.[84] Cowper's ac-count of the growth of war and tyranny, and his mock-heroic "rise and progress" of the sofa in Book I, are both of a kind established in poetry by the Lucretian account of the beginnings of arts and sciences, a kind of episode which was a commonplace of didactic poetry.

Cowper's theology is perhaps not entirely clear-cut. He attacks the deists, of course. Thomson's divine spirit which "pervades, ad-justs, sustains, and agitates the whole" of creation is different from Cowper's Love "that plann'd, and built, and still upholds a world." Cowper's line, evidently suggested by Thomson's, has no hint of divine immanence in nature. But elsewhere Cowper says,

> The Lord of all, himself through all diffus'd,
> Sustains, and is the life of all that lives,

and he also speaks of "a soul in all things," adding "and that soul is God." The immanence of God in nature is in Cowper, as it was in Thomson or Shaftesburian poets like Akenside and Brooke, though often Cowper speaks of the divine as existing apart, as it was the habit of the more orthodox believer to conceive of him. The idea that nature is a teacher, a source of wisdom, recurs also in Cowper.

> Wisdom there, and truth
> Not shy, as in the world, and to be won
> By slow solicitation, seize at once
> The roving thought, and fix it on themselves.[85]

In such lines we are indeed near the ideas, even the manner, of Wordsworth. But Cowper's strong evangelical piety differentiates him sharply from many of the poets of his century who wrote of God in nature. He recognizes the truth of "natural revelation," but he reverses the usual order of the argument when he says, "Acquaint thyself with God if thou would'st taste his works." Natural revelation is not enough; it merely supplements supernatural revelation. It is "grace" which opens to the receptive mind the secrets of the divine in nature. God did not mean that man should "scale the Heav'ns" to find him "in his works"; man is to seek him rather "in his word." Without divine illumination, philosophy vainly searches for God in the universe of divine creation; by the light of such illumination, philosophy "has eyes indeed." The rationalistic approach to revelation is in Cowper completely denied — it can never suffice. The argument also of the deists which would explain away apparent evil as due to our "partial view," Cowper explicitly attacks. Physical evil and moral evil are interrelated; earthquake, famine, plague, and other prodigies of nature are warnings and punishments for sin. With the doctrine of a perfect external harmony, there falls also the related doctrine of a moral harmony and beauty attained through the "moral sense"; the Shaftesburian esthetic pathway to moral order is ridiculed. Here too, divine "grace" is necessary.

Cowper never superseded Thomson as the chief model in descriptive poetry. He did not afford so rounded and universal a panorama as Thomson, and his temperament, more narrow, more dogmatic, and more censorious, did not appeal so widely to public sympathy. Some, indeed, like Anna Seward, actively disliked him.[86] The Task stimulated descriptive poetry, afforded new models, encouraged a less turgid, more natural style in blank verse, and gave new impetus to the search for exactitude and truth, but it did not displace The Seasons in popular favor or influence.

The poems of Robert Burns, which began to appear with the Kilmarnock edition of 1786 and the Edinburgh edition of 1787, had little effect on the traditional descriptive poem. As Burns became more widely known, he stimulated a true reflection of the lives of peasants. Poems like Tam O'Shanter, The Jolly Beggars, Hallowe'en, The Cotter's Saturday Night,[87] The Holy Fair, The Twa Dogs, and such pieces of characterization as Holy Willie's Prayer and Tam Samson's Elegy, encouraged realism. But the de-

scriptive poem clung to its formulas and to the traditional genre
sketches which were its inheritance. And Burns contributed little
to the tendency of the descriptive poem to become more detailed
and even technical in its approach to nature, preserving its objective tone. Burns's influence, as it began to be felt, by Wordsworth
for example, tended to overthrow the old formulas and to encourage new forms and new attitudes toward both nature and the
peasant. This influence was in every way a salutary one; but it did
not make itself immediately felt, and it had to be supplemented
by the much stronger influence, over a long period, of the romantic
school of the next century, before the older type of poem became
more infrequent and finally disappeared.

Two years after Cowper's *Task* appeared, came John Bryant's
Morning (1787),[88] the first part of a projected poem on the parts
of the day; it keeps to the originals of *The Seasons* in its hymn to
the rising sun and its pictures of the herbs, flowers, herds, flocks,
and birds at dawn. An early-morning walk provides landscapes of
a " picturesque " sort.

George Wright, the moralist, appeared again with a number
of descriptive poems in *Retired Pleasures, or the Charms of Rural
Life* (1787). The work is a kind of anthology of prose and verse on
the theme of retirement, drawing upon *The Rambler,* Blair's
Sermons, Young's *Letters on Pleasure,* and verse by Mrs. Carter,
Mrs. Rowe, Dr. Johnson, Young, Browne (*Sunday Thoughts*),
Thomson, Gay, Collins, and others. Presumably by the author are
The Innocent Amusements of a Country Life,[89] a series of genre
sketches of haymaking, sheepshearing, the " noon-day retreat " of
the laborer, and so on; *Summer; or the Rural Prospect,*[90] a com-
bination of local description (the Scottish shore near Solway
Firth) with pictures of the parts of a summer day; *Rural Felicity,*[91]
another adaptation of the " happy-swain " theme; *An Harvest
Scene,*[92] confessedly " imitated from Thomson's Seasons "; and
The Disposition of a Flower Garden,[93] combined precepts and description, somewhat like certain parts of Cowper's Book III.
Wright is not a poet of any consequence, but he seems to have
been a good deal read, and his adaptations are evidence of the taste
for country pictures. As in his earlier work, Wright reflects the
common philosophy of nature in his period, seeing the world of
external phenomena as proof and revelation of the divine. One of
the values of retirement among the scenes of nature is closeness
to the divine as there revealed.

In the same year, a certain " Bob Short " turned Thomson again into couplets, in *The Four Seasons of the Year* (1787). It would be useless to summarize this in any detail. In general, " Short " omits the moral, didactic, " exotic," and narrative episodes, and preserves more detailed descriptions and genre sketches of rural occupations. This choice of circumstantiality in description and of pictures of country pursuits doubtless represents what " Short " considered to be the preferences of public taste. He makes a few additions to Thomson.

Mrs. Elizabeth Steele's *Spring* (1787?), a translation of part of Saint-Lambert, the French imitator of Thomson, together with Thomas Warwick's earlier version of the same part, indicates a belated recognition of the descriptive school across the Channel. Saint-Lambert had long enjoyed the acclaim which greeted his *Saisons* in 1769. Voltaire had praised him as the superior of Thomson and his poem as the best production of French literature in fifty years. French society was full of the " *sentiment de la nature* " which, combined with the taste for natural sciences, turned poets to Vergil, Lucretius, and Thomson as models. But Saint-Lambert's feeling for nature was artificial and vague. When he follows Thomson, he loses the concreteness and exactitude of his model. All melts into vague, undefined fluidity and outlines fade. When he follows Vergil, he follows where Thomson had shown the way. He has a way of combining elements from Vergil and Thomson into synthetic scenes where the original qualities are lost and nothing is gained but a new arrangement of details. He is over-fond of allegorical and mythological figures, which crowd his canvas. The fact is symptomatic. Saint-Lambert is not really a close observer of nature; he is a poet who concocts an idealized countryside out of the English and Scottish materials of Thomson and the Italian ones of Vergil. Mrs. Steele's translation reflects these artificial qualities, though she hardly does justice to the polish of Saint-Lambert's versification.

An aspect of Saint-Lambert's *Saisons* which has considerable interest is their closeness in the expression of religious ideas to the English poems of similar type. The vision of pervasive law in the universe, which is due to science, and the conviction that order and harmony rule, if man could see the whole plan of creation, inspire the poet to faith in a benevolent Deity. He invokes the divine power, " *Esprit universel,*" perceived in nature. Like Thomson, he sees in the sun the " *noble et brillante image* " of the Creator. Nature, "*plein de l'Etre-supreme*," inspires in him the reverence which confirms him in love of virtue.

Mrs. Steele does not translate the interesting *Discours Préliminaire* with which Saint-Lambert prefaced the later editions of his *Saisons*. It is a commentary on the self-conscious formalism which was so large an element in his poetry, and which distinguishes him from the English descriptive poets. Nature has certain characteristic states — *sublime, grande et belle, amiable et riante,* or *triste et mélancolique* — to which the poet suits his episodes, according to analogies between states of mind and states of nature. Principles of agreement and contrast, therefore, provide a rigid formula for descriptive verse, and the poet lays down a system of logical rules for the genre. He warns other poets not to paint the poor peasant, who is unworthy of the Muse; speak of him, he says, show him in action only rarely, and, above all, speak *for* him. It is the antithesis of Wordsworthianism.

Bryant, Wright, " Short," and Mrs. Steele, all published descriptive exercises in 1787. In the same year James Woodhouse wrote his *Autumn and the Redbreast* in tetrameter couplets.[94] Woodhouse contrasts the seasons of the year and writes a celebration of autumn's special charms. He shows more careful observation here than is usual in his verse. His eye is on the object, and if that were enough to produce poetry, his descriptions of such minute phenomena as spider webs, mushrooms, the fall of autumn leaves and their dance, would deserve the term; but his pictures are couched in a lifeless, stereotyped diction.

An interesting contrast to the French Saint-Lambert is James Hurdis, the Sussex curate who later was appointed to the Oxford professorship of poetry and became the friend of Cowper and Hayley. His *Village Curate* (1788) is far removed, in both virtues and defects, from the artifice of *Les Saisons*. Cowper looked upon Hurdis as a "true genius." [95] His poem pictures the life of the author in his Sussex home, through the seasons of a single year. The changes of each month are marked. The unpretentious realism is worthy of note. Hurdis disclaims minute knowledge of botany, but his accounts of the first flowers and leaves of spring are admirably exact. His observations of birds, through the whole poem, the manner of their flight, the distinctive qualities of their songs and calls, their appearance, are worthy of comparison with Thomson and Cowper. He gives a detailed picture of his own garden at Burwash. The pictures of country occupations are no less vivid. The smith at his forge, the stage driver, the reapers, gleaners, and wain drivers of the harvest, the fowler and his pointer, and many characters and scenes of an autumn holiday fair, drawn in full detail, are among the most real rural pictures in English verse. Hurdis does not have many generalized landscapes of a kind that could be called " picturesque." His description is notable, rather, for attention to detail. He is a real lover of the appearances of nature, who can say with conviction that the hop gardens of Sussex are more beautiful than Ranelagh and Vauxhall and who finds a rural fair more fascinating than a fashionable rout.

There is too much moral precept and reflection. Hurdis almost spoils his close observation sometimes by his manner of crowding moral parallels on the reader. The influence of Cowper is apparent in the freedom of Hurdis's blank verse and in the purely associational connection of subject with subject within his chronological divisions. Both he and Cowper, beyond their genre pictures, have their greatest excellence as painters of the animal kingdom, which John Aikin and Pennant had recommended especially to the poets. Another element of interest in Hurdis is the use he makes of nature in urging the common argument from design. Seeing this revelation of God in nature, he feels also an influence from it on the soul of man, an influence which " delights and gives us wisdom," every tree and leaf and flower affording " something to please and something to instruct."

The less interesting, but still more voluminous, George Sackville Cotter, an Irish poet, published his *Prospects* at Cork in 1788.[96] It is another account of the seasons, in four extensive books. His preface protests that " no other poem or writing whatsoever is here imitated," but there are so many close parallels with Thomson that it is hard to acquit him of disingenuousness. He adds much observation of his own, however, and earns consideration as an original writer, especially since he attempts the most complete panorama since Thomson. Spring begins with the revival of nature, " black Winter struggling for his doubtful throne," the beginnings of the labors of the year, the long showers with their preliminary portents:

> the feather'd race
> In thorny hedge their ruffled pinions plume;
> The herds in silence fix'd look up to heav'n,
> Expecting; gentlest voices top the hill,
> That thro' th' aerial stillness distant sound;

The lark that echoed high her shrillest song,
From quiv'ring balance on the misty sky
Descending, swiftly seeks her grassy seat.

The spring gardens, the varied and distinct songs of various birds,
the courtships of the birds, the rural sports of the season, fill out his
outline. His *Summer* has few pictures for which Thomson had not
furnished models. *Autumn* is fertile in genre pictures of the Irish
harvests and field sports, and has more fresh imagery than the other
parts. Birds of the coast, the seal, the porpoise, are sketched, and
the flight of the owl, intent on prey by night. *Winter* is again very
derivative, its wide panorama of scenes usually built up out of the
combination of old themes. The description is sometimes pleasing
enough, though never really strong. Lines like these, describing a
wind stirring the fields, are typical:

All agitative seems;
A floating sea unsettled; while the breeze
Ruffles the margin of the bending corn;
Then onward rolls, till in a tumult all
Concussive shakes; and there as west-winds rise,
Issues a murmur from the rustling ears.
We pensive listen. Gradual swells the sound;
Then wafted far sinks in the parting gust.
Wild-scared ascends the lark, immediate o'er
Her deepen'd covert hov'ring still; — low skims
The twitt'ring swallow o'er the billowy field.
A crowd of greedy rooks low-stooping view
The tossing store beneath, and noisy claim
With unavailing cries the tempting flood.

Cotter makes extensive use of the "excursion of fancy" to northern
and southern lands; he applies the "patriotic panegyric" to Albion and to Ireland; he celebrates retirement, humanitarian sentiment, and the virtues of labor; he shows the usual scientific interest,
discussing the causes of fertility and of thunderstorms. In short, he
extends already familiar outlines. In common with fellow descrip-
tive-poets, Cotter sees in the nature he loves the revelation of God-
head and the demonstration of divine benevolence in order and
harmony. Nature is inseparable from the divine.

Cotter wanted to be an Irish Thomson. David Davidson, in
Thoughts on the Seasons (1789), seems to have wanted to make
Thomson more a Scot than he originally was. His poem is "partly
in the Scottish dialect" and has a savor of Burns, especially in the

tone of its humanitarianism. Most of the description is repetition and the nature theology is conventional. He shows more originality in descriptions of Scottish peasants in their round of labors and recreations, a calendar of the occupations of the year. He likes to interpolate interludes in lyric stanzas — like the picture of Rob and Jeany on the way to the fair, the " elegy " for Willy Clerg the hunter, the nutting song, or the curling match. Sometimes he presents country processes by didactic precepts, as in his instructions for destroying insects that prey on the trees, or in his advice on catching trout and salmon. Local description of the river Dee, Trief Castle, and the prospect from the hill of Screel, is in the " picturesque " taste. The story of Maria, a beautiful field laborer loved by her employer Glenalvon but faithful to her peasant lover Colin, and rewarded by Glenalvon's generous gift of lands, is rather obviously suggested by Thomson's Palemon and Lavinia. Davidson's modest merits are not much improved by the diction he employs, sometimes a hybrid jargon, half Scots and half English.

William Wheatcroft's *Powers of Fancy* (1790) has less merit than a poem like Davidson's. Both are without real imagination or power over language, but the latter has concreteness and realism. Wheatcroft uses the parts of the day as a framework for description and reflection. Much of the poem grows out of the Vergilian " excursion of fancy," and heaps up exotic color in African, Grecian, Italian, and Indian scenes, turning finally to " Happy Britain," praised above all other lands. Wheatcroft wishes for the lyre of Akenside or Thomson, that he may adequately celebrate these scenes, but he is a better reader of the travelers than imitator of the poets.

Baron Haller was a German scientist and poet whose *Die Alpen* is perhaps the best of the German descriptive poems similar to *The Seasons*.[97] His poem was translated in 1794 by a Mrs. Howorth.[98] Knowledge of German in England was still uncommon, and German literature was only beginning to be exploited. *Die Alpen* belongs with Kleist's *Frühling*, Wieland's *Frühling*, Zachariae's *Tageszeiten*, and some of the works of Drollinger, Brockes, Giseke, von Palthen, Dusch, and Hirschfeld, among the Shaftesburian and Thomsonian products of early German romanticism.[99] It is organized about the seasons of the year, and employs themes used also by Vergil and Thomson, applying them to a Swiss setting. The romantic concept of an uncorrupted life of retirement, that of the " happy swain " far from cities and courts, amidst the beauties of

the country and the traditional employments of his contact with
nature, forms the basis of the poem. The occupations of the Swiss
peasants are described. There are characterizations like that of the
hamlet oracle who can foretell the weather and prognosticate coming storms, knows the influences of the moon, and can forecast in
early spring the time of harvest. There is a rustic naturalist who
recounts the virtues of plants, and a centenarian who tells the story
of William Tell and expresses the Swiss hatred of oppression.
Haller tells of the effects of love among these people, of their lack
of false delicacy or affectation, and of their fidelity. Mountain
scenery is an interesting element in the poem, especially a description from Saint Gotthard of the sun scattering a sea of vapors below
and revealing the mountains, streams, and villages. Science is a
prominent feature, especially in accounts of Swiss flowers and
plants and of such phenomena as the caves of crystal formations,
the mineral springs, and a salt stream. Nature turns the poet's mind
to religious contemplation and to the curiosity as to her secrets
which inspires the scientist. Haller is even more concerned to combat the false luxury, the avarice and corruption of society, even
more convinced of the innocence and worth of more primitive ex-
istences, than a Goldsmith or a Thomson, and he does not mingle
this primitivism with progress worship in Thomson's fashion. The
poem seems to owe more to conscious romantic theory than is usual
with English descriptive poets.

James Grahame, the poet of *Birds of Scotland* and the *Rural
Calendar,* made preliminary sketches for the latter in *Spring, Summer,* and *The Redbreast* of 1794.[100] Though Thomsonian, they
show Grahame's merit as one of the most graphic of all the rural
poets. He was not a theorist, but a man who knew nature with
much of the exactness of a naturalist.

The appearance of Grahame and Thomas Gisborne in the same
year is a good augury. In the literatures of lands less rich in poetry,
both would have a recognized, if minor, place. Gisborne was curate
of Barton-under-Needwood, Staffordshire, a country clergyman,
who chose retirement rather than the political career open to
him in youth. He is strikingly like Cowper. Both were by choice
men of retirement, both were intimate lovers of nature, both were
gifted with sensitivity and powers of observation, both had an
evangelical kind of religious fervor. Gisborne had more of the
naturalist's curiosity: Needwood Forest was to him what Selborne
was to Gilbert White. He was also more varied as a writer than

Cowper; his pamphlets against Paley and his sermons were once well known. He was the brother of John Gisborne, whose *Vales of Wever* holds high rank in the prolific company of local poems, and was admired by Wordsworth. *Walks in a Forest* (1795), Thomas Gisborne's long poem, had a good deal of currency, reaching an eighth edition by 1813 and winning wide praise. As finally brought to completion, it is one of the best English descriptive poems.

Gisborne gains by limiting his panorama to the appearances of a forest through the seasons of the year. Forest trees and flowers, the birds, the deer and other animals, the occupations of peasant dwellers there, the changes in sky, forest pools, and landscapes, are his subject matter. He notes the appearance of many flowers and adds botanical notes on them. Birds are just as carefully watched, and he draws on Pennant and Latham in his notes. He paints them with an effort to be graphic and exact:

> With shrill and oft-repeated cry
> Her angular course, alternate rise and fall,
> The woodpecker prolongs; then to the trunk
> Close-clinging, with unwearied beak assails
> The hollow bark; through every cell the strokes
> Roll the dire echoes that from wintry sleep
> Awake her insect prey; the alarméd tribes
> Start from each chink that cleaves the mouldering stem:
> Their scatter'd flight, with lengthening tongue, the foe
> Pursues; joy glistens on her verdant plumes,
> And brighter scarlet sparkles on her crest.

Gisborne is equally exact with the forest animals, hare, deer, wild-cat. He has a description of a weasel attacking a leveret, as graphic as the pictures of nocturnal birds in pursuit of prey. But he is not limited to the kind of observation Pennant would have especially approved. Atmospheric changes interest him: the hazy effect of summer noon on distant woods; the contrast of wooded hills near-by in sunshine, with a flat distance in deep shadow; a shower passing far off over the hills, which disappear and emerge out of the vapors as the rain moves onward; the portents of a snowstorm; and the differences between snow clouds and other formations.

> The clouds advance,
> Not as the vehicles of rain, disposed
> In separate masses, and of varying hue;
> Not as the mansions of rebounding hail,
> Lurid and dark; not as where thunder dwells,

Of wildest forms, scowling, with purple dyes,
And 'gainst the nether stream of air propell'd
By their own currents; but of aspect dun,
Of texture uniform, and blending quick
In one unbroken surface, onward move. . . .
The wind exalts his voice; and sweeping wild
Claps o'er the sounding earth his snowy wings,
And drives through heaven the horizontal storm.

He is very sensitive to color, giving advice to landscape painters on
congruity and gradation of colors, and on the management of high
lights, shade, and middle tints — advice drawn from the principles
of harmony in the autumn tones of the forest.

Gisborne avoids stereotyped genre pictures by keeping to his
forest dwellers or to scenes in his restricted setting: a herdsman
driving his cattle to the Scottish Highlands, woodcutters, charcoal-
burners and fern-burners (with accounts of their processes) , a forest blaze caused by fern fires, a deer-poacher and his methods, and
cottagers gathering fuel. Here, as elsewhere, the poet's virtues are
those of most real and faithful transcription. The people of the
forest are treated without sentimental idealization and without
patronage. He is another humanitarian, defending the peasants,
who are often driven to poverty and theft by the oppressions of the
rich. There are several narratives, true stories — one of the death
of a peasant's family in a forest fire, another of a young emigrant to
America, who rescues from the Indians the girl who becomes his
wife. Though Gisborne says that he means to describe phenomena
common to English forests, Needwood is probably the source of
most of his detail. But there are episodes of explicit local description — Lichfield Cathedral seen at a distance, Dovedale (he cites
Gilpin's praise of it as " picturesquely beautiful ") , and Tutbury
Castle. And the " excursions of fancy " to America, Africa, Lapland, and Norway, have unusual detail, drawn from the travel literature of the period.

Gisborne owes something to Thomson and to Cowper. He often
parallels the former in his themes, though always with independent
treatment. His blank verse owes a good deal to Cowper, who was
his friend, and his loose organization follows the example of *The
Task*. The similarities of their religious views often bring them
close to each other in their exhortations to their readers, and both
look to nature as a source of moral truth. Gisborne finds wisdom
for the guidance of life everywhere in " Nature's ample tone ":

> Wisdom's dictates pure,
> Themes of momentous import, character'd
> By more than human finger, every page
> Discloses.

The poet recognizes the worth of natural revelation and speaks of the wisdom and beauty, evident in nature, which lead the mind to God and teach the heart. There is also the concept of divine immanence: " He fills all space, present throughout." But, like Cowper, Gisborne is an evangelical. God is revealed not only in his works, as deists would insist, but in his word and in the " redemption " offered to man for sin: divine punishment and the need of repentance are always insisted on. The deist's theology and his ethics are alike insufficient. One of Gisborne's prose works was *The Testimony of Natural Theology to Christianity*, in which he contends that Paley did not carry the argument far enough: natural theology establishes not only the existence of God and his attributes but also " the gracious plan of salvation through a Redeemer." Natural theology, he insists, should not only convert an atheist or polytheist into a rational theist but also a deist into a Christian.

Walks in a Forest has positive merits outweighing the diffuseness of its moral passages and the residue of stereotyped mannerisms in its diction and style. Gisborne lacked the gift of finality in phrase and the sense of form, but he is one of the most sensitive and faithful painters of English country life.

Another long poem, partly descriptive, Thomas Cole's *Life of Hubert* (1795), was never completed. Cole calls it " a narrative, descriptive, and didactic poem." Only the first book of a proposed thirteen appeared. A poetic autobiography seems to have been the intention, a narrative including the chief " diversions through the four seasons of the year " and tracing the poet's development through his early education up to his settlement in life as a clergyman. Cole's combination of autobiography with description of nature and ethical instruction, suggests that he might have anticipated some features of Wordsworth's *Prelude*. Perhaps he was influenced by Beattie's *Minstrel*. Very probably the vagueness of his plan, including, evidently, all that life had taught him, was too much for the modest abilities of this poet. But his intention is interesting evidence of what the taste of the time suggested to an ambitious versifier.

The collected *Poems* (1796) of George Harley, the Covent Garden actor, included his *Night*,[101] a long poem in blank verse

which, after some pages of conventional description, turns to a
series of genre pictures of country and city during those hours. The
peasant's return at evening to his cottage and his family is a scene
often painted. So too is the harvest-home festival. All Saints' Eve
and the excitement of a hamlet elopement are more novel in their
details and are sketched at least with real zest. When Harley returns
to the city setting, the suicide, the gamester, the prostitute, and
others allow him scope for an inflated kind of moral exhortation which spoils all effectiveness. The whole poem goes back, of
course, through one of the familiar themes of Thomson's *Winter*
to *L'Allegro* of Milton.

John Bidlake was one of the most prolific of descriptive poets.
The Sea, The Country Parson, The Summer's Eve, and *The Year*
are all long poems produced in the seventeen years of his devotion
to verse. He was a Plymouth clergyman whose preferments, such as
the Bampton lectureship and chaplainships to the Prince Regent
and the Duke of Clarence, never abated his desire for poetic recognition. *The Sea* (1796) has all the advantages of fresh setting which
Gisborne enjoyed, but Bidlake cannot make the same use of them.
He sometimes merely adapts Thomson or Vergil to a seacoast setting. The seasons of winter and summer and the parts of the day
provide a time framework. There is so little that is fresh in the
pictures of these seasons and their effects on the sea and the seacoast
that parts of the poem are dull indeed. Being another amateur of
natural history, however, Bidlake tries to get new imagery in the
accounts of shark, dorado, mackerel, salmon, razor cuttle, shag,
gull, and sea anemone. There are episodes explaining the action of
the tides according to Newton's principles, and conjecturing upon
the " secret springs " of the sea. Since Bidlake was both a descriptive poet and a prominent divine, his attitude toward science is interesting; its importance lies in the fact that in it " true religion "
received a " firm basis " and the " omnipotence of the Deity " was
established by demonstration. Genre sketches, a part of the formula
of descriptive poetry, might have added interest to Bidlake's work,
but not much is done with them. The narrative episodes of Ernesto
and Matilda, and of Telamont and Almeria, are pathetic tales of
lovers and of husband and family separated by death at sea. The
" excursion of fancy " is inevitable — the seas " where round the
pole, his throne eternal frost " uprears " and ever unrelenting
reigns." Bidlake repeats the old praises of commerce and of pioneer
navigators, and he calls upon pomp and affluence to consider — not

the husbandman this time, but the mariner, the gatherer of gulls' eggs on the cliffs, all those who wrest a precarious living from the sea. In spite of its stereotyped outlines, *The Sea* was favorably reviewed by *The Monthly Review, The Critical Review, The Analytic Review, The Monthly Mirror,* and *The British Critic.*

The first of the longer descriptive poems in English which elaborated the usual plan by adopting the month-by-month development implicit in Hurdis's *Village Curate,* seems to have been James Grahame's *Rural Calendar* (1797). This idea was later carried to inordinate lengths by Mant, William Cole, Player, and Partridge, poets whose preoccupation with natural history led them to extravagances of descriptive detail. Grahame has no such faults of excessive zeal; as always, he is an unassuming poet writing with reticence and a modest but real gift for exactitude. The later formula of the "rural calendar" (sometimes so described, with implied recognition, perhaps, of Grahame's priority) is of course simply an extension of Thomson's plan. The poet of the *British Georgics* is here employing much the same materials and with similar qualities of quiet realism. His short episodes contrast the misery and hypocrisy of cities with the charm of country life, urge benevolence and humanity, or attack the tendency he sees in Britain to favor commerce and manufactures at the expense of agriculture.

The Summer's Eve (1800) shows John Bidlake in a more favorable light than does the earlier work, *The Sea.* He has more independence, but the tendency to bathe everything in a pale wash of sentiment is still present. He "ascends an eminence" at sunset, describes scenes near Plymouth, reflects on the happiness of a rural life, and sketches an imaginary village laid waste by war — a contrast to these peaceful scenes. Descending from his hill, he draws a picture of a farm and of the domestic happiness which relieves the toil of a peasant's existence. This suggests the story of Glycine, whose love reclaims the idle and dissipated Morillio. Then Bidlake turns to a less pleasing aspect of country life, to a picture of poor cottagers who would think the joys of rural life a poetic fiction, and to the alehouse which is "the seat of village debauchery." In Part Two, coming darkness leads him to the church where, by moonlight, he contemplates the vanity of pride and the short term of life. The expected conclusion follows, reflections upon a future life. Though most of this is unpromising enough, Bidlake's descriptions do strive for the detailed observation now sought in poetry of nature. Lines like the following show his effort at such observation:

> A busy, ceaseless hum the air invades,
> Of unseen beings, murm'ring in the shades;
> While sullenly the drowsy beetle sings,
> Air flutters with innumerable wings. .. .
> With hardy teeth at his voracious meal,
> I hear distinctly work the varnish'd snail.
> Now the blind Night, enwrap'd in gloom profound,
> Opes all her hundred ears to catch each sound
> That feebly trembles o'er the sleepy air;
> The drop of sickly leaves, soft-falling, rare;
> The chirp half-murmur'd by the dreaming bird,
> 'Mid green boughs by his nestling partner stirr'd;
> The ineffectual gale's scarce-utter'd sighs,
> That hush'd by silence, try in vain to rise.
> Confounded colour sinks upon the plain,
> And growing Darkness spreads her rayless reign.

William Cole, curate of Theberton in Suffolk, in his *Descriptive Review of the Year 1799* (1800), adopted the months as a framework. He cannot be accused of lack of observation or of mere mechanical repetition. The minor poet is often a sensitive person; under the spell of a stronger mind, he may be unaware that his accents and emotions are not altogether his own. Cole's pictures of animals and insects, of the storms of the various months, of portents of changing weather, of the labors of the farm and pastimes of the peasants, have new observation but are never turned into poetry. Two decades later Cole brought out an enlarged version of his poem under the title *Rural Months* (1824), in twelve cantos. The changes in nature and in rural occupations are marked in more detail, and Cole's debt to other poets decreases. Twenty-four years of observation and preparation have made him more worthy of attention, but they have not made him a poet.

Twelve years after *The Village Curate*, James Hurdis printed *The Favourite Village* (1800) on his own private press at Bishopstone. It represented long effort; here, if at all, he would win fame. The favorite village is Bishopstone, Sussex, his birthplace. Part of the poem is local in character, but most of its description is not of appearances peculiar to any single place. It, too, belongs to the large group of panoramas of the year. Hurdis often shows a deficiency in taste, applying a Miltonic diction incongruously to such subjects

as boiling kettles or ocean bathing; his excess of pathetic fallacy
and his awkward, unpoetic polysyllabic words like "assiduous,"
"pituitous," "sequacious" are against him. We smile sometimes
at his style, but we must recognize him as one of the most informed,
exact observers of nature in English poetry. He writes passages of
quiet charm that compensate for others more unequal, awkward,
and crude. Though he owes something to Vergil, Thomson, Cowper, and others, he follows no one closely, and to call him a "pale
copy of Cowper" is uncritical and unjust.[102] The accounts of various activities of harvest, of the fowler's method of trapping birds,
of a port and its labors, of schoolboys on the ice or playing cricket
in spring, of Christmas-carol singers, spring labors in the field, and
a peasant's simple funeral, are less detailed than the pictures of
nature. He observes birds, animals, insects, trees, flowers, changes
in sea and sky, with more delight and greater discrimination. The
many pictures of domestic animals often lead him into the incongruity of subject and manner which is his worst fault; but he is
trying, through the handicaps of a traditional manner, to paint
with something of the feeling of the Dutch genre painters. Hurdis
is one of the best observers of the birds, of which a great number
are pictured with real animation:

> No longer now assembles as of late,
> Gregarious only in the winter hour,
> Bird of the sky baptiz'd, the speckled lark.
> Oft o'er the plain inert or fallow then
> In flight circuitous the nimble flock
> Swam eddying, or with sudden wheel revers'd
> Show'd their transparent pinions to the sun.
> Now earnest as of yore with dewy plumes
> To touch the roof of heav'n, in the first beam
> Of the clear orb apparent, with a spring
> Mounts the sweet warbler, and with upright flight,
> And throat that struggles to make sweeter still
> Exquisite anthem, to the cloud ascends.
> The eye that sees him with strain'd vision soars
> To mark him quiv'ring in the skies above;
> Not seldom, his ascension not observ'd,
> Looks with vain scrutiny the dappled air,
> Nor finds, invisible, the vocal spirit,
> Which fills with ravishment the deep of heaven,
> And chants aerial melody unseen.

There is one unusual passage in Book IV on the nest-building of various birds, the forms of their nests, and their favorite places for building — the sparrow under eaves, the rook high in the elms, the daw in steeples, the marten under cornices or shaded porches, and the finch in forked branches of orchard trees.

Plants, trees, and flowers, as numerous as birds in Hurdis, are painted minutely. Panoramas of sky, ocean, and landscape have the same reality. Even when Hurdis follows old outlines, he makes them his own by adding new observation. The portents of changing weather, for example, are older than Vergil, as old as Hesiod, but Hurdis has done more with this theme than any other poet. Equally familiar themes in his episodes are also made his own by original treatment. There is a scientific account of the physical causes of changing seasons. The religious element in Hurdis is interestingly developed: for him it is especially the exhaustless *beauty* of nature which points to the Deity. He is less the rationalist, convinced by the evidences of order and harmony, than the man of esthetic perception feeling " the manifested God " in the varied beauty of creation, and finding " some remote similitude of Him " in the smallest flower or butterfly.

Quotations partially misrepresent Hurdis. He needs the scope of unhurried development. It would be absurd to claim great merit for him, measured by the most rigorous standards, but in spite of his style he is often successful in doing what he wants to do, to paint nature and the life of the country with graphic precision.

William Holloway's *Peasant's Fate* (1802) and *Scenes of Youth; or Rural Recollections* (1803) are written without the glosses of fiction. *The Peasant's Fate* is like *The Deserted Village* in its thesis, but its form is nearer that of the Thomsonian descriptive poem. Holloway says he intends " to shadow forth the evils arising to the peasantry of this country, from the system of engrossing small farms, and driving the hereditary occupiers to the necessity of embracing a maritime or military life for support, or being reduced to the most abject state of dependence." He shows the former state of the commonable lands and the changes destructive of rural character. His native valley is the scene. There are a number of characterizations in the manner of Goldsmith — of the old and the new type of country girl, the pastor of his youth, the present rector and curate, the squire and his lady. But genre sketches, moral episodes, narrative, description of winter, and " patriotic panegyric" make up a large part of the poem. The recollections of youth are full of sketches of boyish pastimes of the country: bird-catching, fishing, bathing, a rural fair. The story of Reuben, a small farmer driven to a soldier's life, to misery and death by the engrossing of his lands, carries much of the burden of the argument. Holloway laments also the passing of the old relationship between master and peasant, the old indulgence to poor laborers, the encroachments of corrupt manners and of foolish emulation of the world of fashion and luxury. *The Peasant's Fate* is an interesting anticipation of Ebenezer Elliott, whose poems depicting life among the village poor in England, his *Village Patriarch*, *The Splendid Village,* and *The Ranter,* are further removed from the descriptive form.

Scenes of Youth has no thesis. Its descriptions of nature are trite, but it follows the earlier poem in painting occupations of the poet's youth in the village, recounting stories of the countryside, and recalling characters and events of those days. "Childish avocations" and mature pastimes such as bull baiting and cockfighting, cricket, May-Day dances, plowing matches, throwing the sledge, and leaping are described in what seems a conscious search for new imagery. Certainly there are few country occupations left undescribed by 1803. The narratives are drawn from Holloway's experience. "Evan the Parricide" is a hermit near the village. "Walter the Miller's Boy," who achieves success, returns to enjoy the scenes of his youth, and finds himself out of tune with them, points the excellent moral that love of the country and of nature cannot be universal, and requires a mind in harmony with quietness and unchanging beauty. City and country manners are contrasted in pictures of rural and of fashionable weddings, christenings, and funerals. The charity schools and the Sunday schools of the country are praised and recommended. Holloway is no more than a respectable versifier, but he helps to swell the current of rural poetry, now in fullest flood.

In 1803 Thomas Whitby wrote a poem in four cantos, later published as *Retrospection.* It is merely another contribution to the flood of rural verse, but it was written by a man who knew his subject thoroughly. The four seasons are the framework, but the genre pictures are the interesting element. Rural customs celebrating the first of April, Easter, May Day, wakes, "harvest-home," Guy Fawkes Day, and Christmas; diversions like the game "Riding-my-Lord," lifting weights, bull baiting, quoits, wrestling, football, and hunting; and the labors of the year are set down with more realism than art. Whitby is too fond of sentimentalized narrative. Maria, for instance, is struck by lightning as she stands under the shelter of an oak: her father immediately dies of grief. Dame Janet brings together the rustic lovers William and Anna, who marry and care for "Goody Janet" when she is old. "The maniac of the tomb" is another victim of ill-fated love. *Retrospection* tends sometimes toward an idealization of rural themes; it is closer to the mood of Goldsmith's pictures than to that of Crabbe's mordant sketches.

Catching the contagion of rural verse, David Carey wrote a long poem more ecstatic than exact in imagery; *The Pleasures of Nature; or, the Charms of Rural Life* (1803) introduces the Spenserian stanza again into the long episodic poem of the seasons. Carey uses familiar devices — the more general appearances of all the seasons, rural occupations, "excursions of fancy" to Lapland and Mount Etna, pathetic narrative, humanitarian harangues, and celebrations of retirement and of the unique blessings of Britain. He has obviously read the followers of Thomson and Thomson himself. He has also probably read *Tintern Abbey*. He too feels that something of glory and wonder has passed away from nature since his youth. He even anticipates the accents of the *Ode on Intimations of Immortality:*

> Days of my infancy! and are ye fled?
> And will ye never, never more return,
> To bid your light dreams hover round my head
> And bid in ecstasies my spirit burn?
> O, why is life's romantic-colour'd morn
> So short, when so propitious are its beams?
> We tread enchanted ground! the Loves adorn
> The spot, and every hour with pleasure teems!
> Oh! why does it evanish like its mid-day dreams?

He finds consolation in the development of mind and reason that replaces the ecstatic contemplation of youth:

> What though the dream is fled?
> Beam'd from the source of innocence, 'twas bright!
> But reason first, and sense must lend their aid
> His joys, his powers, to estimate aright,
> Ere man can taste the cup of true delight.

John Stagg, "the blind bard of Cumberland," reverted to a sedulous Thomsonism in his *Winter Piece* (1804).[108] This differs

little from the kind of thing written by Samuel Law in 1772, elabo-
rating within the outlines of Thomson's patterns. Again the floods
drive the peasants to the hills, where they watch their little all
swept away, as they had done in *The Seasons* and *Aeneid*. Again
the midnight traveler is lost and meets his death, the fortunate are
admonished to consider their unlucky brethren, the thunderstorm
sweeps over the hills with the usual phenomena in its train. Stagg's
verses have no importance except as another appeal to public taste
for poetry of nature and the country.

E. Warren's *Poet's Day* (1804) had three editions in the year of
its appearance, certainly not because of any exceptional merit. It
is a descriptive and meditative poem on very conventional lines.
Its four books are *Morning, Noon, Evening,* and *Midnight.* Warren tries to reflect nature and even to present minute appearances.
The narratives are after a well-defined formula. Alonza and Al-
mira meet death on the eve of their marriage. The poet hears the
far-off report of a gun and deplores man's tyranny over inferior
creatures. Everything the poet sees is all too likely to suggest its
moral parallel. Evidently seeing no opening for his " patriotic
panegyric," he adds it as a supplement under the title " Eulogy
on Britain." Three editions of so conventional a poem within a
year of its appearance indicate a rather uncritical acceptance of
descriptive verse.

A lengthy but inferior series of morning, noon, and evening
sketches, Robert Couper's *Seasons* (1804), describes typical days
in each part of the year. Couper is another who writes from unfeigned experience and whose descriptions, genre sketches, and
rural tales bear the stamp of reality. It is merely that he is an inferior poet and that his feelings, however sincere, flow into the
molds of literary stereotype. The series fills almost the whole first
volume of his *Poetry Chiefly in the Scottish Language* and attempts novelty only in the verse form employed, the tetrameter-
trimeter quatrain, and in the use of a Scots idiom. Couper concludes his *Seasons* with *An Hymn to the Almighty,* one of his
many points of similarity to Thomson, in which he praises the
Creator, whose sustaining power supports by an unremitting act
the life of all things.

James Grahame's *Sabbath* (1804) was his most popular poem,
reaching a seventh edition in 1812 and appearing at intervals later.
In the second edition, of 1805, he added the four *Sabbath Walks*
in spring, summer, autumn, and winter. The *Sabbath* itself is

partly descriptive. Its main theme is the Scottish Sabbath as observed by the laborer, the town mechanic, the rural churchgoer, the lover of nature, the solitary shepherd boy, the emigrant in the wilds of America, and others. The Sabbath of the persecuted Scottish Covenanters is described in the tone of religious fervor which accounts for much of the popularity of the poem. The realistic pictures of Scottish manners and character and the incidental description have the fidelity characteristic of Grahame. The *Sabbath Walks* combine reflection with description of each season. Each is short, the longest less than eighty lines. Grahame's observation is sharp. He hears the buzz,

> Angrily shrill, of moss-entangled bee,
> That soon as loosed booms with full twang away.

In the early spring he leaves the church and wanders alone in the fields.

> What though the clouds oft lower! their threats but end
> In sunny showers that scarcely fill the folds
> Of moss-couch'd violet, or interrupt
> The merle's dulcet pipe — melodious bird!
> He, hid behind the milk-white sloe-thorn spray,
> (Whose early flowers anticipate the leaf)
> Welcomes the time of buds, the infant year.

One of the few poets who candidly acknowledge imitation of Thomson is Joseph Good, in his *Spring* (1805) .[104] He improvises within the old patterns. There are, for example, the courtships of the birds, their nesting, their ways of teaching the young to fly, the revival of spring flowers and herbs, spring showers and the rainbow. The genre sketches of spring tasks and recreations hardly go beyond their models. Good likes the georgic didactic vein, however, and gives advice on burning weeds to supply salt to the soil, and on the arts of fishing. Scientific episodes explaining the revival of the plants at the spring equinox and the origin of rivers, also occur, and in connection with the theme of science, the motifs of "natural revelation." The "episode of Caelia and Damon" is another instance of "the sorrows of seduction." Good is merely one of the poetasters always drawn into the current of prevailing literary tendencies.

William Cockin, friend of Romney the painter, followed the drift to descriptive verse in *The Rural Sabbath* (1805) . But he is an execrable poet. The stereotyped summer's-day outline is employed, and there is yet another effort to give it new imagery. Whatver his merit as an observer, however, Cockin has made his poem intolerably dull by crowding it with admonitory and moralistic digressions in which all sense of proportion is lost. The diluted-Miltonic cast of his verse is prosaic in the extreme.

Another extreme toward which descriptive poetry might tend is illustrated in William Cooper Taylor's *Seasons in England* (1806). Taylor seems to think that catalogues of country appearances are in themselves poetic. His *Seasons* are calendars of rural changes in weather, general aspects of nature, flowers, plants, trees, birds, tasks of the farmer, pastimes and sports, holidays, and so on. The poem is related to such prose calendars as those of the Aikins, Leigh Hunt, William Howitt, and others, a type of "nature book" increasingly popular. Taylor's glimpses of country occupations include new subjects. The same is true of the descriptions of nature. But Taylor fails because he relies upon mere catalogues, lacking all ability to focus or organize. He reflects the usual view of natural revelation, and he sees "the lot of man" symbolized in nature's scenes, where we may "view imag'd life or moral rules deduce."

James Grahame's *Birds of Scotland* (1806) might be classified either as a descriptive or a didactic poem. It is full of detailed ornithology. But Grahame says it is not "a scientific performance"; he has tried "not so much to convey knowledge, as to please the imagination and warm the heart." Its theme is closely connected with the seasons, since they govern the appearance and departure of most of the birds. The poet develops still further that favorite theme of Thomson, which Hurdis and others had elaborated, "the loves of the groves," and describes minutely the form, plumage, songs and calls, nests, nest-building, haunts, and habits of a large number of birds. Buffon was eloquent on themes like these, and Hurdis and Grahame had read him, as well as Pennant. Grahame's exact descriptions are varied with episodes on the effects of "Monopoly," which drives the small farmer from his lands, the evils of child labor and of slavery, the affectations prevailing in landscape "improvement" (he is a disciple of Uvedale Price and his principles of the "picturesque"), the beauties of Scottish valleys and hills, and the glories of Scotland and her patriotic heroes. These episodes are often tedious, but the descriptions of the birds can be delightful. The suggestions of Pennant and Aikin, and the current taste for natural history, find a logical development in

The Birds of Scotland. Grahame sees the skylark of early spring in the midst of an unseasonable snowstorm:

> Even amid the day-obscuring fall,
> I've marked his wing winnowing the feathery flakes,
> In widely-circling horizontal flight.

He shows its haunts:

> On tree or bush no lark was ever seen:
> The daisied lea he loves, where tufts of grass
> Luxuriant crown the ridge: there, with his mate,
> He founds their lowly house, of withered bents,
> And coarsest speargrass; next, the inner work
> With finer and still finer fibres lays,
> Rounding it curious with his speckled breast.

The eggs of the merle are " five cupless acorns, darkly speck'd "; those of the wren are " small as moorland hare-bell " and dappled " like fox-glove flowers." The peasant foretells the coming shower by the flight of the swallow and martin. The eagle in thunderstorm and snow is vividly described:

> When lowers the rack unmoving, high up-piled,
> And silence deep foretells the thunder near,
> The eagle upward penetrates the gloom,
> And, far above the fire-impregnate wreaths,
> Soaring surveys the ethereal volcanos;
> Till, muttering low at first, begins the peal;
> Then she descends; she loves the thunder's voice,
> She wheels and sports amid the rattling clouds,
> Undazzled gazes on the sheeted blaze,
> Darts at the flash, or, hung in hovering poise,
> Delighted hears the music of the roar.
> Nor does the wintry blast, the drifting fall
> Shrouded in night, and, with a death-hand grasp
> Benumbing life, drive her to seek the roof
> Of cave or hollow cliff; firm on her perch,
> Her ancient and accustomed rock, she sits
> With wing-couch'd head, and to the morning light
> Appears a frost-rent fragment, coped with snow.

Grahame is an unpretentious poet reaching toward a new simplicity in keeping with his rural subjects. Scott and John Wilson (" Christopher North ") were among his sincerest admirers. Byron sneered at him in *English Bards and Scotch Reviewers,* but his merits are real. The loose descriptive form encouraged a diffuseness which is his worst weakness. But Wilson says of Grahame that his verses,

> Kept from the dust, in every cottage lie
> Through the wild loneliness of Scotia's vales,
> Beside the Bible, by whose well-known truths
> All human thoughts are by the peasant tried.
> O blessed privilege of Nature's Bard!
> To cheer the house of virtuous poverty,
> With gleams of light more beautiful than oft
> Play o'er the splendours of the palace wall.[105]

In his *Fisherman's Hut in the Highlands* (1807), Alexander Yeman returned to the series of genre sketches of the seasons. The setting is the rugged northern coast in winter and summer. Since Yeman is not a greatly accomplished poet, we should expect to find his description full of echoes. But his main intention is to draw the attention of readers to the hardships of the highlanders, to the common neglect of them, and to emigration of large numbers to America. There are scenes of the dangerous life of the northern fishermen, their humble cottages, the dread of wife and family while the fisherman is out in storms, the desperate difficulties of winter storm at sea and shipwreck, the summer expeditions southward for work in the harvest fields, and the labors and pastimes of these nomadic workers. In episodes of patriotic feeling, Yeman contrasts the productions and fertility of northern and southern Scotland with those of England. Yeman paints the lives of the highlanders more graphically than does the better-known Anne Grant.[106]

Very characteristic of the period is Mrs. M. H. Hay's *Rural Enthusiast* (1808), a poem in five cantos: *Evening, Sunset, Twilight, Sabbath Morning, Sabbath Evening*. The Enthusiast is a lover of nature and village life, whose excursions and observations the reader follows. The country folk of the poem and its scenes of rural labor and recreation are honestly presented, as is the universal rule by this time, and the descriptions show an enthusiasm wholly conventional. The beauty of nature leads the Enthusiast " to reflections on Nature's God " and on the moral influence exerted upon the soul of the lover of natural beauty.

George Crabbe's *Village* has been spoken of. His later poems demand brief comment also. They are not examples of descriptive poetry, but they probably had their effect upon it. *The Parish*

Register (1807) drew attention again to a highly realistic painter of village life. The new work is still " annals of the poor," but the picture of rural misery, overdrawn in *The Village,* is somewhat relieved by glimpses of content and happiness. One of the characters, Peter Pratt, is an interesting village botanist who gives didactic instructions on the " method of fixing the embryo-fruit of cucumbers." [107] *The Borough* (1810) , another picture of Aldeburgh, is in the same sharply realistic manner. It has more description of nature than its predecessor, an element always exact and precise wherever it occurs in Crabbe: he was deeply interested in natural history, and his description reflects that interest. For exact observation it would be hard to surpass his lines on sea birds, the petrel and the sea gulls.[108] There is also another country naturalist here, the borough weaver,[109] whose keen delight in nature is recorded. Men and manners are the primary subject, of course: borough sects, professions, trades, amusements, clubs, schools, prisons, and the poor. The *Tales* (1812) and the *Tales of the Hall* (1819) continue the manner of the earlier works, except that the tendency to melancholy and unrelieved pictures of misery is constantly softened until it almost disappears. Crabbe's realism, his occasional descriptive excellence, are fully preserved. Descriptive poetry probably felt the influence of Crabbe in both directions, but especially in his truth to actual country life.

Sarah Richardson's *Seasons* (1808) [110] returns to that use of descriptive poetry which the moralist George Wright introduced. Each season is described for the sake of the moral parallels it affords. Her use of description to serve moral precept is merely another indication of the vogue of this type. Similarly, Joseph Blacket's poems, introduced to the world by Samuel Pratt and including the *Morning Landscape, Mid-Day Landscape, Sunset Landscape,* and *Midnight Landscape* (1809) ,[111] are merely repetitive bits of nature description, without distinction and without new observation. Thomas Rhodes' *Spring* (1810) [112] even returns again to the outlines of Thomson and follows the method of improvising within his patterns. There is enough that is new to give Rhodes a claim to more than paraphrase, especially in pictures of rustic employments, more easy to depict than impersonal nature. John Struthers's *Winter Day* (1811) , in three parts, *Morning, Noon,* and *Evening,* is a descriptive and reflective poem quite extended in scope. Struthers had already won a hearing in *The Poor Man's Sabbath* (1806) , published a few weeks before Grahame's

Sabbath. But both his poems, though ambitious, are insipid and derivative. When he describes, Struthers falls back upon the models of better poets; when he paints the employments of men, he sometimes finds new subjects but always writes in a flaccid style of level monotony. Joanna Baillie and Scott interested themselves in Struthers, as another of the "uneducated poets" of the time (he was a shoemaker, like Bloomfield), and his reputation in Scotland was out of proportion to his slight achievement.

Colin Maclaurin, the mathematician, was another Scot who contributed to descriptive verse. Part Three of his *Triumphs of Peace* (1812) [113] is on the Thomsonian model. The poem as a whole is an essay on the benefits of peace, law, and liberty: under this general head, the peaceful triumphs of the field are a subdivision. Maclaurin's thesis is that manufactures and commerce depend on the trade of the farmer, and the arts and sciences on peace and plenty. The descriptive part of the poem is a glorification of the farm and of the country generally. Maclaurin shows no more than a facile, unoriginal talent.

John Bidlake brought his series of descriptive poems to a climax in *The Year* (1813), one of the longest poems the genre produced, rivaling that of the French Roucher. It is another "rural calendar" in twelve parts, one for each month, but Cole, Hurdis, and Grahame are outdone, at least in scope. The poem shows a new richness in Bidlake's observation, achieved through the discipline of natural history; but the style is still hag-ridden by mannerisms; the merits are nullified by the vices of the manner.

The birds are favorites again, and the themes of Thomson, Hurdis, and Grahame are carried further. In his account of autumn months, for example, Bidlake traces minutely the stages of bird migrations. His animals and insects are all drawn with particularity and show the same indebtedness to technical study. The many pictures of the flowers of the year and of the trees and plants, show a wide knowledge of botany, without much ability to turn it into poetry. Developing much further the element of apologetics, which appeared in *The Sea*, Bidlake uses the scientific argument to demonstrate divine wisdom in "the economy of nature"; the sea, the strata of the earth, the elements of air and water, contribute proofs. Both beauty and utility, everywhere in the universe, constitute a harmony in which God is present to the lover of nature, a harmony which can "compose and elevate" the soul. Bidlake unites the esthetic argument for design, prominent with followers of Shaftesbury, with the physico-theological argument from science. The notes indicate Bidlake's debt to writers like Buffon and Gilbert White and to works like the *Encyclopaedia Britannica* and the *Animal Biography*. The descriptions are certainly circumstantial; just as certainly, they are not poetry. Observation — or study of the observation of others — does not suffice for that. The descriptive formula requires genre sketches of the employments of the farmer in the various months. Sometimes these are presented didactically through georgic precepts.

The Year finds much of its episodic matter in georgic tradition. Bidlake's " excursions of fancy " are in the old manner; but he has read the travelers, and he presents pictures of the " sublime " scenery of the Pacific, the Andes, Niagara, Canada, Sweden, and Finland. The " patriotic panegyric " applies most of the time-honored praises to Devonshire. Humanitarianism to animals and to unfortunate men is an old element. The " happy swain " has tended, since Crabbe's *Village*, to disappear; Bidlake shows instead " the abject state of poor laborers," contrasting this with the luxuries and vices of the city. His narrative episodes are in the common vein of " sensibility," stories of domestic fidelity and of lovers who narrowly escape separation by death on the eve of their marriage.

In the later eighteenth and early nineteenth centuries, poetry reflected the more widely diffused knowledge of natural science. The advice given to poets by Pennant and Aikin was a call to the banner of a popular cause. Crabbe and William Cooper Taylor, among other poets, gave interesting pictures of a familiar figure, the amateur naturalist seeking specimens for his collection in country lanes and fields. The vogue of science in Paris, in which almost every intellectual shared, from Voltaire, with his slugs and beetles, to the most obscure hanger-on in the society of fashionable *virtuosité,* had given the contagion of its example. Buffon in France and Pennant in England led in the popularization of natural history, a host of others following each. Such eminent illustrators and engravers as the Bewicks, the Millers (John Sebastian and John Frederick) , Samuel Howitt, and George Ehret, in England, illustrated books on natural history and the country. The race of popularizers increased. William Fordyce Mavor turned his hand to topography, natural history, agriculture, botany, and compilation of " voyages." Priscilla Wakefield adapted natural history to

youthful comprehension; Robert Thornton wrote a long series
of botanical popularizations; Mary Roberts, known now only for
The Annals of My Village, was an excellent teacher of science;
Dionysius Lardner was a rival for any man in volume of production; Edward Newman, the journalist of popular science, edited
*The Entomologist, The Insect Hunter's Year Book, The Phytolo-
gist,* and *The Zoölogist.* " Touring " and seeing the beauties of
England had many points of contact with the vogue for science,
and John Lettsom's *Naturalist's and Traveller's Companion* combined these interests. Other writers followed Gilbert White in not-
ing the phenomena of particular localities in England. J. Leonard
Knapp's famous *Journal of a Naturalist* was a botanical companion
to White's *Selborne.* After the founding in 1790 of the Society for
Promoting Natural History, a number of other organizations
sprang up, facilitating wider dissemination of scientific teaching
— The Society for the Diffusion of Useful Knowledge, the Zoölogical, Astronomical, and Botanical Societies. The Royal Society continued to overshadow all others.

So widespread was the vogue of botanizing, for example, late
in the eighteenth century, that the scandalized Richard Polwhele,
Cowper's facile friend, was shocked into protest in his poem *The
Unsex'd Females* (1798). He views with alarm the common practice among young men and maidens of studying together the Linnaean sexual system of plants, and he predicts dire things for the
future of English morals.

Natural history often combined with simple love of the country
and of rural ways in the voluminous country and village literature
which poured from the presses in the early nineteenth century.
Everyone knows of Mary Russel Mitford, William and Mary
Howitt, and Mary Roberts. Edward Jesse's *Scenes and Tales of
Country Life, with Recollections of Natural History* and his
Scenes and Occupations of Country Life belong in the same company. Thomas Miller's numerous and once-popular works ought
not to be forgotten. Richard Jefferies is but one of many later in
the century.

One popular variety of prose "nature book" had a close connection with descriptive poetry: the calendar of appearances and
occupations of the year, a type of production evidently beginning
with John Aikin's *Calendar of Nature* in 1784. *The Natural
History of the Year* (1798), an enlargement of Aikin's plan by
his son, the scientist Arthur Aikin, had considerable popularity.

Descriptive poets like Thomas Gisborne and Grahame were the predecessors of Arthur Aikin. James Fisher's *Spring Day* (1803) and *Winter Season* (1810) are really long descriptive prose poems, full of Thomsonian pictures and phrases. Even Fisher's episodes are often in the georgic vein, like his account of " countries where winter seizes with despotic sway." Leigh Hunt's *Months* (1821) draws upon the Aikin calendar and White's *Selborne*. It is more "literary" in style than the *Natural History of the Year* and has less scientific content, but it follows the same plan. Bourne Draper's *Sketches from the Volume of Creation as Displayed in the Seasons of the Year* (1830) is descriptive and moralistic. William Howitt's *Book of the Seasons; or the Calendar of Nature* (1831) has " an original article on the general appearances of nature in each month " together with " all their poetic and picturesque features " found " in the garden, the fields, and the waters," besides " a complete table of the migrations of birds; a copious list of garden plants which come into flower in the month; a botanical calendar . . . an entomological catalogue; a notice of rural occupations, and finally, one of angling." Mary Roberts's *Annals of My Village* (1831) has " a calendar of nature for every month in the year." Thomas Miller's *Beauties of the Country* (1837), his *English Country Life* (1859), and other works through a long and productive career, grew out of the rural-calendar type. Mary Howitt's *Children's Year* (1847) and *Pictorial Calendar of the Seasons* (1859), the latter embodying Aikin's work; the anonymous *Book of the Months, and Circle of the Seasons* (1844), illustrated by Harvey; and Leonard Jenyns's *Calendar of Periodic Phenomena in Natural History* (1852), are other examples of a long-popular genre in prose, which ·sprang out of and finally replaced the descriptive poem. Thomas Miller is typical in the announcement of his aim, in the preface to *English Country Life:*

The author has attempted to embody in this volume whatever is most beautiful or poetical in country life and scenery; to exhibit the most pleasing and interesting features of natural history, without giving all the dry details of the learned naturalist; to show the beauty of plants, flowers, and trees, openly and simply as they grow, in a clear and common light, without enacting the part of the botanist; and to render that descriptive and readable, which has too often only found a place in the table of the calendar. . . . He has also portrayed old customs and festivals as they, to his knowledge, existed in many a village in merry England in his boyish days.

These numerous writers, the predecessors of W. H. Hudson, Thoreau, and Burroughs, had a ready audience and gradually took the place once preëmpted by the descriptive poets. Rural description never entirely escaped from the dominance of the *Georgics* and the *Seasons* until it began to develop as a popular variety of prose.

But, though prose was to take the place of descriptive poetry, the first three decades of the nineteenth century produced much verse in that genre, which continued true to the objective attitude toward nature, following Thomson or Cowper rather than Wordsworth or Byron. David Hurn's *Months* and *Description of an Autumnal Calm and Storm* (1813) [114] are examples of how even a farmer (for Hurn was one) looked at nature through the eyes of Thomson and Cowper. The second of these poems makes much of the Vergilian theme of portents of storm, a constant favorite, adding many new details obviously from Hurn's own observation: the dampness of harness, the croaking of ravens, rooks overspreading the land, the increased audibility of small sounds, pigeons mute on the house-tops, and so on. *The Months* is another catalogue, in a variety of verse forms, of appearances and occupations of the year. The anonymous *Autumnal Reflections* (1813) is a very stereotyped contribution to descriptive and reflective verse, conventional and unoriginal in all respects. The same may be said of Thomas Grinfield's *Seasons* (1815). [115]

An effort to supply new imagery from the country into which many Scottish highlanders had gone, Ann Cuthbert Knight's *Year in Canada* (1816) combines description of nature and sketches of occupations with episodes of a humanitarian and moral sort. The description often resembles Thomson's, but there is an effort to observe freshly, as in the account of the quick and luxuriant vegetation of spring, in contrast with the tardiness of the season in Scotland. The Canadian harvest, the running of the maple sap, winter pastimes, and other occupations are described. The peasants themselves are characterized — and their Indian neighbors. But the poet sets down new images in a frayed and faded style.

Another very extensive poem, Henry Hudson's *Hours* (1817), is mainly a recombination of old elements. The four books, *Morning, Noon, Evening,* and *Night,* are each a series of contrasts between these "hours" as seen in the different seasons, in different lands, in city and country, and among various occupations. The notes indicate Hudson's large debt to travel literature. His style, like Bidlake's, often spoils the effect of the observation he tries to set down. Natural history is a minor element, but both verse and notes show Hudson's interest in it. The narratives run true to type, as in that of a distracted maiden whose lover was lost at sea, or that of the old negro who sees his son borne away to slavery.

Ewald Christian von Kleist's *Frühling* was translated by Georg Egestorff as *Kleist's Vernal Season*,[116] and went into a second edition in 1818. This is one of the few indications of English interest in the descriptive poetry of the Continent, and Kleist attracted a very inferior translator indeed. Egestorff's translation is based on Kleist's recasting of the poem, the version of 1756. The poem itself is a conventional exercise in its genre, with echoes of Vergil and Thomson, and a strong admixture of primitivism and religiosity. But Kleist had genuine first-hand observation. His religiosity, like Thomson's, takes the form of celebration of the Creator manifest in his works, as glorious in the bird or insect as in the sea or the sky. Kleist's reflection of teleological argument and his worship of God in the creation, were elements of common occurrence in German descriptive poetry after the publication of *Frühling*.

John Clare was an authentic " peasant poet." He had his day of glory when the periodicals acclaimed him and patrons and literary leaders sought him out. Even the *Quarterly Review,* which about the same time " killed poor Keats," praised Clare highly. *The Gentleman's Magazine,* the *Anti-Jacobin Review,* the *London Magazine,* and others welcomed him. One of his songs was set to music by Corri and sung at Covent Garden by Madame Vestris. His patrons and friends included the Prince Regent, Lord and Lady Milton, the Marquis of Exeter, Scott, Lamb, Henry Cary, Allan Cunningham, Darley, Gifford, and Montgomery; but he lived to experience neglect, extremes of poverty and sickness, and finally madness. The story is almost unendurably tragic. His fame has been revived today, partly because of the recent Georgian vogue for pastoral verse but also because of the real merit of his best work; and a number of editors have revived his published verse and winnowed the extensive manuscript material.

Clare was first turned to poetry by the profound impression made on him by Thomson's *Seasons.* As a youth, he twice walked fourteen miles to buy a copy of these poems, with a few pence gathered together with difficulty. Though traces of Gray, Collins, Burns, Keats, Wordsworth, and Shelley, are evident in Clare, Thomson never ceased to be the most formative influence. Except for *The Village Minstrel* and *The Shepherd's Calendar*, he wrote no extended descriptive poems, and he always preferred lyrical stanzas to blank verse or couplets. Nevertheless, a large part of his work uses the themes and methods of the long descriptive poem, objective in its approach to nature.

His love of nature was the most absorbing thing in his life; he is naïve, objective, unreflective. Technical shortcomings, often awkward, sometimes even strengthen the effect of spontaneity and sheer impulse. At his worst, Clare is feeble, mawkish; at his best, the limpid and crystalline verse is a delight. Love of nature made him a student of natural history. In the diary of 1824–25, we find him planning *A Natural History of Helpstone* (his native village), and writing for it essays on the sexual system of plants, the fungus tribe, mildew, and other subjects.[117] Evidently he hoped to emulate White of Selborne. We see him buying colors to make sketches of "curious snail horns, butterflies, moths, sphinxes, wild flowers, and whatever my wanderings may meet with that are not too common." [118] He goes " bird nesting and botanizing." [119] He visits and exchanges data with Artis and Henderson at Milton Park, both of them students of natural history.[120] The wife of the Bishop of Peterborough sends him a microscope " to assist in his observations in entomology." [121]

His *Poems Descriptive of Rural Life and Scenery* (1820), which brought him into immediate favor, include no extended descriptive poems. But there is little which is not in the tradition of Thomson and Cowper, the difference being that where others combined these elements into episodic poems in blank verse, Clare uses lyrical stanzas for shorter, unified pictures. *Noon, Summer Evening,* and *Summer Morning,* combine description of nature and genre sketches of peasant employments. *The Village Funeral* and *The Harvest Morning* are vivid genre sketches. *The Robin* again shows that bird in winter seeking the haunts of men. The *Address to Plenty* is the old humanitarian appeal to the rich, in winter, to consider those less fortunate. *Crazy Nell* is another of the episodes of ill-fated love, especially numerous since Cowper's " Crazy Kate." The sonnets to the primrose, the glowworm, the ant, and such others as *A Winter Scene, Evening, Approach of Spring,* and *Summer,* are like unassembled elements of a typical descriptive poem. What *is* Clare's is the rare quality of his observation and the unaffected simplicity of his style.

The poems of his *Village Minstrel* (1821), in two volumes, show a very marked advance. The title poem is autobiographical and descriptive, running to 119 Spenserian stanzas. With Clare's *Shepherd's Calendar*, it approaches nearest to the plan of the typical descriptive poem. But all the stage properties of "relief" drawn from the storehouse of georgic episode, disappear; even the reflective element is reduced to a minimum. Clare seems to borrow a little from Bloomfield, but he is immeasurably superior as a poet. "Lubin," Clare himself, is drawn as in childhood he observed the changes of the seasons and village life. Clare later surpassed the pictures of birds and insects and changes of weather in this poem, but it is doubtful whether he ever did more vigorous pictures of peasants. He puts Northamptonshire dialect in their mouths and does not gloss over their crudities and coarseness. "The statute," a rural festival, appears in all its details; the old women who glean in the harvest fields are sharply etched; the coarse sports of "harvest-home" are recounted. The other poems of 1821, like those of 1820, are, in the main, on traditional themes. *The Gypsy's Camp, The Woodsman, Rustic Fishing,* and *The Cress Gatherer,* are genre pictures. *Description of a Thunder Storm, Autumn, Sunday Walks, Recollections after an Evening Walk,* and others, are equally traditional in outline. But the lines often convey sharp sensation. Clare sees dandelions "gilt with dew, like suns with showers," [122] the breeze "with feather-feet, crimping o'er the waters," [123] sunbeams that "filtering small, freckling through the branches fall," [124] the "antique mullein's flannel-leaves." [125]

The breaking up of the elements of the descriptive poem into shorter forms, usually in stanzaic measures, was a tendency fairly constant among the minor poets of the later eighteenth and early nineteenth centuries. John Clare may stand as an example of this numerous class; many others described country scenes, country people, farm labors, village pastimes, the changes of the year. Anna Seward, Robert Galloway, Mrs. Barbauld, John Stagg, Alexander Balfour, James Scadlock, Ewen Machlachlan, and Richard Gall, are among their number. Leigh Hunt's *Juvenilia* (1801) shows this tendency, and the nineteenth century produced poets of a similar kind: William and Mary Howitt, James Crease, Robert Nicoll, Bernard Barton, William Barnes, Ebenezer Elliott, and many others. The poets who have best painted the country, down to our own time, owe a debt to the descriptive tradition in poetry and to the prose literature of country life which began to spring up late in the eighteenth century and early in the nineteenth. The broadening and deepening of the tradition of country realism in verse has continued to our own day; Thomas Hardy, Edward Thomas, Robert Frost, and others, are its heirs.

Humphrey Woolrych's *Winter* (1824) has scarcely a passage not imitated from *The Seasons,* though the preface protests, " It has never been the intention of the author of this poem, to rival the graceful talents, or emulate the established excellence of Thomson." Woolrych is really a belated John Huddlestone Wynne. Descriptions of nature, genre sketches, even such episodes as the " patriotic panegyric," and the " excursion of fancy " to regions of northern winter, show only a sedulously imitative quality. Thomas Shaw's shorter *Seasons* (1824) [126] is also quite unimportant.

Edward Moxon, later the publisher of Wordsworth, Knowles, and Tennyson, contributed to descriptive verse in *The Prospect* (1826), which has a number of village scenes well drawn, another " rural walk," pictures of peasant festivities, and episodes drawn from recollections of those buried in the churchyard. He too must include the familiar figure of the crazed maiden whose lover was lost at sea. But he is not without originality in his village scenes.

John Clare's *Shepherd's Calendar* (1827) follows the month-by-month outline, familiar in poetic and prose " calendars." As in Clare's earlier work, there is little that is new in subject or plan; but his unaffected simplicity and closeness of observation are unchanged. The evidences of his study of natural history appear again; the same graphic sense in rural scenes gives them their suggestion of Dutch realism. It might seem that descriptive verse had touched almost all possible themes, but Clare finds new detail for his animated sketches of country labors and diversions. His feeling for words has improved; he speaks of " bright glib ice," the almanac's "wisdom gossip'd from the stars," the crane "cranking a jarring, melancholy call," the young lambs on April hillsides " like spots of ling'ring snows." Sometimes he can be both as musical and as vivid as in the first stanza of *November:*

> The landscape sleeps in mist from morn till noon:
> And, if the sun looks through, 'tis with a face
> Beamless and pale and round, as if the moon,
> When done the journey of her nightly race,
> Had found him sleeping, and supplied his place.
> For days the shepherds in the fields may be,
> Nor mark a patch of sky — blindfold they trace

The plains, that seem without a bush or tree,
Whistling aloud by guess to flocks they cannot see.

John Gisborne's *Vales of Wever* had already won recognition and the praise of even Wordsworth, who was not conspicuous for praise of other poets of nature, when his *Reflections* (1833) appeared, " a poem descriptive of events and scenery connected with the different months of the year." Any merit of observation is outweighed by the bulky mass of his hackneyed " reflections." He has what we are accustomed to call " the poet's eye for Nature," without being really a poet. There is all the exactitude he sought to convey, but he does not rise above prose. The non-descriptive elements of the poem lack interest. The narratives are realistic rural tales, with the usual bias toward a pathetic kind of " sensibility," both of them harmonious in tone with the descriptive elements out of which they grow. But the historical and moral essays are more difficult to justify; they seem to be fragments of unrelated poems coerced into inharmonious association. Yet in spite of the indictment against him as a poet, John Gisborne belongs among the literary descendants of Gilbert White, as does his brother Thomas, both of them studious observers of nature in the localities where they lived. But he might have written to better purpose in prose.

John Clare's last book during his lifetime, *The Rural Muse* (1835), had little success, though it is his best. The popularity of purely descriptive verse was declining. Clare's poems are on subjects like those he treated earlier, but his command of his medium constantly improved. There is a delightful series of poems on old themes of bird lore, full of fresh notations and sensitive expression. Objective genre sketches of country occupations are many and vivid. Sonnets increase in number. Clare uses this form in an individual way, leaving out all reflection and making it simply a clear outline sketch of a flower, a tree, or a sudden shower. He lies under the trees to hear "the laugh of summer leaves above." [127] He notices pebbles in the brook that are worn as smooth "as hermits' beads by gentle floods." [128] Grasshoppers "still wear the short night. weary with their fretting song." [129] He listens to the beetle that " wakes inquiries ever new " and the " droning dragon-fly on rude bassoon." [130] Clare's unpublished manuscripts have been selected from, since Cherry's edition of 1873, by a number of editors: Norman Gale, Arthur Symons, Edmund Blunden, and Alan Porter.[131] The striking qualities of *The Rural Muse* persist in much of the posthumously printed work.

The year of *The Rural Muse* saw the appearance of a voluminous "rural calendar" in two volumes, *The British Months* (1835) by Bishop Mant. His *Months* are those of a naturalist; his object is to show in detail the changes of the year as they affect the birds, animals, trees, plants, and flowers, and in these changes to assert natural revelation of the divine. He differs from earlier writers of "calendars" in being far more detailed than any. He differs also in that, though there are genre sketches of rural occupations and accounts of methods (even georgic precepts), these are entirely subordinate to the exhaustive calendar of natural history. There are hundreds of birds in *The British Months*. Mant notes their times of appearance and disappearance, their form and plumage, their songs and calls, the times of day when their song is heard, their courtships, their nest-building, the materials of their nests and where they are built, the singularities of their habits, their manner of flight, their ways of rearing their young, their peculiarities in migration. Flowers are as minutely treated. Mant even regrets the impossibility of including all the flowers of June. Trees and plants are also treated with minuteness and inclusiveness. In short, Mant is the poet *par excellence* of the amateur natural historian and of the orthodox believer in natural revelation. It was inevitable, given the advice of Pennant and Aikin, the mounting interest in science and in themes of natural revelation, and the long line of predecessors in descriptive verse, that a Mant should have appeared. It was well that this limited formula should have exhausted itself in such an encyclopedic crescendo. The long descriptive poem had already served its purpose, in fostering love of the country and of nature. Both were now commonplaces; otherwise Mant's poem would have been impossible. It represents all the old formulas of the descriptive genre gone to seed, top-heavy, verging on dissolution.

Yet several of the longest poems in the genre were still to come. There was, for example, *Home: or, the Months* (1838), by John Player of Saffron-Walden, another "rural calendar" in twelve parts, which its author says were "nearly finished upwards of twelve years since." Player's pictures of nature are many, and his observation is faithful enough, but the essential element of poetry is lacking. The subject matter of seasonal changes, traced in month-by-month transitions, of birds and insects, wild flowers and garden flowers, the crops, peasant labors and diversions, rural holidays, and so on, follows familiar lines, a difference being that

Player makes a closer connection than usual with a particular locality, and turns the poem to praise of " domestic life " in the country.
He is another devotee of natural history. There is much description of places, and his rural fair and country market are interestingly drawn. Plain, honest sketches like Player's have a certain
quiet appeal, like that of the Howitts, but unpretentious prose
would have been better.

The first book of George Garioch's *Association* (1839), a poem
on the association of ideas, is a descriptive poem of the seasons, full
of further development of old themes. Garioch adds nothing really
new, and writes in an anachronistic kind of blank verse. He is a
typical instance of the tenacious hold of literary tradition on unoriginal minds. Joanna Baillie's *Fugitive Poems* (1840) include *A
Winter's Day* and *A Summer's Day*,[132] both of them the familiar
episodic combination of description and genre pictures of peasant
life. Dilnot Sladden's *Spirit of Beauty* (1840), its third book praising the beauties of the seasons and the parts of the day, is as traditional as Garioch's work. *The Seasons* (1842) of " Piscator "
(George Pulman),[133] in the dialect of East Devon, included in his
volume of angling sketches, is equally derivative and unimportant.
The Seasons Moralized (1847), by " J. C.," returns to the method
of George Wright, turning description to ends of moral instruction.

Thomas Aird is a very belated Thomsonian. His *Old Bachelor
in the Old Scottish Village* (1845) was a popular series of prose
" delineations of Scottish character and . . . descriptive sketches of
the various seasons," [134] which belongs with the productions of the
Howitts, Mary Roberts, and others. *A Summer's Day* and *A Winter's Day*, both of 1848,[135] are relics of another age, eloquent testimony to Thomson's survival against the rivalry of the romantic
generation. Aird was another devotee of natural history and can
be pleasing in the quality of his observation; but he had no ear and
his blank verse is little more than stiffly scanned prose.

The " rural calendar " in verse did not end with Mant and
Player. As late as 1862 Samuel Partridge's *Our English Months* is
only less extensive than Mant's two-volume work. The preface
says:

I have written the following pages from a conviction that, notwith-
standing much that is taking place among us in the right direction, the
book of nature is still, to multitudes both of our villagers and towns-
men, one of far less suggestiveness and improvement than it might be,
for want of more observant habits and discriminative intelligence.

Partridge is returning to the example of earlier decades in trying to enlist verse under the banner of natural history. He differs little in plan from his predecessors, except that he interpolates occasional lyrics in his blank verse. There is more natural history in Partridge than in any other descriptive poet except Mant. Like Mant, he continually points out evidences of design and divine benevolence. Old Vergilian and Thomsonian elements still survive in full strength, though they are no longer defined limits for the poem.

The decade of the 1870's saw the old descriptive form still surviving in sporadic productions like John Lloyd's *Rural Hours* (1870), which recounts the scenes, labors, and diversions of the seasons. There is even the georgic didactic element. James White's *Seasons* (1873) are in stanzaic forms, but their content follows old patterns; and Oliver Raymond's *Seasons* (1878), in irregular rhymed measures, is still based on formulas which, a century before, had been long-established.

Few poetic forms in English verse have had so tenacious a life as the Thomsonian descriptive poem developed from the *Georgics* of Vergil. It represents a long-enduring effort to assimilate the growing observation and knowledge of nature and the country into poetry. Its greatest popularity was contemporaneous with the greatest popular interest in natural history. It produced no first-rate poets, and few second-rate ones. Its scientific bent became a too self-conscious effort to extend the boundaries of poetry; and the present writer, at least, is in agreement with the rejection of pure description as proper subject matter for extended poems. The writers in this tradition were too often convinced that exactness of observation was in itself necessarily poetic. But the extraordinary persistence of the type is the best testimony to the dominant position of Thomson in literary tradition over a long period; to the general interest in nature among English readers; and to the fact that observation of nature, reflection of country life, and a definite philosophy of nature, did not wait for the maturity of the famous poets of the English romantic school.

VII

A NOTE ON LOCAL VERSE

Ever charming, ever new,
When will the landscape tire the view!
The fountain's fall, the river's flow,
The woody valleys, warm and low;
The windy summit, wild and high,
Roughly rushing on the sky!
The pleasant seat, the ruined tower,
The naked rock, the shady bower;
The town and village, dome and farm,
Each giving each a double charm,
As pearls upon an Aethiop's arm.

Dyer

POETRY describing places has a long history, from the time of its classical examples, through the Middle Ages and the Renaissance to the days of Denham, Pope, and Dyer, and long after them. The "local poem," the "topographical poem," the "loco-descriptive poem," as it has been variously called, is separate in origin from the kinds of verse discussed above. A detailed history of the genre has been written by Mr. R. A. Aubin.[1] The purpose of the present note is merely to suggest how topographical poetry, like other forms in the eighteenth century, showed a tendency toward confusion of genres, and felt the influence over a long period of time of the georgic and the Thomsonian descriptive types. It would be strange if this had not been true. Local poetry was descriptive, and Thomson and Vergil were models toward whom descriptive writers tended to gravitate. Local poetry also felt the need of "relief" in episodes of various kinds, all the more as it became broader in scope and subject matter after the mid-century. The dominant types of longer poem employing episodes of different kinds, were the georgic or quasi-georgic didactic and the descriptive.

Local poetry was perhaps the most prolific of all types in the eighteenth century. It left, however, few examples which have had permanent recognition. Denham, Pope, Dyer, Goldsmith, Crabbe, and a few others before Wordsworth are still read, but on the whole this local verse has deservedly fallen out of favor. Yet it is very instructive as a reflection of its period. Its very existence is a refutation of the old notion that interest in nature and the country languished during the eighteenth century, and many of its poets re-

flect the constant extension of the bounds of English poetry during
the period.

From the beginning of their history, local poems fall into fairly
well defined groups: those, like Drayton's *Poly-Olbion*, dealing
with an entire district or extended locale; those, like Jago's *Edge-
Hill* or Booker's *Malvern*, dealing with a limited locality (hill
" prospects," towns, estates, parks, castles, rivers or lakes, or natural
phenomena like the Giant's Causeway in Ireland) ; and those, like
James's *Iter Lancastrense*, based on a journey or tour. Of these the
second is most important and most numerous. The third is usually
informal and often humorous. But our purposes will best be served
not by any division as to types or even by extended consideration of
individual poems. It is enough to indicate the original differ-
entiation of local poetry from the types already considered and
its tendency, especially after 1750, to adopt elements drawn from
didactic and descriptive verse. From 1770 to 1830 both the popularity of the type and the prevalence of new influences are at their
height. With such a definition of limits as indicated, it will not be
possible to show the important bearing of poems like Goldsmith's
Deserted Village or Crabbe's *Village* and *Borough* upon local
poetry.

The classical examples of the local poem are not of primary importance, but a few of them may be mentioned. The poem *Aetna*
(55–44 B.C.), of uncertain authorship, is not predominantly descriptive. Hyginus' *De urbibus Italicis*, of the Augustan period, had
no perceptible influence. Horace's Satire v of Book i is a " journey." Ovid and Propertius [2] also wrote poems of this type. There
are other such poems in Latin, from the later years of the empire
and from the Middle Ages. The *Mosella* of Ausonius (*c.* 371), perhaps with the *Georgics* as a source, praises the life of the husbandman and touches the didactic strain in an account of the fish of that
river. It includes several genre pictures and expressions of the pride
of place characteristic of later poets, but no one would contend that
Ausonius offered a model of primary importance. Ausonius was
imitated by Namatius in his *Itinerarium* (*c.* 417), and there were
other obscure writers of the *iter*. Ausonius' *Ordo urbium nobilium*
and Claudian's *Aponus* are on cities.

Anglo-Saxon literature knew an approximation of the type in
The Ruin. Wright and Halliwell reprint the early *Characteristics
of Counties* and the versified geography of *Recapitulatio omnium
terrarum civitatumque*.[3] Camden's *De connubio Tamis et Isis*,

Churchyard's *Worthiness of Wales*, Drayton's *Poly-Olbion*, Jonson's *To Penshurst*, and a number of the poems of Taylor, the "water poet," are later examples.

Drayton's *Poly-Olbion* anticipates many features of later local verse. Aubin analyses these in detail. History and topography are the main subjects. There are stories, mainly historical or legendary: Bevis, Locrine, Godiva, Guy of Warwick, etc. Moral or philosophical episode is scanty. There is a little didacticism, showing certain processes, but there is no indication of classical models in these few lines. Personal panegyric is sparingly present. There are short descriptions of stag hunting, hare hunting, and falconry. A "hill prospect" is described. Praises of retirement appear. The occasional pictures of country occupations and labors are short and lack detail. Speculation on scientific subjects is present, anticipating Thomson to some extent. Drayton's description of nature is highly formalized and artificial.

But local poetry immediately after Drayton, in John Taylor, Ben Jonson, Richard James, Carew, Vaughan, Marvell, Waller, and Charles Cotton, seems to show little evidence of his influence. As time went on, the popularity of *Cooper's Hill* and *Windsor Forest* made Denham and Pope the usual models. *Cooper's Hill* begins with a "prospect" seen from a hill, and includes panegyric, invective, historical matter, praise of retirement, moral reflections, praises of the Thames and of commerce, and a description of a stag chase. Denham's description merely indicates broad outlines, and is full of personifications and conventionalized classical allusions. The success of *Cooper's Hill* stimulated all varieties of local poetry in the late seventeenth and early eighteenth centuries. Davenant, Cotton, Tickell, and William Harrison, among others, wrote in the genre. But Pope's *Windsor Forest* in 1713 gave local poetry its greatest stimulus in the early years of its history. Pope's subjects are description of nature, very vague and general in character, historical reminiscence, rural sports, narrative of Lodona transformed to a river (Loddon) by Diana, praise of retirement, the poets of Windsor groves, panegyric of Granville and his daughter, the English rivers and English commerce, Queen Anne's preservation of peace, and the poet's own "humble Muse." The formulas of Denham and Pope tended to become fixed in local verse.

John Dyer's *Country Walk* (set at Abergasney, his brother's country seat) and *Grongar Hill,* both of 1726,[4] bring to the type genuine feeling for nature. *Grongar Hill* includes some themes common later, that of departed grandeur (inspired by ruins) , the catalogue (of trees, here) , the motif of retirement, and the eloquent lines on Peace and Pleasure which live " on the meads and mountain heads." Unfortunately, Dyer seems to have had less influence than either Denham or Pope.

The effect of Thomson on local poetry was far-reaching. Aubin says *The Seasons* " lacks the most vital element [of local verse], the description, namely, of a specific locality which is definitely named," but there is of course the " prospect " from " thy hill, delightful Shene," which includes, among other scenes, London, Harrow, Windsor, the Thames, Twickenham, Hampton, Clermont, and " Esher's groves." There is, to be sure, little specifically local description in Thomson, but the natural connections between types of descriptive verse brought the local poem under Thomsonian and georgic influence as time went on. Local verse was one of the most stereotyped forms English poetry ever knew, one of the slowest to change. The old models long continued in force; but new tendencies gradually crept in as blank verse began to share the field with the heroic couplet, as the type moved toward larger scale and longer episodes, as description moved toward more faithfulness and exactitude, as interest in the life of the country grew. It was not until the later eighteenth century that newer tendencies became really dominant over the old, but their effects continued well into the next century. In Chapter IV above (The Poetry of Country Occupations) , we have already noticed the materials borrowed by later poets from georgic and Thomsonian tradition. The local poets borrow in much the same way as writers of didactic poems or poems on divisions of time, except that usually their borrowings are less matters of fundamental plan than of detail, or of episode. It is impossible here to do more than indicate the general outlines of such indebtedness. Sometimes georgic precepts are given. The scope afforded to description of phenomena of general occurrence in nature (as opposed to aspects strictly of topography and place) is usually a mark of influence from other genres. The time divisions of the seasons and the parts of the day are employed by many poets after 1750. It would be reasonable to suppose these features carried over from other forms, even if the marks of imitation were not frequently unmistakable in the phrasing of the lines. The realistic genre sketches of country occupations, of the life of the peasant, which had appeared in undeveloped form in

Drayton and Cotton, are expanded by many poets. Scientific fact and speculation becomes a stock theme, as in Vergil or Thomson and their imitators; after the use of natural history had been developed in other descriptive poets, local poets also felt the influence of this effort toward new closeness of observation. Specifically georgic themes, dating back to Vergil, were rather common: exotic episodes, usually contrasting the torrid zone and extreme northern lands; patriotic panegyrics, often following the outlines of Vergil's praise of Italy or Thomson's lines on England and on Scotland; moral episodes, often borrowing freely from Vergil's " *Labor omnia vincit* " and his " *O fortunatos nimium* " passages, among others, or from Thomson's amplifications of these. The use of pastoral narrative by Thomson and his followers in the service of sympathetic emotions, the "inward harmony" of benevolence, was very often emulated in local verse. These tales of the countryside are quite different in tone from the legendary and historical narratives of Drayton or the neo-Ovidian inventions of Pope or Garth. The whole emphasis on benevolence, "social feeling," the "inward harmony" of virtue, strong too in writers of local verse, had been first conspicuously elaborated in poetry by Thomson. The use of physico-theological materials also, and the tendency toward worship of nature as a reflection of the divine, and toward recognition of an immanent divine life in nature influencing man's moral being, appear in local poets and frequently seem to echo *The Seasons*.

To show in detail how local poets follow the lead of writers in other genres would be tediously repetitious of preceding chapters. Many such poets remain quite distinct, following rather the earlier models of local verse, Pope or Denham or another. I shall therefore merely add certain examples of the kinds of mixture of genres spoken of above, although others will be referred to in the notes following.

The Didactic Episode. — First, then, as to the episodic use of didactic elements. The pure georgic of farm occupations is reflected by poets who give advice on such subjects: by John Wilson (*Clyde*, 1764) [5] and James Woodhouse (*Leasowes*, 1764) , [6] who use the old Vergilian theme of the dangers the seed of the grain must survive; by Joseph Budworth (*Windermere*, 1798) , who instructs readers on planting trees and flowers; by John Leyden (*Scenes of Infancy*, 1803) , [7] who advises shepherds on the care of flocks; and by Anna Liddiard (*Mount Leinster*, 1819–20) , who includes a short Irish georgic on draining bogs and cultivating potatoes. Landscape gardening, which gave rise to the georgics of Mason and Knight, was also the subject of a similar kind of instruction in Henry Jones's *Clifton* (1767), Richard Jago's *Edge-Hill* (1767), and James Woodhouse's *Norbury Park* (written in 1789).[8] A short cynegetic is included in James Cririe's *Loch Kettrin* (1803).[9] The kind of didacticism of industrial processes found in Dyer and other writers of English georgics seems to be begun in local verse by Richard Jago (*Edge-Hill*), who praises almost equally the mansions of the aristocracy, the commerce of the middle classes, and the labor of the lower classes. He seems to have tried to emulate Dyer in what he writes of Coventry silk manufactures and the processes of mining and iron working. John Leslie (*Phoenix Park*, 1772), George Woodley (*Cornubia*, 1819), and even John Allen (*Matlock*) as late as 1848, celebrate other industries and manufacturing processes in the didactic manner.

Seasons of the Year. — When the local poets began using the seasons of the year among their common formulas, they began to move toward themes like Thomson's, toward description of phenomena of general occurrence in nature. The story is repeated again. They at first follow Thomson closely, learn to observe by seeing through his eyes, by adding to his outlines. They develop more independence as time goes on, but the habit is strong, and Thomson (and Vergil) do not cease to be formative influences until the old forms of local verse begin to disappear. The use of the seasons as a structural device in the organization of local poems is almost invariably the mark of Thomsonian influence and, incidentally, of Vergilian. Nevertheless, local poetry sometimes shows interesting and abundant observation. Richard Rolt's *Cambria* (1749) describes the progression of the seasons in Wales and is strongly Thomsonian. There had been earlier treatments of particular seasons, of course, as in Samuel Shepherd's *Leixlip* (written in 1739), which shows a fondness for winter imagery. The most noteworthy of the local poems including imagery of the seasons, came later, however. William Crowe (*Lewesdon Hill*, 1788) has a modest picturesqueness of phrase and sounds the note of the genuine country tradition. Anne Grant (*Highlanders*, written in 1795),[10] J. Mackay (*Quebec Hill*, 1797), and Joseph Budworth (*Windermere*, 1798) are noteworthy before 1800. After that date James Cririe (*Loch Kettrin*, 1803), the John Leyden of *Scenes of Infancy, Descriptive of Teviotdale* (1803), who excels in exact observation, and Noel Carrington (*Dartmoor,* 1826), deserve more attention than it is possible to give them here. Men like Rolt, Crowe, Budworth, Leyden, and Carrington made real contributions to the growth of a full and varied appreciation of nature. There were others also who must be dismissed without discussion.[11]

Parts of the Day. — The poets who used time divisions of parts of the day are more numerous than poets of local seasons. Frequently Milton's *L'Allegro* and *Il Penseroso* are models. But more often Thomson is again the source: his *Summer* traces the transitions of a single day. Here again the story is the same, obvious free-hand tracing of his outlines leading to greater independence in observation and originality in treatment. Wetenhall Wilkes (*Kilikeen,* 1741),[12] William Harrod (*Sevenoke,* 1753), and Richard Jago (*Edge-Hill*) may represent for us the stage of tyro imitation. But John Wilson's *Clyde* had already shown independence and real merit of an exact, graphic kind. Michael Bruce (*Lochleven,* 1766)[13] should also be singled out; his death at twenty-two brought to an end the promise of real accomplishment. Later there were such poets as John Leslie (*Killarney,* 1772); Luke Booker (*Knowle Hill,* 1789), who had elements of vitality in his close knowledge of nature and country life; John Gisborne (*Vales of Wever,* 1797), a local poet praised by Wordsworth, one whose eye was certainly keener than that of many a better poet; Thomas Shoel (*Mileshill,* 1803); and the Noel Carrington (*Banks of Tamar,* 1820, and *Dartmoor,* 1826) whose graceful talent was well suited to the charm of his native Devonshire. After 1770 close observation grows more common in local verse, and there are many others who would repay the attention of readers interested in the spread of a tradition of nature-and-country verse.[14]

The Genre Sketch. — The genre sketch of country life, usually of rural occupations, had appeared in local verse before Thomson. Such sketches are found in undeveloped form in Drayton and Charles Cotton. Country sports had been described by Denham, Pope, and their followers. But *The Seasons* gave an elaborated panorama of the principal occupations and relaxations of country life through the year; and from 1730 on, many poets in didactic, descriptive, and local verse carried on this tradition of genre painting. Often there is an obvious debt to Thomson's pictures; in other cases the poets owe nothing directly to him, but continue a tradition in which he was the most conspicuous forerunner. After 1750 this element became fairly common in local verse; by 1800 there were few aspects of country life which remained untouched: after 1800 this kind of writing increased still further. What remained for such a poet as Wordsworth was a deeper psychological study of rural character, rather than any new reflection of the external life of the country.

Before 1750 Wetenhall Wilkes shows unusual interest in peasant life, especially in his *Hounslow Heath* (1748). Richard Rolt (*Cambria*), much influenced by Thomson, is also noteworthy before the mid-century. After this date poets of country life abound in these pictures, often pleasing in their graphic quality. William Harrod (*Sevenoke*) and John Wilson again, the Greenock schoolmaster (*Clyde*), excel in such painting. We should expect sharp glimpses of village life in poets like Michael Bruce (*Lochleven*) and John Scott (*Amwell,* 1776); we find a quality of realism which looks forward to Crabbe and Wordsworth. New pictures of the northern herring fisheries and of the highlander's winter life are in Luke Booker's *Highlanders* (1787?); his *Knowle Hill* is also interesting. William Crowe, Anne Grant, J. Mackay, John Gisborne, and Joseph Budworth, already spoken of for their description of nature, are also among the best painters of country life. It is impossible to do more than hint at the growth of this element in country verse after 1800. Again, poets interesting for fresh treatment of nature excel others as painters of rural life. Scottish writers like John Leyden, James Cririe (*Scottish Scenery,* 1803), and David Landsborough (*Arran,* 1828) are among the best of these. There was the Irish William Hamilton Drummond (*Giant's Causeway,* 1811), an outstanding local poet who sketched the life of the wild Antrim coast; there were the Englishmen Thomas Noble (*Blackheath,* 1808), Robert Bloomfield (*Banks of the Wye,* 1811), Joseph Cottle (*Dartmoor,* 1823), and William Lisle Bowles (*Banwell Hill,* 1828) — all poets who treated country life and character with authentic truth, though not always with real poetic merit. Among these later poets, I have found David Landsborough's Ayrshire sketches especially appealing: the folk of Lamlash Bay, the clans going over the glens to church, the services in Gaelic, country recreations, the fishing fleet in Lannox Bay where the devout fishermen sing hymns in chorus, and the ships passing off the coast with their sailors listening to the music from Lamlash church. Other poets also contributed to this mounting tide of rural realism in verse.[15]

Scientific Facts or Theories in Episode. — The kind of episode in which poets, deviating from description, outline current scientific facts or theories, as Thomson discussed the origin of rivers, the supposed force of the sun under the earth, the causes of meteors, or the nature of ice and frost, was probably taken over into local verse pretty generally from descriptive and didactic poetry, where it often occurred. Thomson and his followers seem to have set the example for much wider treatment of such themes than local verse had known before. Form and tone in such episodes, and sometimes even subject, are much the same, whether in georgic, descriptive, or local verse. Among local poets who include such episodes are George Keate, the naturalist and antiquary (*The Alps*, 1763); John Wilson (*Clyde*), who discusses the generation of insects and the spawning of salmon; Richard Jago (*Edge-Hill*), writing on the formation of mountains and of bodies of water, and on other themes; Edward Davies (*Blaise Castle*, 1783); and Luke Booker (*Malvern*, 1798), who speculates on the healing properties of Malvern springs. Geological subjects are the most common; theories of the formation of mountains, rivers, ocean bed, and other phenomena of the earth, are elaborated by Brian Broughton (*Reflections*, 1801),[16] James Cririe (*Scottish Scenery*), William Drummond (*Giant's Causeway*), George Woodley (*Cornubia*), John McKinley, (*Giant's Causeway*, 1819), David Landsborough (*Arran*), and John Allen (*Matlock*). Drummond almost rivals Erasmus Darwin as a poet of science. His third book is largely a defense of Huttonean theories for the formation of the Giant's Causeway, basaltic columns at Port Noffer on the Irish coast. Other poets are at least amateurs of astronomy, like Thomas Noble (*Blackheath*), of optics or botany, like John Holland (*Pleasures of Sight*, 1829 — partly a local poem), or of other branches of science.[17]

Use of Natural History. — The poets who used natural history as a means to more vivid and exact description appeared later in this genre than in descriptive verse on divisions of time. Scott of Amwell, Keate, and Booker, however, were versed in natural history; and John Wilson, Bruce, and Crowe, among others, show close observation like that of poets who seem more conscious of a scientific approach. But Gisborne and Budworth, late in the century, make a wider use of natural history. John Gisborne's *Vales of Wever* (1797), which Wordsworth praised, shows a wide technical knowledge and some freshness in its descriptions of trees and birds, for example, though it is too diffuse for real effectiveness. Joseph

Budworth's *Windermere* (1798) is the poem of a trained observer of nature in the lake country. His keenness of perception and his knowledge appear in his notes also, and have the appeal of exactness unpretentiously phrased. After 1800 local poets more often give evidence of the study of natural history which Pennant and Aikin had recommended to descriptive writers. James Cririe (*Scottish Scenery* and *Loch Kettrin*), Nathaniel Howard (*Bickleigh Vale*, 1804), and Fortesque Hitchins (*The Sea-Shore*, 1810) are examples. John Leyden's *Scenes of Infancy* (1803) is one of the most interesting poems of the time for minute observation sharpened by close knowledge of science. The Irish poets Drummond and McKinley, who wrote on the Giant's Causeway, apply exact knowledge to the description of animate nature of the seacoast. Drummond's *Clontarf* (1822) also reveals him as one of the poets most thoroughly committed to the alliance of poetry and science in this period. Like other descriptive verse, local poetry shows an especial fondness for subjects of ornithology and the themes Thomson suggested to so many later poets: Gisborne, Budworth, Leyden, Noble, Hitchins, and McKinley are examples. The best work of Noel Carrington, his *Dartmoor* (1826), shows the lover and close student of nature and is especially pleasing in describing birds like the moorland lark or the ring ouzel of the falls of Lyd. William Lisle Bowles is a curious and observant student of nature in his local verse. And David Landsborough, the Ayreshire naturalist (*Arran*, 1828) who added nearly seventy new species of plants and animals to Scottish records, is another excellent example of the alliance of science and poetry.

The Exotic Episode.— It would be tedious to discuss all the local poets who use the exotic episode, usually describing remote tropical or far northern regions and often contrasting these with each other, on which Thomson lavished so much color and which he elaborated from Vergil's example in the *Georgics*. Later poets who use such episodes, strongly recommended by John Aikin to the descriptive writers, often show the popularity of the travel literature of the period, sometimes citing the records of travelers in the footnotes usually accompanying the longer local poems. Such episodes are often, also, further evidence of the tendency toward natural history in verse. The interest in lives of humble folk appears also, in genre pictures of the common people of other lands.[18]

The Patriotic Panegyric. — Like the exotic episode, the Vergilian and Thomsonian patriotic panegyric was a model for local poets. Vergil's eloquent praise of Italy in *Georgic* ii and Thomson's praises of England and Scotland, emulative of and partly imitative of Vergil's lines, were natural models for local poets writing similar eulogies of the natural beauties and resources, the local cultures and traditions of England, Scotland, Ireland, Wales, or even Devonshire or Kent. The same outlines are often followed, though special sources of local pride, not suggested by any model, may be included.[19]

The Moral Episode. — The moral episodes of Vergil's *Georgics,* especially the praise of the life of the husbandman in contrast with the life of cities and courts (Vergil's " *O fortunatos nimium,*" etc.) and the praise of labor and its accomplishments in changing the world man inhabits (" *Labor omnia vincit,*" etc.) , are often echoed by local poets, as by didactic and descriptive ones. It is not always possible, of course, to separate echoes of Vergil or Thomson, in the first case, from echoes of Horace, Lucretius, Seneca, and many, many others who have written praises of " retirement." The poets who seem closest to Vergil or Thomson are indicated below.[20]

The Narrative Episode. — Thomson used narrative episodes with pastoral setting in the interest of " social feeling," " benevolence," " the inward harmony of virtue." These narratives were among the most popular features of *The Seasons;* they were imitated by the descriptive poets and by certain didactic ones. In local verse a similar use of narrative episode points again to a relationship after 1750 between descriptive, didactic, and local genres. Tales with the same narrative outlines as those of Thomson are, of course, not often found. John Leslie's tale of the beautiful peasant girl (*Phoenix Park*) , descendant of " Donaghoe the Great," led forth by her highborn lover to " higher scenes more suited to her worth," is much like Thomson's story of Palemon and Lavinia. William Carr (*Rosstrevor,* 1810) seems to have Thomson's Damon and Musidora in mind in his episode of the country maids bathing in the stream. Thomson's Celadon and Amelia, country lovers separated when she is struck by lightning, are among the many fate-crossed lovers of these episodes. Often these lovers meet death together, as do Archibald Maxwell's Florimond and Aurelia (*Portsmouth,* 1755) , George Keate's Matilda and Rodolpho, William Hurn's Felix and Calista (*Heath Hill,* 1777) , David Landsborough's Norman and Mary, and others in Pye's *Faringdon Hill,* Cririe's *Scottish Scenery,* and Budworth's *Windermere.* The separations of lovers by death are the most common of all themes

in narrative episodes of local verse. In most cases — and far too
often — the girl, who lives on, goes mad and wanders the seaside
or the highroads. This kind of episode is especially common after
Cowper's story of Kate in *The Task*, crazed after her lover is lost
at sea. Stories of lovers separated and of madness include those of
Michael Bruce's Levina, Joseph Budworth's youth who roams
the mountains " no longer in his perfect mind," John Penwarne's
William and Mary (*Contemplation*, 1807), Francis Skurray's
soldier's widow wandering the Portsmouth highroad (*Bidcombe
Hill*, 1808), Fortescue Hitchins's Edwin and Ellen, Cyrus Red-
ding's Ethelia (*Mount Edgcumbe*, 1811), John McKinley's Ellen,
and William Roscoe's Emeline (*Contemplative Days*, 1834).
Other pathetic tales of lovers' separations are those of Mark
Foster's Eugenio and Serena (*Scarborough*, 1770), Nathaniel
Howard's Edmund and Eliza, Luke Booker's Laetitia (*Knowle
Hill*), and John Leyden's youth and two maidens who were
rivals for his love. Bowles (*Banwell Hill*) and Edward Cooke
(*Kensington Gardens*, 1840) have episodes of desertion, madness,
and death. But these belong to another group on the theme of
seduction and its consequences, often stories highly overwrought
in their pathos. Such tales are told by Luke Booker (Louisa and
Hilario in *The Highlanders*), Francis Skurray, John Lewes (the
"lost maid of Buttermere" in *Keswick Scenery*, 1811),[21] Noel
Carrington (Eugenio and Eliza in *Banks of Tamar*), and Henry
Atkins (Susan Bertram in *Isle of Wight*, 1834). Stories like these
are of course very different from the traditional historical and
legendary narratives of local verse. Most of them are examples of
appeal to " social feeling," rather than of strictly realistic treatment of character and setting. After 1800 more realism did appear
in poets like Budworth, Carrington, Landsborough, and Atkins.
Many of the poets who tell these stories tell them as authentic
tales of particular localities, but their interest as examples of
literary traditionalism remains, whether or not they are founded
on fact.

   Themes of Benevolence and Humanitarianism. — Thomson's
narratives belonged, on one side, to the ethical element in his poem.
They were attempts to inspire the social feelings and benevolent
emotions which for him were the essence of virtue. Themes of
benevolence and humanitarianism were constant among local poets
and were indeed the common property of poets in the period.
Thomson apart, Goldsmith, Gray, Cowper, Crabbe, and Burns

also affected the local poets in themes like these. There are frequent panegyrics of philanthropists and reformers (the Howards
and the Wilberforces) of the age, exhortations to the wealthy and
proud to pity those less fortunate, and condemnations of the chase,
all much in the vein of Thomson. But these are details. More important is the growing evidence in local poetry of interest in the
lives of humble folk, of concern with the betterment of conditions among the agricultural and industrial poor, of acceptance of
the ethical importance of social feelings. Among local poets most
notable for concern with social betterment were Luke Booker,
Joseph Cottle, Anne Grant, Joseph Budworth, John Penwarne,
Thomas Noble, William Drummond, Mary Lloyd (*Brighton*,
1809), Anna Liddiard, William Lisle Bowles, and John Leyden.

Divine Immanence in Nature. — Local poetry includes a good
deal of that expression of reverence for the divine revealed in
nature, which was so characteristic of the poetry of the eighteenth
century and which appears in varying forms in such poets as Thomson, Mallet, Akenside, Savage, Cooper, Brooke, and Grahame. The
expression of this idea constantly turns toward the concept of divine immanence, whether this presence is conceived of as something akin to Thomson's "Soul of Being" and "Essential Presence," as a universal principle of law guiding and supporting the
whole, in the terms of analogy to the sun's influence in nature, or
in some vaguer concept of omnipresence. Local poetry expresses
these ideas less often than does the more general descriptive form,
and this expression seems to come later, perhaps because the more
generalized themes were a step toward a synthesis of the meaning
of nature. But the idea of divine revelation in the harmony or
beauty of the universe is found in such local poets as Bruce, Jago,
Woodhouse, Keate, Lane (*Cliffden* and *Vale of Wycombe*), Cottle, Broughton, Shoel, Penwarne, Drummond, and Noble. Michael
Bruce, echoing the ideas of divine presence and benevolent design, probably caught them from Thomson, since his *Lochleven*
shows other signs of debt to *The Seasons*. Jago's *Edge-Hill* concludes with a statement of faith in universal harmony contrived
by "the all-comprehensive mind," to understand which would
"all apparent evil turn to good." William Lisle Bowles speaks of
"the ideal spirit that abides unseen" in "rocks, and woods, and
solitudes." In his *Coombe Ellen*, the sublimity of nature leads
him to a contemplation of God's presence there; the poem breathes
a spirit of fervent nature worship. Joseph Cottle (*Malvern Hills*)

sees "in every blade of grass" the God who formed the universe. Nature "bids mankind learn goodness from herself," exerting an influence over man's moral nature. Thomas Reed's *Hastings* (1824) has an interesting "Hymn to Deity" praising God as the author and informing spirit of all things, revealed in his creation. William Hamilton Drummond, a local poet who was both an explorer of science and a disciple of the religion of nature, expresses well, in his *Giant's Causeway* (1811), the elements of natural revelation, divine harmony and beauty, and immanence in nature, which had appeared more or less fully in other local poets:

> In every wing that cuts th' aerial tides,
> In every fin that through the ocean glides,
> In every shell that studs the sea-beat strand,
> And bud and flower which western gales expand,
> Such beauty mingles with such reach of thought
> As nought, save power divine, could e'er have wrought;
> He, only He, with wisdom's store replete,
> He, in whose essence all perfections meet.
> E'en these bleak rocks deep stablished in the brine
> Declare the sovereign architect divine. . . .
> In all we see an omnipresent God;
> And every cause in Nature's ample reign
> Forms but a link of that unmeasured chain
> Which holds earth, seas, and skies, and worlds unknown
> High in stupendous poise from God's eternal throne.
> O Thou who rul'st o'er ocean, earth and air,
> Whose sovereign power but willed and all things were;
> While Nature's devious wilds my thoughts explore,
> Teach me to love thee, honour, and adore,
> In thee to hail the animating soul
> That forms, supports, adorns, pervades the whole.[22]

It was not until, roughly, about 1840 that the old types of long episodic local poem were recognized as outmoded and tended to disappear. Poetry of place did not, of course, disappear, and is never likely to do so. But the local poems of Byron, Tennyson, or Arnold are far removed from the forms and themes of the eighteenth century, which served their purposes in their turn.

CONCLUSION

PRECEDING chapters have told the story of the beginning, growth, and changes of a literary tradition. There are doubtless other examples of the types of poetry discussed. But complete record is less important than a general view of developing tendencies. The story has been that of the origin and growth in England of a georgic tradition in poetry, of its various mutations, and of the complementary, indeed inseparable, growth of the descriptive form introduced by Thomson, an offspring of the georgic.

The importance of the descriptive and didactic school in the reflection of knowledge and appreciation of nature and country life in poetry is evident. The dominance of classical models early in the century and the devotion of English and European eclogue writers to an artificial concept of Arcadian simplicity, had their result: the *Georgics* became the model through which a more realistic country tradition might develop. Obviously, to try to accommodate rural, agricultural, and even, in part, industrial England of this period within a literary form of the age of Augustus Caesar was to attempt the impossible. But in the growth, out of georgic influence, of the related descriptive and didactic forms, a tradition of honest representation of nature and of country life did emerge. In the didactic poems, in spite of imitativeness, often incongruous " elevation " of style, and disunity, there is, whenever they touch country life, a ruling spirit of truth. The poems of country occupations from Laurence, Somervile, Smart, Dyer, and Dodsley, to Cowper, Bloomfield, and Grahame are examples of growing realism. In these and in the episodes of descriptive poems there developed an interest in the peasant himself. This was inherent from the beginning; it is present in the *Georgics*. The decades from 1780 to 1810 show a culmination of this interest in the peasant with the appearance of a whole throng of poets of the country, men like Cowper, Crabbe, Hurdis, Davidson, Booker, Cotter, Grahame, the Gisbornes, Burns, Bloomfield, Holloway, Leyden, Noble, Yeman, and Wordsworth. But Thomson, Rolt, Smart, Dodsley, Wilson, Dyer, Stevenson, and the adapters of Thomson's plan from the forties to the eighties, were their forerunners. Wordsworth's theory of the countryman as the best subject for poetry reflecting permanent truths of human nature, came when interest in such character was at its height and when exploitation of the country in verse had reached flood tide. In the eighteenth century, interest in the man of the country grew from various causes: humanitarian sentiment, the primitivistic reaction toward simplicity and nearness to nature, even from democratic political theory. But an important literary tendency lay also in the development of such interest as poets found it in Vergil and Thomson. The genre sketch of peasants and of country pursuits, the treatment of common people of other lands, constant elements in georgic and descriptive poetry, grew in fullness and reality. Country life in general, in both kinds of poem, is reflected with a realism in sharp contrast to the mood of pastoral artifice.

The old conception of the eighteenth century as one in which the English love of nature mysteriously disappeared, no longer has any sanction. The period of the Restoration and two decades of the next century were marked by conventionality and superficiality in this respect, and time was required to break down these urban limitations; but after Gay, John Philips, Dyer, and especially James Thomson, there was a growing knowledge of nature, and a feeling of personal relationship to it, which reached a climax in poets of the romantic generation. Many factors contributed to this intimacy and knowledge. The assimilation of natural science during the century, and the theology of natural revelation, are of primary importance. The growth of landscape painting, the popularity of landscape prints, and that taste for the " picturesque " seen in William Gilpin, Uvedale Price, Richard Payne Knight, Arthur Young, and others, testify to a taste for broad, general scenes rather than to any love of minute observation. The same is true, on the whole, of the many accounts of tours, most of them in prose, which the century produced. The travel literature of the period shows a taste for exotic landscape and sometimes for a knowledge of the natural history of other lands, as well as of the life of their people. Shaftesbury's ecstatic love of sublimity and beauty and his belief in a perfected universe where all aspects of nature are good or beautiful, had a widespread effect, as did the nostalgic primitivism and search for simplicity exemplified by Rousseau. Other manifestations were the love of landscape gardening and the efforts of the English school, in revolutions of method and in a fascinating warfare of controversy, to approximate more closely a true taste for unadulterated nature. The social prestige and political power of the landed class, which brought the drift of Whig trading leaders to the land, was a social influence of paramount importance in all forms of English interest in the country and its life. One of the most vital factors has hardly been investigated by students of the period — the gradual improvement of the turnpikes, which allowed easier access to the country and stimulated the taste for tours and for country life. Most of these factors favored especially a love of landscape, of scenes of broad scope. The extra-literary influence which most encouraged minute observation was the growth of interest in natural history. In earlier pages we have seen this interest grow to full expression in poetry in the 1780's, increasing in force up to 1810, though some of its most detailed examples are, of course, later. The example of Thomson especially, and of Dyer, Cowper, and others stimulated precise observation; but these tendencies were intensified by poets who turned to the discipline of natural history. Poets like Hurdis, Cotter, the Gisbornes, Grahame, Bidlake, Darwin, Evans, and Tighe, besides others who wrote of places, had expressed this popular taste for more than two decades before *Lyrical Ballads* appeared, and they continued to do so until the old objective descriptive poetry slowly faded before the triumph of new forms in the more romantic poets. These contributions to knowledge and love of nature, the interest in science and natural revelation, the taste for landscape and for " picturesque " scenes, for exotic color, for landscape gardening and agriculture, for the beauty of individual trees, flowers, birds, and animals, were all reflected in the poetry of a country tradition which took its form from Vergil and Thomson. The number of poets who merely tried to refine or enlarge upon Thomson's notations is large. They illustrate the dominance of Thomson's model in men's minds and suggest the favor which might have rewarded a successful rival. Those who, like Wynne or Wright, merely recast Thomson, are only footnotes to his fame and indications of the popular preferences among his many themes. But Gay, Browne, Mallet, Ralph, Savage, Bruce, Dyer, Rolt, Akenside, John Scott, John Wilson, Stevenson, Falconer, Crowe, Mason, Cowper, Leyden, Hurdis, Budworth, the Gisbornes, Bidlake, Bloomfield, Bowles, Drummond, Grahame, Cririe, and Clare, are all poets who made their own contributions to a fuller knowledge and appreciation of the external world.

Almost all poets of the tradition here studied, excepting those who depart from subjects of the countryside entirely, show a real feeling for nature, even those who merely reflect rural sports. The didactic poets of country occupations show this feeling, but most of them are not remarkable for detailed natural description. They presented, in however derivative and oblique a form, the ancient tasks and pastimes of country life. But the descriptive poets show great variety of observation. The phenomena of clouds and winds and atmosphere, Coleridge's "goings-on" in the sky, for the observation of which Professor Myra Reynolds finds little evidence before Wordsworth and Shelley,[1] were described by Thomson, Ralph, Savage, Foot, Cowper, Thomas Gisborne, Hurdis, and Bidlake. The ocean, which, she says, "waited for Turner, Byron and Shelley," was painted by Falconer, Kirkpatrick, Hurdis, Fletcher, Cotter, and Bidlake. Taste for the grand and "sublime" in storms, in winter, in violent aspects of tropical and extreme northern phenomena, was almost constantly present, amplified in later years through the travelers and tourists. Close observation of flowers, trees, animals, and the habits and songs of birds, was not lacking in earlier years, as, for example, in Thomson, Ralph, Savage, Rolt, John Scott, Stevenson, and Wilson; but it was from 1780 onward that the desire for minuteness was most strongly encouraged by the vogue of natural history, and came to a striking climax just before Wordsworth entered on the scene.

Various factors brought the decline of the descriptive genre. Romantic subjectivity found other forms, especially the kind of lyric in which the poet and the nature he described were merged. The popular "nature books" in prose which sprang up early in the nineteenth century and increased rapidly, began to take the place of lengthy poems on such subjects. How far the decline of descriptive verse was due to critical theory, is problematical. The theories of Lessing and Burke discouraged the genre on grounds of esthetic propriety, while the effect of the so-called "Byron-Bowles controversy" was probably unfavorable.

Burke approached the subjectivist attitude when he said, "The truth is, all verbal description, merely as naked description, though never so exact, conveys so poor and insufficient an idea of the thing described, that it could scarcely have the smallest effect, if the speaker did not call in to his aid those modes of speech that mark a strong and lively feeling in himself." [2]

Coleridge gave the whole question a brilliant answer when he said that "images, however beautiful, though faithfully copied from nature . . . became proofs of original genius only as far as they are modified by a predominant passion . . . or when they have the effect of reducing multitude to unity, or succession to an instant, or lastly, when a human and intellectual life is transferred to them from the poet's own spirit." [3]

De Quincey is more narrowly subjectivist: " The fact is, that no mere description, however visual and picturesque, is in any instance, poetic *per se*, or except in and through the passion which presides." [4]

Lessing had taken Aristotle's *Poetics* as his guide, considering it "as absolutely valid as Euclid." The objects of poetic imitation are, in the Aristotelian term, the actions of men. Lessing's distinction between the plastic arts and poetry, in *Laokoon*, assumed the truth of this principle, and condemned descriptive poetry as an invasion of the provinces of other arts, especially painting.

Bowles's controversy on descriptive poetry was waged over a period of years; the final salvo was fired in 1825. The Wiltshire parson faced, one after another, Campbell, Octavius Gilchrist, the *Quarterly Review*, Lord Byron, the *London Magazine*, McDermot of the *Pamphleteer*, the *New Monthly Magazine*, and William Roscoe, the historian.[5] Hazlitt in the *London Magazine* (June, 1821) upheld Bowles's " invariable principles of poetry." But the cloud of witnesses who rose against Bowles, the redoubtable Byron among them, probably hurt his cause among those not disposed to examine logic too closely. Bowles defended description in poetry, and his " invariable principles " included these:

Works of Nature, speaking of those more beautiful and sublime, are more sublime and beautiful than works of art; therefore more poetical. . . . The descriptive poet, who paints from an intimate knowledge of external nature, is more poetical, supposing the fidelity and execution equal, not than the painter of human passions,[6] but the painter of external circumstances (manners) in artificial life; as Cowper paints a morning walk, and Pope a game of cards!

He can be even more dogmatic, and we often hear made explicit the assumptions of the older descriptive school:

No one can stand preëminent as a great poet, unless he has not only a heart susceptible of the most pathetic or most exalted feelings of nature, but an eye attentive to and familiar with every external appearance that she may exhibit, in every change of season, every variation of light and shade, every rock, every tree, every leaf in her solitary places. He who has not an eye to observe these, and who cannot at a glance distinguish every diversity of every hue in her variety of beauties, must so far be deficient in one of the essential qualities of a poet.

Bowles found Pope "deficient" and Cowper, of course, accomplished. Much controversy turned on this "talent for the picturesque." Campbell rightly objected,

This botanizing perspicacity might be essential to a Dutch flower-painter. Sophocles displays no such skill and yet he is a genuine, a great and affecting poet.

Byron categorically denied all of Bowles's principles, with more rhetorical virtuosity than logic. Indeed, Bowles's defense of his original principles, in spite of his over-statements of them in the heat of battle, was never overthrown by his opponents. But the effect of the controversy was probably damaging to descriptive poetry, sufficiently so, at least, to discourage long poems of the older type.

Wordsworth was direct heir to the tradition of descriptive verse. Both as a poet of nature and as a poet of rural life and character, he is indebted to his predecessors. It is significant that, of his earliest poems, *An Evening Walk* is conventionally in the manner of descriptive poems on parts of the day, and *Descriptive Sketches* is a quite orthodox piece of local verse. The framework of description in the former is rounded out by the usual digressions into moral reflection, autobiography, humanitarian sentiment, local tradition, and narrative of sensibility. The many sensory impressions give promise for future accomplishment but are in no way new to the genre. Even the diction is convention. *Descriptive Sketches* is equally true to type. As his genius developed, Wordsworth often continued to work through inherited descriptive traditions. The *Memorials of a Tour on the Continent* and *Memorials of a Tour in Italy* follow the already fixed tendency to break up the extended digressive *iter* into unified short poems. The *Yarrow Revisited* volume of 1835, commemorating two tours in 1831 and 1833 in Scotland and on the English border, does this also, the old outlines of description, local legend, history, and moral reflection remaining. The *River Duddon* sonnet sequence follows the old device of tracing the course of a river to the sea, with digressive themes like those common to topographical verse. The sonnets differ, however, in being less inclusively topographical; in touching such elements as history, panegyric, local scene, and local tradition with a lighter hand; and in being selective and personal rather than inclusive and impersonal. Wordsworth brought into local verse the selective faculty of artistic taste, what it had long needed. The poems later brought together in *Memorials of a Tour in Scot-*

land, 1803, and *Memorials of a Tour in Scotland in 1814,* originally
published in various years, are on themes suggested by places
and incidents connected with his itineraries. Wordsworth trans-
mutes local verse into poetry in such lines as those of *At the
Grave of Burns, Yarrow Unvisited,* and the *Address to Kilchurn
Castle.*

It is impossible to think of Wordsworth apart from his character
as a poet of place. Who has had more love of particular places or
more of the faculty for distilling their qualities into language? The
poems *On the Naming of Places,* lines in *Tintern Abbey, The
Prelude* and *The Excursion, The Simplon Pass, The Pass of Kirk-
stone, View from the Top of Black Comb, By the Side of Rydal
Mere, On a High Part of the Coast of Cumberland,* and sonnets on
the valleys of Westmoreland, on Grasmere, and on the woods of
Rydal — these are local poetry at its best. The way had been prepared for Wordsworth by innumerable poets who celebrated almost
every hamlet, hill, stream, and valley of England; in the flood of
local verse which inundated the readers of the latter half of the
eighteenth century. He excels them all, not so much because he
was a mystic who saw the deepest significance in nature, nor because he had keener sensory observation than they, but rather because he had at his best a finer gift of artistic selection; the plastic,
unifying stress of an essentially lyrical impulse; and, most important of all, the final poetic gift, sway over language. He added
also, it is true, a definite psychological theory, locality being the
starting point for a chain of Lockian sensations and Hartleyan
associations; but this too was of secondary importance.

The kind of descriptive verse directly developed out of Thomson's *Seasons* also culminated in Wordsworth. Beyond *An Evening
Walk* and perhaps the *Evening Voluntaries,* the matter of time
divisions as a framework did not figure in Wordsworth's verse.
It was high time, in any case, that the days and seasons should cease
to give the outlines of descriptive poetry — not that these were any
more unnatural than the topographical devices of local poetry, but
that in both cases form had become formalism. But the descriptive
poem had opened the way for this new poet and must have helped
to form his mind. Especially noteworthy is the emphasis on close
observation. This cult of precision, with all its researches into
branches of science, its effort to assimilate a fuller knowledge of the
universe, created an esthetic atmosphere which helped to make
Wordsworth what he was and to make his victory as a writer easier.

Qualities we attribute to Wordsworth as a nature poet, exact faithfulness to reality, wealth of sensory notations, were precisely those sought by Grahame, Cowper, Hurdis, the Gisbornes, and a host of others. Some of them, like Grahame and Clare, excel Wordsworth in observation, however much they fall short of him elsewhere. In comparison with men like Grahame, Crabbe, Thomas Gisborne, and Clare, Wordsworth was as certainly *not* a naturalist as he *was* a poet. There is a great deal of minute knowledge in poems like *To the Small Celandine, The Parrot and the Wren, A Wren's Nest, Love Lies Bleeding, To a Snowdrop,* and others. But the more common occurrence of this sort of notation in poems of the " fancy " than in those of the " imagination " is significant. Minute points of rare observation awaken the sense of novelty and stimulate the fancy; the imagination broods rather on the more familiar as it appears in moments of intense emotion, when natural objects have startling vividness as if set against some strange effect of light like those before a storm. At all events, Wordsworth owes much to the emphasis placed by lesser poets on the faculties of observation. He did not immerse himself in natural history in order to enrich his observation. He tended rather to draw away from science, because what really engrossed him was the avenue nature afforded into transcendentalism. But there are memorable notations of the beauty of landscape, sky, clouds, atmosphere, sounds, forms of objects, colors, motions — innumerable phenomena of the changing year.

It would probably be impossible to say how much Wordsworth's " aesthetic application of sentimental democracy " [7] owes to humanitarianism and literary primitivism, and how much to French revolutionary doctrine. But this much is clear. Both descriptive and georgic verse had long treated peasant life with sympathy and realism. Wordsworth's own account of how his early interest in the life of shepherds was fostered by his sense of " this sanctity of Nature given to man," illustrates how love of nature stimulated interest in men close to nature. Throughout the eighteenth century, many forces tended toward the kind of " sentimental democracy " Wordsworth represents. Among these was the discovery of man near to nature, by poets whose first concern was often for nature herself. Of these poets Wordsworth was the most conspicuous, and he is most successful in the treatment of peasants when he is most free from the tyranny of theories.

One of the important phases of the poetry of the eighteenth

century was its reflection of the assimilation of new scientific materials into thought and literature. A subject which I hope to discuss at a later time is the relation of this assimilation of science, a
large factor in eighteenth-century thought, to the formation of
romantic attitudes toward nature. We have seen a relation between minute techniques of science and the cult of exact observation in poetry. The relation between science and the romantic
"religion of nature" is perhaps even more important. The mind
of Wordsworth, for example, and his philosophy, are what they
are, in part because of this assimilation of natural science in the
preceding century.

The "new science" had an immediate bearing on religious
thought in the seventeenth and early eighteenth centuries. Its testimony was used in the defense of religion by Ralph Cudworth,
Robert Boyle, William King, Henry More, Bishops Stillingfleet
and Parker, and others in the seventeenth century. The " physico-
theological" and "astro-theological" works of John Ray and
William Derham were widely read and were still familiar to men
like Wordsworth and Coleridge. Gilbert Burnet's *Defence of Natural and Revealed Religion* (1737) abridges the Boyle Lectures
of such men as Bentley, Whiston, Clarke, Derham, and Woodward,
lectures often full of the themes of natural revelation.[8] The literature of the subject is extensive, in both verse and prose. Interest
in this literature, which represented various shades of belief, continued through the century and is illustrated also by many translations from foreign writings in this field.

Natural revelation was welcomed by the orthodox in the warfare
against doubt and atheism. There was warrant for it in the Bible
and in orthodox theology: did not the heavens declare the glory of
God and the firmament show his handiwork? But the oppositions
of science and religion were implicit in it, and it seemed to many to
make all other revelation unnecessary. It led away, too, from the
idea of a personal God to vague, shifting concepts of universal
spirit, embodied natural law, universal beauty, and the subtleties
of pantheistic and panentheistic belief. When God was widely
thought of under various concepts as immanent in his creation,
faith found its way into new mists of doubt, and divine authority
began also to lose definition. In the long conflict of science and
religion, of rationalism and mysticism, the lines were drawn tighter;
the issue was joined, first on one front and then on another.

The rationalism of those who opposed supernatural revelation had many points of contact with more orthodox positions. In this fact lay one of the dangers to orthodoxy. A follower of Shaftesbury or Bolingbroke and a more orthodox Newtonian would have agreed on premises of a universal order, harmony, and beauty of benevolent design, though their emphasis on one or other of these qualities would have differed; on the revelation of God in nature *to* reason and to the esthetic faculties of man; on the universal chain of causes and effects which lead to the First Cause. Shaftesbury himself and the Newtonians alike can speak of God as if he were immanent in his creation, though both would have professed belief in a personal God. If the revelation of God lies in nature, it is an obvious step to the idea of God's immanence there, a step often taken in the literature of the eighteenth century. The expression of this may be less the negation of a personal God than the tendency in moments of poetic fervor to embrace concepts more harmonious with the awesome vastness of creation. But God is seen in the universe and in man as part of it. Shaftesbury speaks of him as a permeating spirit appealing to man's spiritual faculties. Thomson thinks of him as the " Essential Presence" that pervades, supports, and sustains the universe as the sun ("best image of thy Maker ") pervades and sustains the solar system; but this presence is the great soul of being, accessible to the soul of man. Newton thought God present " to his world in space, as it were in his sensorium." [9] A few poets speak as if God and nature were one (pantheism), others as if God included nature (panentheism). Erasmus Darwin speaks of divine immanence as the embodiment of natural law, which includes the evolutionary principle. More orthodox poets and the men of Evangelical cast, William Stevenson, George Wright, Cowper, Thomas Gisborne, speak of God as immanent spirit but insist upon the necessity for "faith," " grace," or "redemption." Through the century runs the thought of an influence from nature on the moral being of man, sometimes crudely conceived merely in terms of moral analogies latent in phenomena, but often the natural consequence of the idea of an immanent divine life accessible to man in the life of nature. Nature does not simply " harmonize [man's] heart " and " serene his soul"; it guides his moral being and inspires him with wisdom and reverence. For the Shaftesburians, of course, this moral influence came as an inward " responsive regularity and sympathetic order" bestowed through the divine beauty and harmony in external nature.

It is unnecessary to point out all the poets whose "religion of nature" has been glanced at in earlier pages. They are numerous, but there were others who wrote in other forms and have not been spoken of, or but indirectly. But the relationship of descriptive poetry to nature makes its reflection of religious attitudes particularly interesting. The ideas of natural revelation are among its common themes; its reflection of teleological argument is constant. Among the poets in whom one finds various expressions of divine immanence are Thomson, Mallet, Savage, Bruce, Stevenson, Akenside, Wynne, Cowper, Hurdis, Grahame, Thomas Gisborne, Bidlake, Bowles, Cottle, and Drummond. The influence of nature on the moral being of man appears in Thomson, Mallet, Savage, Bruce, Stevenson, Jago, Akenside, Wright, Aikin, Mason, Cowper, Hurdis, Thomas Gisborne, Bowles, Cottle, and others. The concept of such influence is usually the corollary of the idea of divine immanence.

The "religion of nature," "romantic nature-worship," was a product of the eighteenth century, owing much to the scientific and rationalistic movements of the period. The colors in which it appears in Wordsworth are hardly peculiar to him; they had appeared earlier in the century which sought to assimilate new scientific knowledge and to transmute it into belief and faith. Though Wordsworth is anti-rationalistic, as were Stevenson, Cowper, Gisborne, and others, revelation was for him in his best period natural revelation — but revelation involving mystical insight. It was the mystical temperament and the genius of a great poet which Wordsworth added to ideas already widespread when he dedicated himself to poetry. Through Locke's sensationalism and Hartley's associationalism, he added, too, a theory and a technique of the mystical experience. But nature speaks to him and he to nature through a communion of like with like, through the immanence of the divine in his soul and in nature. This immanent spirit influences his spirit because they are related to each other and share the same pervasive life. It is of little importance, perhaps, to raise the questions whether Wordsworth was a panentheist, as a recent writer would have him,[10] and whether he strayed very far from at least a nominal orthodoxy of High-Church Anglicanism. It is the method of Procrustes. Certainly the religion of nature, revelation in nature, divine immanence in man and nature, and the communion of man's spirit with divine life in nature, are the essence of his earlier creed. He gave the religion of nature its most poetic expression, drawing into one body of belief elements found in the intellectual atmosphere of his younger years, elements which were his own only in so far as we make peculiarly our own whatever satisfies our profoundest needs.

APPENDIX
TRANSLATIONS OF DIDACTIC POETRY INTO ENGLISH TO 1850

The purpose of the following list is to suggest the extent of interest in didactic poetry in languages other than English, down to 1850. Translations from the *Georgics* are given as fully as possible. A number of the imitators of Vergil are included. Lucretius and the classical and neo-Latin poets of "natural philosophy" appear also. But other didactic writers are excluded, for obvious reasons.

'A. F." [Fraunce or Fleming?], *The Buckolicks of P. V. M. . . . together with his Georgicks,* 1589.

George Chapman, *Georgicks of Hesiod,* 1618.

J. Brinsley, *Virgil's Eclogues, with his Booke De Apibus,* 1620. [*Georgic* iv.]

Thomas May, *Virgil's Georgicks,* 1628.

Abraham Cowley, *A Translation out of Virgil. . . . from Georgic ii.* (?)

Richard Crashaw, "Out of Virgil, in Praise of Spring" (*Delights of the Muses,* 1646) . [From *Georgic* ii.]

Henry Vaughan, *Georgic* iv (*Delights of the Muses,* 1646) .

Mrs. Lucie Hutchinson, A translation of Lucretius. British Museum Add. MSS., 19,333, n.d.

John Ogilby, *The Works of P. V. M.,* 1649. His " second English Virgil," 1654.

Christopher Wase, *Gratii Falisci Cynegeticon,* 1654.

John Evelyn, *Essay on the First Book of Lucretius,* 1656.

Thomas Sprat, *The Plague of Athens,* 1659. [From Lucretius, Book vi.]

Sir Robert Howard, " The Fourth Book of Virgill " (*Poems,* 1660) .

John Evelyn (the younger) , *Rapin of Gardens,* 1673.

Sir Edward Sherburne, *The Sphere of Marcus Manilius,* 1675. [Book i.]

Thomas Creech, *T. Lucretius Carus . . . Done into English Verse,* 1682.

John Sheffield, Earl of Mulgrave, " Part of Virgil's Fourth Georgick " (Dryden's *Miscellany Poems,* Part I, 1684) .

Mr. Chetwood, " The Praises of Italy, out of Virgil's second Georgic " (Dryden's *Miscellany Poems,* Part I, 1684) .

Thomas Creech, "Part of Virgil's Fourth Georgick " (Dryden's *Miscellany Poems,* Part II, 1685) .

John Sheffield, Duke of Buckingham, *Part of the Story of Orpheus.* (?) [From *Georgic* iv.]

Sir Charles Sedley, *The Fourth Book of Virgil.* (?) [*Georgic* iv.]

Nahum Tate, *Syphilis . . . by Fracastorius,* 1686.

Charles Cotton, "Essay upon Buchanan's First Book" (*Poems*, 1689).

"J. O.," C. Cleve, N. Tate, and Aphra Behn, "Six Books of Plants" (*Second and Third Parts of the Works of Mr. Abraham Cowley*, 1689).

John Dryden, "Select Translations out of Lucretius" (Dryden's *Miscellany Poems*, Part III, 1693).

John Dryden, "Amor omnibus idem . . ." (Dryden's *Miscellany Poems*, Part III, 1693). [*Georgic* iii, 209–85.]

Henry Sacheverell, "Part of Virgil's First Georgick" (Dryden's *Miscellany Poems*, Part III, 1693).

Joseph Addison, "A Translation of all of Virgil's Fourth Georgick, except the Story of Aristaeus" (Dryden's *Miscellany Poems*, Part IV, 1694).

John Dryden, *The Works of Virgil*, 1697.

Thomas Creech, *The Five Books of M. Manilius*, 1697.

Luke Milbourne, "The First Book of Virgil's Georgics" (*Notes on Dryden's Virgil*, 1698).

Richard Maitland, Earl of Lauderdale, *The Works of Virgil*, 1700 (?), 1708–9 (?).

"J.C.," A translation from Buchanan's *De sphaera*. Harl. MSS., 4628, No. 15, n.d.

James Gardiner, *Rapin of Gardens*, 1706.

Joseph Trapp, "The Description of the Prodigies Which Attended the Death of Julius Caesar" (Dryden's *Miscellany Poems*, Part VI, 1709). [From *Georgic* i.]

Anon., *Lucretius: a Poem against the Fear of Death*, 1709. [Lucretius iii, 830–1094.]

Anon., *Callipaedia . . . Translated from the Original Latin. By Several Hands*, 1710. [Quillet.]

N. Rowe, G. Sewell, S. Cobb, and W. Diaper, *Callipaediae . . . to Which Is Added Paedotrophiae*, 1710. [Quillet and Sainte-Marthe.]

William Hamilton, *The Corycian Swain*. (?) [From *Georgic* iv.]

William Oldisworth, *Callipaediae . . . from Cladius Quilletus*, 1719.

William Diaper and John Jones, *Oppian's Halieuticks*, 1722.

Anon., *Silkworms*, 1723. [Vida.]

William Benson, *Virgil's Husbandry*, 1724. [*Georgic* ii.]

William Benson, *Virgil's Husbandry*, 1725. [*Georgic* i.]

George Sewell and others, Addison's Latin verses (*Miscellanies . . . by Addison*, 1725).

John Rooke, A translation of Vida's *De bombyce* (*Select Translations*, 1726).

Walter Harte, "Episode of Orpheus and Eurydice" (*Poems*, 1727). [From *Georgic* iv.]

William Pattison, "Orpheus and Eurydice" (*Poetical Works*, 1728). [From *Georgic* iv.]

Thomas Cooke, *Works of Hesiod,* 1728.

H. Travers, A translation of Ford's *Piscatio* (*Miscellaneous Poems,* 1731).

Joseph Trapp, *The Works of Virgil,* 1731.

William Cooke, " The Country Life from Georgic ii " (*Musae Juvenilis,* 1732).

Tipping Silvester, Ford's *Piscatio* and Bisse's *Microscopium* (*Original Poems and Translations,* 1733).

John Mawer, *Oppian's Cynegeticks,* 1736.

Jabez Hughes, Lines from Aratus (*Miscellanies in Verse,* 1737).

Anon., *The Dove-Cote,* 1740. [From Vanière, Book XIII.]

Joshua Dinsdale, *The Modern Art of Breeding Bees,* 1740. [From Vanière, Book XIV.]

John Martyn, *The Georgicks of Virgil,* 1741.

Elijah Fenton, Lines from Oppian of Cilicia. [Quoted in T. Cooke's edition of Vergil, 1741.]

James Hamilton, *Virgil's Pastorals . . . also his Georgicks,* 1742.

Anon., *T. Lucretius Carus of the Nature of Things,* 1743.

Michael Curtius (?), *Columella of Husbandry,* 1745. [Book X is in verse.]

Anon., " O fortunatos nimium, etc., Paraphrased " (*Poems,* 1748). [From *Georgic* ii.]

Anon., *The Georgics of Virgil,* 1750. [*Georgic* i.]

Thomas Gibbons, " Part of Fourth Georgic " (*Juvenilia,* 1750).

Samuel Pullein, *The Silkworm,* 1750. [Vida.]

Christopher Pitt and Joseph Warton, *The Works of Virgil,* 1753. [*Georgics* translated by Warton.]

George Jeffreys, Books I and XIII of Vanière (*Miscellanies,* 1754).

James Beattie, " Selections from Georgics " (*Original Poems and Translations,* 1760).

James Beattie, " Selections from Lucretius " (*Original Poems and Translations,* 1760).

Anon., A translation of Ford's *Piscatio* (*Gentleman's Magazine,* XXXV, 184, April, 1765).

Robert Andrews, *The Works of Virgil Englished,* 1766.

Thomas Nevile, *The Georgics of Virgil,* 1767.

Brockill Newburgh, " A Translation of Some Parts of Virgil's Georgics " (*Essays, Poetical, Moral, and Critical,* 1769).

Walter Harte, *The Episode of Orpheus and Eurydice* (?). [From *Georgic* iv.]

John Gray, " Part of Georgic iv " (*Translations,* 1778).

John Nichols, *Select Collection of Poems,* 1780. [Includes passages from the *Georgics* by earlier translators, Chetwood, Creech, Temple, and Sacheverell, and from Lucretius by Sir Robert Howard.]

Anne Penny, " Lines from Aratus' Phaenomena ". (*Poems,* 1780).

William Mills, *The Georgics of Virgil*, 1780.

Capel Lofft, First and second *Georgics* (see *Monthly Review*, LXXII, 345, May, 1785).

Anon., *Delille's Gardens*, 1789.

Vicesimus Knox, "Evening the Forty-second" (*Winter Evenings*, 2d ed., 1790, I, 363–67). [Lines from Sainte-Marthe.]

William Melmouth, *The Whole Genuine Works of Virgil*, 1790 (?).

R. Comerford, "Georgic I" (*Anthologia Hibernica*, 1794).

W. S. Landor, "The shell assuaged his sorrow" (John Forster, *Walter Savage Landor*, 1874, I, 24). [Lines from the Orpheus passage, *Georgic* iv, wr. 1794.]

Gilbert Wakefield, "Lucretius, Book II" (*Poetical Translations*, 1795).

Percy Smythe, *The Episode of Aristaeus*, 1795. [From *Georgic* iv.]

Caleb Alexander, *The Works of Virgil*, 1796.

Arthur Murphy, *The Bees*, 1797. [Vanière, Book XIV.]

Henry Tytler, *Paedotrophiae*, 1797. [Sainte-Marthe.]

William Roscoe, *The Nurse*, 1798. [Tansillo's *Balia*.]

Mrs. Montolieu, *The Gardens*, 1798. [Delille.]

Anon., Lines from Delille's *Homme des champs* (*Monthly Review*, XXXIII, n.s., 470–82, December, 1800).

Erasmus Darwin, Vergil's lines on grafting from *Georgic* i, and part of Edward Tighe's Latin lines on broccoli (*Phytologia*, 1800).

William Collier, "Lines from Lucretius" (*Translations*, 1800).

William Sotheby, *The Georgics of Virgil*, 1800.

John Maunde, *Rural Philosopher*, 1801. [Delille's *Homme des champs*.]

W. P. Greswell, "Lines from Fracastoro's Morbus Gallicus" (*Memoirs of Politianus*, etc., 1801).

Thomas Owen, *Palladius De re rustica*, 1803.

John Carey, *Dryden's Virgil Revised and Corrected*, 1803. An "improved edition" in 1819.

John Good, *The Nature of Things*, 1805. [Lucretius.]

John Belfour, *Music*, 1807. [Yriarte's *Música*.]

Charles Boyd, *Virgil's Georgics*, 1808.

William Drummond, *First Book of T. Lucretius Carus*, 1808.

William Stawell, *The Georgics of P. V. M.*, 1808.

J. R. Dease, *The Georgics of P. V. M.*, 1808.

John Duncombe, *Fishing*, 1809. [Book XV of Vanière.]

John Walker, "Translation of the Georgic of Hesiod" (*Poems*, 1809).

Anon., *Gastronomy*, 1810. [Berchoux.]

—— Davidson, *The Works of Virgil Translated into English Prose*, 1810.

Thomas Busby, *The Nature of Things*, 1813. [Lucretius.]

Charles Elton, *Specimens of the Classical Poets*, 1814. [Including selections from Hesiod, Aratus, Nicander, Nemesianus, Vergil, Gratius, Manilius, and Oppian.]

" J. G.," Addison's *Gesticulantes* and *Sphaeristerium* (*Miscellanea,* 1818).

Hans Busk, *The Banquet,* 1819. [Adaptation of Berchoux.]

John Ring, *A Translation of the Works of Virgil,* 1820.

Anon., *Virgil, Translated into English Prose,* 1821.

William Smart, *Virgil,* 1822. [Complete works.]

John Thelwall, "Delille's *Homme des champs,* Chant I " (*Poetical Recreations of the Champion,* 1822).

Robert Hoblyn, *A Translation of the First Book of the Georgics,* 1825.

A. W. Wallis, *Select Passages from the Georgics of Virgil,* 1833.

Isaac Butt, *The Georgics, Translated into English Prose,* 1834.

J. M. King, *The Georgics,* 1843.

William Sewell, *The Georgics,* 1846.

James Banks, *The Works of Hesiod,* 1848.

Henry Owgan, *Bucolics and Georgics of Virgil,* 1848.

J. Lamb, *Phenomena and Diosemeia,* 1848. [Aratus.]

John Watson, *Lucretius on the Nature of Things,* 1848.

William Bathurst, *The Georgics,* 1849.

R. and C. R. Kennedy, *The Works of Virgil,* 1849.

James Mongan, *Lucretius, Book I,* 1850.

NOTES

It has seemed unnecessary to include a formal bibliography which, in the present case, would add to the bulk of the book rather than to its usefulness. Primary sources are clearly indicated in text or notes; secondary sources are cited in notes. Line references to the works of Thomson and Cowper in the following pages are to the Oxford editions of 1908 and 1913 respectively. References to Vergil's works are to the edition of Benjamin Hall Kennedy (London, 1895). Abbreviations used refer to publications, as follows: E. E. T. S. = *The Early English Text Society; P. M. L. A.* = *Publications of the Modern Language Association of America; D. N. B.* = *The Dictionary of National Biography.*

CHAPTER I

1. *Popular Treatises on Science, Written during the Middle Ages . . . Edited from the Original Manuscripts, by Thomas Wright,* London, 1841.
2. *Instructions for Parish Priests, by John Myre.* Ed. by Edward Peacock. E. E. T. S., No. 31, London, 1868.
3. *The Boke of St. Albans . . . With an Introduction by William Blades,* London, 1901. Dame Juliana's *Vénerie* is a rhymed version, with certain additions, of the older French *Vénerie de Twety.* Another version of this, evidently of the fifteenth century, is edited in *Reliquiae Antiquae,* I, 149 ff.
4. *Palladius on Husbondrie. . . . Edited by Barton Lodge, with a Rhyme Index.* Ed. by S. J. H. Herrtage, London, 1873-79.
Mark Liddell edited the translation from the MS. of Earl Fitzwilliam, unknown to Lodge and Herrtage, which fills in certain gaps in the Colchester MS. See Mark Liddell, *The Middle English Translation of Palladius De re rustica . . . Part I, Text,* Berlin, 1896.
5. *Archaeologia: or Miscellaneous Tracts Relating to Antiquity, pub. by the Society of Antiquaries of London,* London, 1894, pp. 157 ff.
6. See Edith Rickert, *The Babees' Book,* London, 1923. Introduction.
7. Edited by Frederick J. Furnivall. E. E. T. S., No. 32, London, 1868.
8. See Rickert, *op. cit.*
9. *The Mirrour of Good Maners Conteining the Four Cardinal Vertues.* Spenser Society Publications, No. 38, Manchester, 1885.
10. See *Regimen sanitatis Salernitanum . . . with Introduction and Notes by Sir Alexander Croke,* Oxford, 1830.
11. Croke, *op. cit.*
12. *The Governayle of Helthe . . . with Introductory Remarks and Notes, by William Blades,* London, 1858.

13. *Art of Longevity, or, A Diaeteticall Institution,* London, 1659. 1659.
14. Ἐπιλοιμια 'επη, *Or, the Anatomy of the Pestilence . . . By William Austin,* London, 1666.
15. *The Compound of Alchymy, or the Ancient Hidden Art of Archemie,* London, 1591.
16. *Theatrum Chemicum Britannicum. Containing Severall Poeticall Pieces of Our Famous English Philosophers, Who Have Written the Hermetique Mysteries,* London, 1651.
17. *The Tryall of Travell . . . By Baptist Goodall, Merchant,* London, 1630.
18. *The Praise of Hemp-Seed . . . By John Taylor,* London, 1620. *Drinke and Welcome . . . Compiled First in the High Dutch Tongue, by . . . Huldricke Von Speagle . . . and Now . . . Amplified, and Translated . . . by John Taylor,* London, 1637.
19. *Minerva, or the Art of Weaving; Containing the Antiquity, Utility, and Excellency of Weaving . . . By R.C.,* London, 1677.
20. Information as to these poets and others of similar kind has never been presented completely, so far as I know. See, however, D. Murarasu, *La Poésie néo-latine,* Paris, 1928; and Abbé Vissac, *La Poésie latine en France au siècle de Louis XIV,* Paris, 1862 (?). And on the general subject of *Georgics* imitation on the Continent, see also M. C. Lilly, *The Georgic. Hesperia,* Supplementary Series: Studies in Eng. Philology, No. 6, Baltimore, 1919; P. L. Ginguené, *Histoire littéraire d'Italie,* Paris, 1824; Felippo Re, *Della poesia georgica degli Italiani,* Bologna, 1809; and L. Girardelli, *Dei poema georgici nostrali,* Goriza, 1900.
21. See H. B. Charlton, *Castelvetro's Theory of Poetry,* Manchester, 1913.
22. Castelvetro, *Poetica d'Aristotele vulgarizzata et sposta,* Vienna, 1570; J. C. Scaliger, *Poetices libri septem,* Lyons, 1561; Minturno, *L'Arte poetica,* Venetia, 1564 and *De poeta,* Venetiis, 1559; Fracastoro, *Naugerius, sive De poetica dialogus,* Venetiis, 1555; Patrizzi, *Della poetica,* Ferrara, 1586; Tasso, *Discorsi dell' arte poetica,* 1587, and *Discorsi del poema eroico,* Napoli, 1597 (?).
23. J. E. Spingarn in *Literary Criticism in the Renaissance* (New York, 1925), from which some of my facts here are drawn. See also Charlton, *op. cit.*
24. See Girolamo Frascatoro, *Naugerius, sive De poetica dialogus. With an English Translation by Ruth Kelso and an Introduction by M .W. Bundy,* " University of Illinois Studies in Language and Literature," Vol. IX, No. 3. Urbana, 1924.
25. Kelso and Bundy, *op. cit.,* p. 68.
26. *Ibid.,* pp. 68–69.
27. *Ibid.,* pp. 71–72.

28. Puttenham, *Arte of English Poesie*, 1589. See G. Gregory Smith, *Elizabethan Critical Essays,* Oxford, 1904, Vol. I.

29. *Ibid.,* p. 46.

30. Thomas Lodge, *A Defence of Poetry*, 1579. *Ibid.,* II, 71. For St. Paul's knowledge of Epimenides (the lost work *On Oracles*) see Titus 1: 12; of Aratus (the *Phaenomena*) see *Acts* 17: 28.

31. Sir Philip Sidney, *An Apologie for Poetrie*, 1595. *Ibid.,* II, 152.

32. Francis Meres, *Palladis Tamia*, 1598. *Ibid.,* I, 322.

33. Henry Peacham, *The Compleat Gentleman*, 1622. See J. E. Spingarn, *Critical Essays of the Seventeenth Century*, Oxford, 1909, Vol. I.

34. Henry Reynolds, *Mythomystes, c.* 1633. See Spingarn, *op. cit.,* Vol. I.

35. *Ibid.,* I, 162–63.

36. Thos. Hobbes, *Answer to Davenant's Preface to Gondibert*, 1650. *Ibid.,* II, 55–56.

37. Sir William Temple, *Of Poetry*, 1690. *Ibid.,* Vol. III.

38. On the subject of French critical influence, see A. F. B. Clark, *Boileau and the French Classical Critics in England*, Paris, 1925. On the general subject of criticism in the seventeenth century, see A. Bourgoin, *Les Maîtres de la critique du XVIIᵉ siècle*, Paris, 1889; and F. Vial and Louis Denise, *Idées et doctrines littéraires du XVIIᵉ siècle*, Paris, 1906.

39. *Monsieur Rapin's Reflections on Aristotle's Treatise on Poesie . . . Made English by Mr. Rymer; by Whom Is Added Some Reflections on English Poets*, London, 1694.

40. Thomas Pope Blount, *Censura celebriorum authorum: sive tractatus in quo varia virorum doctorum de clarissimis cujusque seculi scriptoribus judicia traduntur*, Londini, 1690.

41. Thomas Pope Blount, *De re poetica: or, Remarks upon Poetry with Characters and Censures of the Most Considerable Poets, Whether Ancient or Modern. Extracted Out of the Best and Choicest Criticks*, London, 1694.

42. *Ibid.,* p. 33.

43. *Ibid.,* p. 32.

44. *Ibid.,* pp. 77–78.

45. *Ibid.,* p. 78.

46. *Ibid.,* pp. 142–43.

47. *Ibid.,* p. 143.

48. *Ibid.,* p. 144.

49. See Charles Symmons, *Life of John Milton*, London, 1822, pp. 134–42.

50. See Abraham Cowley, *Essays, Plays and Sundry Verses. Ed. by A. R. Waller*, Cambridge, 1906, pp. 243–58.

51. See C. R. Weld, *History of the Royal Society*, London, 1848, I, 42, 49.
52. Waller, *op. cit.*, p. 258.
53. See Wm. Bray, *Memoirs of John Evelyn . . . Comprising his Diary from 1641 to 1705–6, and a Selection of His Familiar Letters*, London, 1827, IV, 376–78.
54. *Diary*, May 30, 1667.
55. See C. S. Duncan, *The New Science and English Literature in the Classical Age*, Menasha, Wis., 1913, on which I have drawn *passim* for details concerning the Royal Society.
56. Bray, *op. cit.*
57. Thomas Sprat, *The History of the Royal-Society of London, for the Improving of Natural Knowledge*, London, 1667.
58. *Ibid.*, pp. 415–17.
59. *Parallel of Poetry and Painting*, see Scott-Saintsbury, *Works of John Dryden*, Edinburgh, 1882 etc., XVII, 316.
60. See J. W. Draper, *Aristotelian "Mimesis" in Eighteenth Century England*. P. M. L. A., XXXVI, No. 2, pp. 372–400, June, 1921.
61. A. F. B. Clark, *op. cit.*
62. As examples, wholly or in part, of the types mentioned, see:
Sir Aston Cockain, *Art of Love*, in *Small Poems of Divers Sorts*, 1658.
John Sheffield, Duke of Buckingham, *Essay on Satire*, wr. 1675.
John Sheffield, Duke of Buckingham, *Essay on Poetry*, 1682.
Sir William Soames, *The Art of Poetry . . . made English*, 1683 (Boileau).
Wentworth Dillon, Earl of Roscommon, *Essay on Translated Verse*, 1684.
John Oldham, *Horace's Art of Poetry, Imitated in English*, 1684.
John Wilmot, Earl of Rochester, *Allusion to the Tenth Satire of First Book of Horace*, 1685.
Samuel Wesley, *Epistle to a Friend Concerning Poetry*, 1700.
Charles Hopkins, *The Art of Love*, 1700.
Anon., *The Art of Love. Paraphrased from Ovid*, 1701.
William King, *The Poet Banter'd, or Ovid in a Vizor*, 1701.
Thomas Uvedale, *The Remedy of Love. In Imitation of Ovid*, 1704.
William King, *The Art of Cookery*, 1705 (?).
William King, *The Art of Love, in Imitation of Ovid*, 1709.
William Coward, *Licentia Poetica Discuss'd*, 1709.
Alexander Pope, *Essay on Criticism*, 1711.
George Granville, Lord Lansdowne, *Essay upon Unnatural Flights in Poetry*, 1712.
" J. B.," *The Art of Beauty*, 1719.
Christopher Pitt, *On the Art of Preaching*, 1724 (?).

Walter Harte, *Essay on Painting*, 1727.

James Bramston, *The Art of Politicks*, 1729.

Edward Young, *Epistle to Pope. From Oxford*, 1730.

"Martinus Gulliverianus," *The Art of Beauing*, 3d ed., 1730.

Aaron Hill, *Advice to Poets*, 1731.

James Miller, *Harlequin-Horace: or, the Art of Modern Poetry*, 1731.

Robert Dodsley, *The Art of Preaching*, 1735 (?).

James Miller, *The Art of Life. In Imitation of Horace's Art of Poetry*, 1739.

Anon., *The Art of Poetry*, 1741.

Anon., *The Art of Architecture*, 1742.

William Whitehead, *The Danger of Writing Verse*, 1741.

Anon., *Essay on the Theatres*, in *Harleian Miscellany*, Vol. V. 1745.

John Brown, *Essay on Satire*, 1745.

Aaron Hill, *The Art of Acting*, 1746.

"A Gideonite," *The Art of Stock-Jobbing*, 1746.

Ralph Schomberg, *Tetrorhapsodia, or a Physical Rhapsody*, 1751.

John Armstrong, *Taste, an Epistle to a Young Critic*, 1753.

"A Comedian," *An Essay on the Stage; or, the Art of Acting*, 1754.

Nathaniel Weekes, *On the Abuse of Poetry*, 2d edition, 1654.

Anthony Moore, *An Essay on the Art of Preaching*, 1758.

Henry Fielding, *The Lover's Assistant*, 1759 (in prose).

"E. P. Philocosm" (Ellis Pratt), *Art of Dressing the Hair*, 1770.

John Byrom, *An Epistle to a Friend, on the Art of English Poetry*, in *Miscellaneous Poems*, 1773.

James De La Cour, *A Prospect of Poetry*, 1778.

"Samuel Smilewell," *The Art of Joking*, 1780 (?).

John Scott, *On Painting, to a Young Artist*, 1782 (?).

Joseph Fawcett, *The Art of Poetry*, in *Poems*, 1798.

John Penn, *The Art of English Poetry*, wr. 1798.

Martin A. Shee, *Rhymes on Art*, 1805 and *Elements of Art*, 1809.

C. B. Ash, *Essay on the Art of Acting*, in *Poetical Works*, 1831.

63. See Edward Malone, *Critical and Miscellaneous Prose Works of John Dryden*, London, 1800, II, 263.

64. Joseph Trapp, *Praelectiones poeticae*, Oxonii, 1711–19, I, 17.

65. *Ibid.*, II, 92.

66. *Ibid.*, p. 97.

67. *Ibid.*, p. 102.

68. First printed by J. L. Austin in an English translation in his *Thomas Tickell and the Eighteenth Century Poets*, London, 1931, pp. 198–209.

69. *Ibid.*, p. 209.

70. Christopher Pitt and Joseph Warton, *Works of Virgil in English Verse*, London, 1753.

71. Translations from the *Georgics* are listed in the Appendix.

72. British Museum Add. MSS., 19,333.

73. See William Upcott, *Literary Remains of John Evelyn*, London, 1834: on Gratius, p. 795, on Columella, p. 431, and on Cowley, pp. 786 and 799, where he translates from *Liber plantarum*.

74. Upcott, *op. cit.*, p. x; and Bray, *op. cit.*, IV, 19–22.

75. Bray, *op. cit.*, IV, 247–48.

76. See Alexander Chalmers, *Works of the English Poets*, VI, 638. On the general subject of Lucretius in England in this period, see T. F. Mayo, *Epicurus in England (1650–1725)*, 1934.

77. Chalmers, *op. cit.*, VI, 604.

78. Reprinted 1683, 1714, 1715, 1722, 1744, 1766, etc.

79. *Dryden's Miscellany Poems*, Part III, London, 1693.

80. See Charles Cotton, *Poems on Several Occasions*, London, 1689.

81. Harl. MSS., 4628, No. 15.

82. *The Second and Third Parts of the Works of Mr. Abraham Cowley . . . The Third Containing His Six Books of Plants . . . now Made English by Several Hands*, London, 1689.

83. *Rapin of Gardens . . . English'd by Mr. Gardiner*, London, 1706.

84. *Callipaediae: or, an Art How to Have Handsome Children . . . To Which Is Added Paedotrophiae, or, the Art of Nursing and Breeding Up Children*, London, 1710. The last three books of Quillet were translated by Sewell, Cobb, and Diaper. In the same year appeared a second anonymous version of Quillet: *Callipaediae . . . Translated from the Original Latin . . . By Several Hands*, London, 1710.

85. William Diaper and John Jones, *Oppian's Halieuticks, of the Nature of Fishes and Fishing of the Ancients*, Oxford, 1722.

86. John Rooke, *Select Translations*, London, 1726.

87. Samuel Pullein, *The Silkworm*, Dublin, 1750.

88. See Appendix of Translations, pp. 219–23.

Chapter II

1. W. P. Mustard, "Virgil's Georgics and the British Poets," *American Journal of Philology*, XXIX (No. 113), 1–32, 1908.

2. *The Silkwormes, and Their Flies: Lively Described in Verse, by T. M. . . . For the Great Benefit and Enriching of England*, London, 1599.

3. *Ibid.*, p. 38.

4. See *A New System of Agriculture* . . . *By John Laurence*, London, 1726, pp.161–67.
5. *Ibid.*, pp. 165–66.
6. Dennys' *Secrets of Angling* is reprinted in Arber's *English Garner*, Vol. I, 1877. Other editions are those of T. Westwood, London, 1833, and of "Piscator," *Bibliotheca Curiosa*, Edinburgh, 1885. Westwood lists still other editions in his introduction.
7. See M. C. Lilly, *op. cit.*, pp. 150–51.
8. *Ibid.*, p. 153.
9. The halieutic, ixeutic, and cynegetic. See below, notes to Chapter IV, note 1.
10. In *The Northern Atalantis: or York Spy* . . . *The Whole Interspers'd with Several Diverting Poetical Amusements. Second Ed. Corrected*, London, 1713. It appeared also, credited to King, in *Original Poems and Translations by Mr. Hill, Mr. Eusden, Mr. Broome, Dr. King, etc.*, London, 1714.
11. John Nichols, *The Works in Verse and Prose of Leonard Welsted*, London, 1787, pp. 1–3.
12. *Georgic* i, 324 ff. and 351 ff.
13. *Georgic* ii, 458 ff.
14. Chronologically out of position, but included here as another piece of humorous adaptation.

CHAPTER III

1. See, for example, the fourteenth of Lyttelton's *Dialogues of the Dead*, where Boileau speaks of Thomson to Pope.
2. See M. M. Cameron, *L'Influence des saisons de Thomson sur la poésie descriptive en France*, Paris, 1927.
3. See below, notes on Chapter VI, note 99.
4. Otto Zippel, *Entstehungs- und Entwicklungsgeschichte von Thomson's "Winter,"* Berlin, 1909; and *Thomson's Seasons, Critical Edition, Being a Reproduction of the Original Texts with All the Various Readings of the Later Editions, Historically Arranged*, Berlin, 1908.
5. William Hinchliffe, *Poems; Amorous, Moral, and Divine*, London, 1718.
6. C. A. Moore, "A Predecessor of Thomson's Seasons," *Modern Language Notes*, XXXIV (No. 5), 278–81, May, 1919.
7. *Georgic* i, 129–35; and *Georgic* ii, 338–40. *Cf.* Thomson, *Spring*, 243 ff.; and Hinchliffe, *Spring*, 1–31.
8. *Georgic* iii, 322–38. *Cf.* Thomson, *Summer*, 432–97; and Hinchliffe, *Summer*, 34–39.

9. Thomson, *Summer*, 516 ff.; and Hinchliffe, *Summer*, 40–63.
10. *Georgic* i, 208–9.
11. Hinchliffe, *Autumn*, 9–10.
12. Thomson, *Autumn*, 23–24.
13. *Georgic* i, 318–20. *Cf.* Thomson, *Summer*, 1114–15; and Hinchliffe, *Autumn*, 89–90.
14. *Aeneid* ii, 305–8. *Cf.* Thomson, *Autumn*, 342–50; and Hinchliffe, *Autumn*, 95–131.
15. *Georgic* iii, 478–566. *Cf.* Thomson, *Summer*, 1026–91; and Hinchliffe, *Autumn*, 36–49.
16. Thomson, *Winter*, 720–59; and Hinchliffe, *Winter*, 53–73.
17. *Georgic* iii, 360. *Cf.* Thomson, *Winter*, 724–25; and Hinchliffe, *Winter*, 67.
18. Thomson, *Winter*, 544–616; and Hinchliffe, *Winter*, 89–112.
19. Hinchliffe, *Summer*, 40–43.
20. Thomson, *Autumn*, 1030–32.
21. Willis argues well for the idea that Thomson planned all four of his *Seasons* at the time of writing *Winter*. See W. Willis, *Thomson's Winter: Being a Reproduction of the First Edition, with an Introduction*, London, 1900.
22. Mustard, *op. cit.*
23. Elizabeth Nitchie, *Vergil and the English Poets*, " Columbia University Studies in English and Comparative Literature," New York, 1919.
24. G. C. Macaulay, *James Thomson*, London, 1908.
25. Logie Robertson, *Seasons and Castle of Indolence*, Oxford, 1891.
26. Otto Zippel, *Thomson's Seasons. Critical Edition*, Berlin, 1908.
27. *The Northern Star, or Yorkshire Magazine*, London, 1817, etc., I, 343–47, 432–38, 505–8; II, 9–16, 118–22.
28. The word " magisterial" is a commonplace of *Georgics* criticism, describing the authoritative manner of the lawgiver, assumed by Vergil in his precepts.
29. See *Georgic* i, 197–203; *Georgic* iii, 63–68; and *Georgic* iii, 511–14.
30. *Georgic* iv, 219–227.
31. These figures are taken from R. D. Havens, *The Influence of Milton on English Poetry*, Cambridge, 1922. Havens draws them from a Caxton Head Catalogue (No. 556), which lists nearly 150 different editions, and from the British Museum Catalogue and the *Cambridge History of English Literature*.
32. R. D. Havens, " Primitivism and the Idea of Progress in Thomson," *Studies in Philology*, XXIX (No. 1), 41–52, Jan., 1932. As this book is prepared for the press there is announced also *Prim-*

itivism and the Idea of Progress, by Lois Whitney. Johns Hopkins University Press, Baltimore, 1934.

33. See Léon Morel, *James Thomson, sa vie et ses oeuvres,* Paris, 1895, Chapter VI.

34. H. P. Drennon, *James Thomson and Newtonianism,* " University of Chicago Abstracts of Theses, Humanistic Series," VII, 523–28, Chicago, 1930.

    H. P. Drennon, *James Thomson's Contact with Newtonianism and His Interest in Natural Philosophy. P. M. L. A.,* XLIX (No. 1), 71–80, March, 1934.

35. C. A. Moore, *Shaftesbury and the Ethical Poets in England, 1700–1760. P. M. L. A.,* XXXI (No. 1), n.s. XXIV, 264–325, 1916.

    C. A. Moore, " The Return to Nature in English Poetry of the Eighteenth Century." *Studies in Philology,* XIV (No. 3), 243–91, July, 1917.

36. Gainsborough's " Musidora " and Theophilus Clarke's " The Lovers " and " The Pensive Girl." See *D. N. B.*

CHAPTER IV

1. κυνηγετικος = pertaining to the chase; ἰξευτής = a fowler; ἁλιευτικός = of fishing.

2. The exclusion of scientific poems like Blackmore's *Creation,* Brooke's *Universal Beauty,* and Moses Browne's *Essay on the Universe* is arbitrary, but in so far as they turn to classical poetry for a model, it is primarily to Lucretius.

3. Abraham Markland, *Pteryplegia; or, the Art of Shooting-Flying,* London, 1727.

4. In *Works of Mr. Henry Needler. Second Edition,* London, 1728. First printed 1724.

5. For the background of the fisherman's pastoral as a type, see H. M. Hall, *Idylls of Fishermen,* " Columbia University Studies in Comparative Literature," No. 13, New York, 1914. For Browne's debt to this tradition, see pp. 165–81.

6. *Poems on Various Subjects. Written by Mr. Moses Browne,* London, 1739, p. 20 (note).

7. Third edition. London, 1773.

8. Book I, 106–17. *Cf. Georgic* i, 373–91.

9. *Miscellanies,* London, 1754. *The Country Farm,* Book I, pp. 163–210; Book XIII, pp. 210–30.

10. XVIII, 205–6.

11. See *The Monthly Review,* XXXVII, 315, Oct., 1767.

12. To Alexander Dyce, January 12, 1829.

13. *Monthly Review*, XVI, 328–40, April, 1757. *Critical Review*, III, 402–15, April, 1757.

14. John Scott, *Critical Essays on Some of the Poems of the Several English Poets*, London, 1785.

15. Nathan Drake, *Literary Hours*, Sudbury, 1798, pp. 137–72.

16. See Paget Toynbee, *Correspondence of Gray, Walpole, West and Ashton*, Oxford, 1915, II, 91.

17. See page 103.

18. See Anderson, *British Poets*, LIX, 12.

19. See George Birkbeck Hill, *Boswell's Life of Johnson*, Oxford, 1887, II, 453–54.

20. *Critical Review*, XVIII, 270–77, Oct., 1764.

21. William Stevenson, *Original Poems*, London, 1765, I, 187–219.

22. In a letter to Richard Graves dated March 7, 1757, from the Leasowes, Shenstone says, " I remember a poem of yours, called —————, upon the present taste in gardening; which you will not wonder if my late employments make me wish once more to see." On December 23, 1743, he had written to Graves of his pleasure in reading a poem of the latter, as a title for which he suggested " The Villa, a Poem; containing a Sketch of the present Taste in Rural Embellishments, written in 1740." It is possible that an earlier poem of Graves is here finding publication.

23. William Mason, *The English Garden*, Book I, 1772; Book II, 1777; Book III, 1779; Book IV, 1782, all printed in London.

24. Notice the edition of Mason with extensive commentary and notes by W. Burgh: *The English Garden*, York, 1783.

25. Kent, Southcote, and Brown are treated in E. M. Manwaring's excellent *Italian Landscape in Eighteenth Century Poetry in England*, New York, 1925.

26. See *Les Saisons*, Amsterdam, 1773, pp. 37–39. *Les Saisons* first appeared at Paris in 1769.

27. See *Cambridge History of English Literature*, Vol. XIV, Chapter VII.

28. Ralph Straus, *Robert Dodsley*, London, 1910.

29. Charles Welsh, *A Bookseller of the Last Century*, London, 1885.

30. By Benjamin Martin, the instrument-maker and general compiler. See D. N. B.

31. See John Scott, *Critical Essays on Some of the Poems of the Several English Poets. With an Account of the Life and Writings of the Author by Mr. Hoole*, London, 1785.

32. H. Pearson, *Doctor Darwin*, London, 1930, pp. 204–7.

33. The poets who employed themes of " natural revelation " and " physico-theology " represent different shades of belief. Among such poets the following may be cited:
Richard Blackmore, *The Creation*, 1712.

Richard Collins, *Nature Display'd*, 1727.

Samuel Edwards, *The Copernican System*, 1727.

Henry Baker, *The Universe*, 1727.

Robert Gambol, *The Beauties of the Universe*, 1732.

Henry Brooke, *Universal Beauty*, 1735.

Moses Browne, *An Essay on the Universe*, 1739.

Samuel Boyse, *Deity*, 1739.

Bevill Higgons, *Poem on Nature*, 1736.

Capel Lofft, *Eudosia*, 1781.

Joseph Wise, *The System*, 1781.

William Sotheby, *Extracts from a Manuscript Poem on the Elements*, 1825.

34. J. T. Desaguliers, *The Newtonian System of the World*, Westminster, 1728.

Richard Glover, *Poem on Sir Isaac Newton*, London, 1728.

James Thomson, *Poem Sacred to the Memory of Sir Isaac Newton*, London, 1727.

35. Mark Akenside, *Hymn to the Naiads*, wr. 1746.

Henry Jones, *Philosophy*, Dublin, 1746; and *Inoculation*, Bath, 1768.

John Walters, *Botany*, in *Poems*, Oxford, 1780 (?).

36. See C. A. Fusil, *La Poésie scientifique de 1750 à nos jours*, Paris, 1918.

37. See Louis Bertrand, *La Fin du classicisme et le retour a l'antique dans la seconde moitié du XVIIIᵉ siècle et les premières années du XIXᵉ en France*, Paris, 1897, Chapter I.

38. Pearson, *op. cit.*, p. 115.

39. Canto II, 307 ff.

40. Canto II, 313 ff.

41. See L. Rice-Oxley, *Poetry of the Anti-Jacobin*, Oxford, 1924.

42. *Anti-Jacobin*, Nos. XXIII, XXIV, and XXVI; April 16, April 23, and May 7, 1798.

43. See pages 144–49.

44. John Aikin, *Poems*, London, 1791, pp. 52–57.

45. See Christopher Hussey, *The Picturesque*, London, 1927.

46. *Poetical Works of Henry Brooke . . . and His Life. By C. Brooke*, Third Edition, Dublin, 1792, I, 417–32.

47. *Quarterly Review*, XIV, 533, Jan., 1816.

48. See Hussey, *op. cit.*, Chapter V, Part 4.

49. *Poems*, Dublin, 1797, pp. 1–23.

50. *Monthly Review*, XXXIII, n.s., 470–82, Dec., 1800.

51. See Appendix, pp. 219 ff.

52. Tomás de Yriarte, *La Música*, Madrid, 1779.

53. See *Oeuvres Complètes de Jacques Delille*, Paris, 1840, p. 5.

54. See, here and above, Bertrand, *op. cit.*, Chapter V.

55. Erasmus Darwin, *Phytologia; or the Philosophy of Agriculture and Gardening*, London, 1800, pp. 429–30, 431, 560–63, 391, 412–13.
56. Robert Southey, *Attempts in Verse by John Jones . . . with an Essay on the Lives and Works of Our Uneducated Poets,* London, 1831. See also C. B. Tinker, *Nature's Simple Plan*, Princeton, 1922.
57. See Chapter VI.
58. *European Magazine,* XLII, 424–26, Dec., 1802.
59. Book I, 1806; Book II, 1808; Book III, 1813, all printed at Shrewsbury.
60. Cantos I and II, 1808; Cantos III and IV, 1811, all printed at London.
61. *The Task,* Book I, 534 ff.
62. See pages 176–78.
63. H. P. Lipscomb, "Virginia Georgics," *American Journal of Philology,* XLIII (No. 171), 228–37, 1922.
64. "The Hop Garden; a Modern Georgic in Two Cantos," in *Blackwood's Magazine,* September and October, 1908. Canto II printed also in Courthope's *Country Town,* London, 1920, pp. 60–71.
65. V. Sackville-West, *The Land,* London, 1926.
66. From *The Land,* by V. Sackville-West, reprinted by permission of Doubleday, Doran and Co., Inc.

Chapter V

1. Alexander Chalmers, *Works of the English Poets,* XI, 74.
2. T. J. Mathias, *La Salute, o l'arte di conservarla,* Napoli, 1824.
3. Thomas Warton, *Ex poemate De ratione salutis conservandae.*
4. Thomas Warton, *Ex poemate De voluptatibus facultatis imaginatricis.*
5. *Spectator Papers,* Nos. 411–21.
6. The British Museum Catalogue lists forty-four editions, including those in Falconer's collected works.
7. Comments of James Stanier Clark in his 1803 edition of *The Shipwreck.*
8. George Birkbeck Hill, *Boswell's Life of Johnson,* Oxford, 1887, II, 171.
9. Book I, 1774; Book II, 1775; Book III, 1776, all printed at London.
10. Part I, 1774; II, 1775; III, 1777.
11. Book I, 1796; Books I and II, 1803, all printed at London.
12. In Thomas Downey, *Naval Poems,* London, 1813, pp. 3–111.

CHAPTER VI

1. See Chapter IV.
2. In *Poems on Several Occasions by Mr. Mallet*, London, 1743.
3. See Zippel, *op. cit.*
4. James Ralph, *Night*, London, 1729, pp. ii–iii.
5. See Zippel, *op. cit.*
6. *Poems on Several Occasions. By Samuel Wesley*, London, 1736, pp. 151–56.
7. Michael Bruce, *Elegy Written in Spring*.
   John Scott, *Written in Winter, The Approach of Spring, Written in the Hot Weather* (1757), *Written in Harvest, Written at the Approach of Winter*.
   Mark Akenside, *Ode on the Winter Solstice* (1740).
   Thomas Warton, *Pleasures of Melancholy* (1745), and his odes *On the Approach of Spring* (1753) and *The First of April* (1777).
   John Cunningham, *Day*, etc., in his *Day, and Other Pastorals* (1761).
   William Woty, *An Evening Piece*, and *To Winter*, in *Blossoms of Helicon* (1763). See also *The Harvest* (contributed by W. Sharp).
   Cuthbert Shaw, *Odes on the Four Seasons* (1760).
   John Logan, *Ode Written in a Visit to the Country in Autumn*, and *Ode Written in Spring*.
   Anna Seward, *The Hay-Field, Ode to the Sun* (1780), *Amusements of Winter* (1779), and *The Terrestrial Year*.
   Mrs. Barbauld, *On the Backwardness of Spring* (1771), *Ode to Spring, A Summer Evening's Meditation*, and *Autumn, a Fragment*.
   W. L. Bowles, *The Sylph of Summer*.
   See also Francis Fawkes, *Autumnal Ode* (1754), *Vernal Ode* (1754), *Ode on Winter*, and *Ode to Summer;* William Hamilton, *Ode III* (" Now spring begins her smiling round . . ."); and Thomas Brerewood's " pastoral ballads " *Spring, Summer, Autumn*, and *Winter* (G. Pearch's *Collection of Poems*, 1775).
8. Edward Stephens, *Poems on Various Subjects*, London, 1759, pp. 152–57.
9. Francis Leighton, *The Muse's Blossoms*, London, 1769, pp. 47–58.
10. Anon., *Reflections on the Ruins of an Ancient Cathedral . . . Second Edition*, Chelmsford, 1770, pp. 15–20.
11. R. Valpy, *Poetical Blossoms*, Guilford, 1772, pp. 10–15.

12. Samuel Bentley, *Poems on Various Occasions*, London, 1774, pp. 29–40

13. Joseph Wise, *Miscellany of Poems*, London, 1775, pp. 48–54.

14. Anon., *Sylvae*, Guilford, 1776, pp. 48–54.

15. Elizabeth Fell, *Poems*, London, 1777, pp. 61–80.

16. Ewan Clark, *Miscellaneous Poems*, Whitehaven, 1779, pp. 92–105.

17. John Hoy, *Poems on Various Subjects*, Edinburgh, 1781, pp. 1–21.

18. Robert Alves, *Poems*, Edinburgh, 1782, pp. 65–77.

19. J. H. Colls, *Poems*, Norwich, 1786 (?), pp. 135–38.

20. J. Macgilvray, *Poems*, London, 1787, pp. 11–22.

21. Hugh Mulligan, *Poems*, London, 1788, pp. 44–55.

22. G. S. Cotter, *Poems*, Cork, 1788, I, 10–31.

23. T. S. Dupuis, *Miscellaneous Poetry*, London, 1789, pp. 32–37.

24. Peter Newby, *Poems*, Liverpool, 1790, I, 97–134.

25. William Mavor, *Poems*, London, 1793, pp. 191–96, 231–32.

26. Henry Man, *Miscellaneous Works*, London, 1802, II, 87–90.

27. William Richardson, *Poems and Plays*, Edinburgh, 1805, I, 31–34; II, 3–17.

28. G. M. Woodward, *The Fugitive*, London, 1805, pp. 44–55.

29. J. M. Lacey, *The Farm House*, London, 1809, pp. 27–38, 107–9.

30. William Hersee, *Poems*, Chichester, 1810, pp. 128–32.

31. Patrick Brontë, *Cottage Poems*, Halifax, 1811, pp. 43–46.

32. W. Allston, *Sylphs of the Seasons*, London, 1813, pp. 7–41.

33. Patrick Brontë, *The Rural Minstrel*, Halifax, 1813, pp. 71–76.

34. M. W. Hartsonge, *Ode to Desolation*, London, 1815, pp. 1–9.

35. Thomas Crossley, *Poems*, London, 1828 (?), pp. 73–75, 76–80.

36. William Calder, *Poems*, Edinburgh, 1838, pp. 26–31.

37. *Pleasures of Melancholy*, 136–53.

38. *Ibid.*, 126–30. Cf. *Summer*, 912 ff.

39. *Ibid.*, 227–40. Cf. *Winter*, 799 ff.

40. Cf. *Il Penseroso*, 1 ff. and *Winter*, 894 ff.

41. *A Banquet of the Muses: or, the Miscellany of Miscellanies . . . Printed for Jacob Bickerstaff*, London, 1746, pp. 5–20.

42. *Ibid.*, p. 19.

43. The question of Thomsonian imitation in American descriptive poetry is approached in Miss Adelaide Schneider's *Influence of Thomson's Seasons on American Poetry in the Eighteenth Century* (Unpublished Columbia Master's dissertation, 1929).

44. *A Collection of the Most Esteemed Pieces of Poetry . . . Printed for Richardson and Urquhart*, London, 1770.
   A Collection of Poems, in Four Volumes, by Several Hands . . . Printed for G. Pearch, London, 1775.

45. William Stevenson, *Original Poems on Several Subjects*, London, 1765, I, 3–125.

46. *Ibid.*, I, 161–86.

47. [F. N. C. Mundy], *Poems*, Oxford, 1768.
48. See J. W. Mackail, *Studies of English Poets*, London, 1926: "The Poet of the Seasons," pp. 83–109.
49. *Poems on Various Subjects. By a Young Gentleman*, London, 1776, pp. 60–83.
50. Thomas Pennant, *British Zoölogy*, Warrington, 1776, Vol. I, Preface.
51. *Ibid.*, I, xi.
52. *Ibid.*, I, 315.
53. See Barrington's "Experiments and Observations on the Singing of Birds," Pennant's *British Zoölogy*, Vol. II, Appendix V.
54. Charles Welsh, *A Bookseller of the Last Century*, London, 1885.
55. Ralph Straus, *Robert Dodsley*, London, 1910.
56. Ralph Straus, *The Unspeakable Curll*, London, 1927.
57. Walpole says (Walpole to Zouch, Jan. 3, 1761) that Hill made fifteen guineas a week working for the booksellers, and that he was working at one time on six large works on botany, husbandry, and science, which were published weekly.
58. *Diary*, Sunday, Jan. 19, 1873.
59. *Poetical Works of Anna Seward; with Extracts from Her Literary Correspondence*, Ed. by *Walter Scott*, Edinburgh, 1810. Letter of April 15, 1790, to Mrs. Piozzi.
60. Anna Seward's letters. *Ibid.*
61. H. Pearson, *Doctor Darwin*, London, 1930, Chapter VII.
62. See C. S. Duncan, *op. cit.*, Chapter IV.
63. See notes to Chapter IV, note 48.
64. See C. E. Norton, *The Poet Gray as a Naturalist*, Boston, 1903.
65. Walpole to Mann, May 6, 1770.
66. See page 18.
67. See Benjamin Stillingfleet, *Miscellaneous Tracts*, London, 1775, pp. 3–35.
68. The Columbia University Library possesses British editions of 1778, 1779, 1781, 1792, 1793, 1794, 1799, 1802, 1803, 1811, and 1819, and American editions of 1802, 1808, 1812, 1814, which include Aikin's essay as a preface. The British Museum catalogue lists another such edition, of 1791 (Hamburg). The New York Public Library has another American edition, of 1804.
69. Ann Seward, *op. cit.*, VI, 180–81.
70. See Chapter VII.
71. C. A. Martin, *A Bibliography of Gilbert White of Selborne*, London, n.d.
72. See Martin, *op. cit.*
73. The verses are added after Letter XXIV to Pennant. See Martin, *op. cit.*
74. Martin, *op. cit.*

75. Lines appended after Letter XLI to Barrington. See Martin, *op. cit.*

76. Benjamin West, *Miscellaneous Poems,* Northampton, 1780, pp. 40–43, 54–56.

77. Thomas Warwick, *Abelard to Eloisa* . . . *and Other Poems,* London, 1784, pp. 30–36.

78. See M. M. Cameron, *op. cit.*

79. *Task,* VI, 6–10.

80. *Ibid.,* I, 192–96.

81. *Ibid.,* I, 368–86; VI, 134–42.

82. *Ibid.,* I, 697–748; II, 206–54; V, 460–508.

83. *Ibid.,* I, 600–31.

84. *Ibid.,* II, 88–132.

85. *Ibid.,* VI, 114–17. See also VI, 182–83.

86. See, for example, Anna Seward, *op. cit.,* VI, 166–69.

87. *The Cotter's Saturday Night* is a more detailed treatment of the theme of the peasant's leisure hours at home with his family, which had been a part of georgic tradition since Vergil.

88. John Bryant, *Verses,* 2d edition, London, 1787, pp. 42–55.

89. George Wright, *Retired Pleasures, or, the Charms of Rural Life,* London, 1787, pp. 153–57.

90. *Ibid.,* pp. 157–61.

91. *Ibid.,* pp. 168–77.

92. *Ibid.,* pp. 186–87.

93. *Ibid.,* pp. 250–53.

94. See *Poetical Works of James Woodhouse,* London, 1896, II, 193–97.

95. James Hurdis, *The Village Curate,* London, 1810. See *Account of the Author,* p. xiii.

96. George Sackville Cotter, *Poems,* Cork, 1788, Vol. II.

97. There is a difference of opinion as to whether Haller knew *The Seasons* when he wrote *Die Alpen.* See L. M. Price, *English-German Literary Influences,* "University of California Publications in Modern Philology," Vol. IX, Chapter VI, Berkeley, 1920.

98. Mrs. Howorth, *Poems of Baron Haller,* London, 1794. Morgan notes this translation, and also *Haller. Translated by Mrs. Howard,* 1793, querying whether these may not be the same. See B. Q. Morgan, *A Bibliography of German Literature in English Translation,* "University of Wisconsin Studies in Language and Literature," No. 16. Madison, 1922.

99. See Knut Gjerset, *Der Einfluss von James Thomson's "Zahreszeiten" auf die deutsche Literatur des achzehnten Jahrhunderts,* Heidelberg, 1898; Max Koch, *Uber den Beziehungen der englischen Literatur zu der deutschen im 18 Jahrhunderts,* Leipzig, 1883; Charles Joret, *La Littérature allemande au 18ᵉ siècle dans*

ses rapports avec la littérature française et avec la littérature anglaise, Aix, 1876; and L. M. Price, *op. cit.*

100. James Grahame, *Poems*, Paisley, 1794, pp. 17–23, 24–25, 41–42.

101. George Harley, *Poems*, London, 1796, pp. 26–107.

102. See the account of Hurdis in D. N. B.

103. John Stagg, *Miscellaneous Poems*, Carlisle, 1804, pp. 17–36.

104. Joseph Good, *Poems on Several Occasions*, Sherborne, 1805 (?), pp. 5–23.

105. *Lines Sacred to the Memory of the Rev. James Grahame*, in John Wilson, *Isle of Palms and Other Poems*, New York, 1812, p. 323.

106. Mrs. Anne Grant, *The Highlanders*. See *Poems on Various Subjects*, Edinburgh, 1803.

107. *Poetical Works of George Crabbe*, London, 1908 (Oxford Edition), p. 58.

108. *Ibid.*, p. 112.

109. *Ibid.*, p. 141.

110. Mrs. Sarah Richardson, *Original Poems*, London, 1808, pp. 113–32.

111. *Specimens of the Poetry of . . . Joseph Blacket*, London, 1809, pp. 93–101.

112. Thomas Rhodes, *Poetical Miscellanies*, Coventry, 1810 (?), pp. 114–23.

113. *Poetical and Dramatic Works of Colin Maclaurin and George Maclaurin*, Edinburgh, 1812, II, 127–312.

114. David Hurn, *Rural Rhymes*, Spalding, 1813, pp. 6–24, 25–30.

115. Thomas Grinfield, *Epistles and Miscellaneous Poems*, London, 1815, pp. 91–95.

116. Morgan (*op. cit.*) says of Georg Heinrich Christoph Egestorff that he was a native German whose command of English was hardly sufficient to equip him for the various translations he attempted from Kleist, Klopstock, and others.

117. J. L. Cherry, *Life and Remains of John Clare*, London, 1872 (?), pp. 81–88.

118. *Ibid.*, p. 85.

119. *Ibid.*, p. 86.

120. *Ibid.*, p. 89.

121. *Ibid.*, p. 65.

122. *Cowper Green.*

123. *Cowper Green.*

124. *Solitude.*

125. *Cowper Green.*

126. Thomas Shaw, *Recent Poems*, Huddersfield, 1824, pp. 20–28.

127. *Shepherd's Tree.*

128. *The Flitting.*

129. *Summer Evening.*

130. *Summer Images.*
131. Norman Gale, *Poems by John Clare*, Rugby, 1901.
 Arthur Symons, *Poems by John Clare*, London, 1908.
 Edmund Blunden and Alan Porter, *John Clare, Poems Chiefly from Manuscript*, London, 1920.
 Edmund Blunden, *Madrigals and Chronicles. Being Newly Found Poems Written by John Clare*, London, 1924.
 The recent " life " by J. W. and Anne Tibble, *John Clare,* London, 1932, has new information on the poet.
132. Joanna Baillie, *Dramatic and Poetical Works*, London, 1853, pp. 772–75, 775–78.
133. G. P. R. Pulman (" Piscator "), *Rustic Sketches*, Taunton, 1842, pp. 42–59.
134. *Poetical Works of Thomas Aird*, Edinburgh and London, 1878, p. xxiii.
135. *Poetical Works of Thomas Aird*, Edinburgh and London, 1848, pp. 150–69, 205–12.

Chapter VII

1. Robert A. Aubin, *The Topographical Poem.* (Unpublished Harvard University doctoral thesis, 1927.) The present writer collected his materials on local poetry before seeing Mr. Aubin's work. The first pages of this chapter owe a good deal, however, to his researches. A number of poems cited by him, which might be relevant to my purpose, I have been unable to see.
2. Ovid, *Tristia*, I, 10; Propertius, III, 21 (this merely proposes a journey).
3. Thomas Wright and J. O. Halliwell, *Reliquiae antiquae*, London, 1841–43.
4. Dyer's *Country Walk* appeared in Savage's *Miscellaneous Poems and Translations*, London, 1726; and his *Grongar Hill* in D. Lewis's *Miscellany Poems by Several Hands*, London, 1726. For an earlier version of the latter in " Pindaric " measures, see G. Greever, " The Two Versions of ' Grongar Hill,' " *Journal of English and Germanic Philology*, XVI (No. 2), 274–81, April, 1917.
5. See John Leyden, *Scottish Descriptive Poems*, London, 1803.
6. James Woodhouse, *Poems*, London, 1764, pp. 38–109.
7. John Leyden, *Poetical Works*, London, 1875, pp. 120–30.
8. James Woodhouse, *Norbury Park*, London, 1803.
9. James Cririe, *Scottish Scenery*, London, 1803, pp. 175–228.
10. *Poems . . . by Mrs. Grant*, Edinburgh, 1803, pp. 21–109.
11. Note the use of seasons also in the following local poems: Weten-

hall Wilkes, *Hounslow Heath*, 1748; John Missing, *Titchfield*, 1749; Joseph Atkinson, *Killarney*, 1750 (?) ; Henry Pye, *Faringdon Hill*, 1774; John Scott, *Amwell*, 1776; Rev. Cameron, *Panana* (*Poems*, Edinburgh, 1780) ; John Hawthorne, *River Bann*, *Combe Village*, and *Combe Camp* (*Poems*, Salisbury, 1779) ; T. Davis, *Eastham Hill*, 1796; Thomas Peacock, *Genius of the Thames*, 1810; the anonymous *Sketch from Nature*, 1814; Thomas Pringle, *Autumnal Excursion*, 1819; John McKinley, *Giant's Causeway*, 1819; and James Henry James, *Banks of the Wye*, 1856.

12. Wetenhall Wilkes, *An Essay on the Pleasures and Advantages of Female Literature*, London, 1741. His *Three Poetical Landscapes*, including *Kilikeen*, pp. 59–77.

13. Bruce's *Lochleven* was first printed in the *Edinburgh Magazine* in 1766, and later included in *The Works of Michael Bruce*, Edinburgh, 1865.

14. Note the use of time divisions of parts of the day, also, in these local poems: Mark Foster, *Scarborough*, 1770; William Mavor, *Blenheim*, 1787; John Jackson, *Gilsland Wells*, 1797; Edward Gardner, *Barrow Hill* (*Miscellanies*, Bristol, 1798) ; William Fox, *La Bagatella*, 1801; Nathaniel Howard, *Bickleigh Vale*, 1804; John Hodgson, *Woodlands* (*Poems*, London, 1807) ; George Baker, *Tenby*, 1807; Francis Skurray, *Bidcombe Hill*, 1808; Thomas Noble, *Blackheath*, 1808; Mary Lloyd, *Brighton*, 1809; Fortesque Hitchins, *The Sea-Shore*, 1810; William Carr, *Rosstrevor*, 1810; William Hamilton Drummond, *Giant's Causeway*, 1811, and *Clontarf*, 1822; Arthur Brooke, *Durovernum*, 1818; James King, *Poem on Leigh Park*, 1829; Brian Broughton, *Copse Grove Hill*, 1829; William Stanley Roscoe, *Contemplative Days* (*Poems*, London, 1834) ; Henry Stokes, *Vale of Lanherne*, 1836.

15. See similar genre sketches in these poems: Wetenhall Wilkes, *Kilikeen*, 1741; Joseph Atkinson, *Killarney*, 1750 (?) ; E. Coopei, *Bewdley* (*Collection of Elegiac Poesy*, London (?) , 1761) ; James Woodhouse, *The Leasowes*, 1764; Richard Jago, *Edge-Hill*, 1767; the anonymous *South-Downs*, 1793; John Fitchett, *Bewsey*, 1796; William Lane, *Cliffden*, 1792 (?) , and *Vale of Wycombe* (*Poems*, London, 1798) ; W. L. Bowles, *Coombe Ellen*, 1798; Nathaniel Howard, *Bickleigh Vale*, 1804; John Hodgson, *Woodlands*, 1807; John Penwarne, *Contemplation*, 1807; Francis Skurray, *Bidcombe Hill*, 1808; Mary Lloyd, *Brighton*, 1809; Fortesque Hitchins, *The Sea-Shore*, 1810; William Carr, *Rosstrevor*, 1810; the anonymous *Sketch from Nature*, 1814; Charles Ash, *Adbaston*, 1814; George Woodley, *Cornubia*, 1819; Anna Liddiard, *Mount Leinster*, 1819–20; John Holland, *The Village of Eyam*, 1821; John McKinley, *Giant's Causeway*, 1819; Henry Atkins, *Isle of Wight*, 1834; Henry

Stokes, *Vale of Lanherne*, 1836; Robert Banks, *The Ploughman*, 1836; George Henderson, *Scenes of Boyhood*, 1840; Samuel Browning, *Devona* (*Poems*, London, 1846) ; Edward Davies, *Dartmoor Days*, 1863.

16. *Six Picturesque Views in North Wales*, London, 1801, included six engravings in aquatint by Alken, and the poem *Reflections on Leaving That Country*, by Brian Broughton.

17. See also Sarah Hamilton, *Beauties of Vegetation; with . . . Sketches of Norwich, &c.* (*Liberation of Joseph and Other Poems*, London, 1827) ; James King, *Leigh Park*, 1829; Henry Stokes, *Vale of Lanherne*, 1836.

18. See the use of exotic episodes in the following poems: the anonymous *Essay on Halifax*, 1761; Richard Jago, *Edge-Hill;* J. Mackay, *Quebec Hill;* John Gisborne, *Vales of Wever;* W. H. Drummond, *Hibernia*, 1797; W. L. Bowles, *Coombe Ellen;* Romaine Thorn, *Retirement* (*Poems*, Cork, 1808) ; John Penwarne, *Contemplation;* Thomas Noble, *Blackheath;* Alexander Glas, *River Tay*, 1810; Sarah Hamilton, *Beauties of Vegetation;* James King, *Leigh Park;* William Roscoe, *Mount Pleasant* (*Poetical Works*, Liverpool, 1853) .

19. See the use of such episodes, apparently inspired by the traditional models, in Richard Rolt, *Cambria;* Joseph Atkinson, *Killarney;* Anne Christian, *Cambridge*, 1756; Richard Jago, *Edge-Hill;* Henry Pye, *Faringdon Hill;* William Williams, *Head of the Rock*, 1775; Luke Booker, *The Highlanders;* J. Mackay, *Quebec Hill;* John Jackson, *Gilsland Wells;* John Leyden, *Scenes of Infancy;* Romaine Thorn, *Retirement;* W. H. Drummond, *Hibernia*, *Giant's Causeway*, and *Clontarf;* Alexander Glas, *River Tay;* Cyrus Redding, *Mount Edgcumbe*, 1811; Francis Webb, *Somerset*, 1811; John Holland, *Sheffield Park*, 1820; Noel Carrington, *Banks of Tamar;* David Landsborough, *Arran;* Brian Broughton, *Copse-Grove Hill;* Charles Crocker, *Kingley Vale*, 1837; William Roscoe, *Mount Pleasant;* James Henry James, *Banks of the Wye.*

20. Among those closest to Vergil's " *O fortunatos nimium* " passage, or Thomson's expansion of it, are Richard Rolt, *Cambria;* the anonymous poet of *Essay on Halifax;* George Keate, *The Alps;* Richard Jago, *Edge-Hill;* the anonymous poet of *South-Downs;* Edward Hamley, *Portsdown* (*Poems*, London, 1795) ; Brian Broughton, *Reflections;* Nathaniel Howard, *Bickleigh Vale;* Alexander Glas, *River Tay;* William Carr, *Rosstrevor;* Cyrus Redding, *Mount Edgcumbe;* Noel Carrington, *Banks of Tamar.* Among those closest to Vergil's " *Labor omnia vincit* " passage, or Thomson's expansion of it, are the anonymous poet of the *Essay on Halifax;* Michael Bruce, *Lochleven;* Anna Liddiard, *Mount Leinster;* Sarah Hamilton, *Beauties of Vegetation;* Joseph·Cottle, *Dart-*

moor. Compare too W. L. Bowles's eulogy of "Culture" in *Coombe Ellen.*

21. John Lewes, *Poems,* Liverpool, 1811, pp. 91–99.
22. W. H. Drummond, *Giant's Causeway,* Belfast, 1811, pp. 100–2.

CONCLUSION

1. Myra Reynolds, *Nature in English Poetry between Pope and Wordsworth,* Chicago, 1909.
2. Edmund Burke, *A Philosophical Enquiry into the Origin of Our Ideas of the Sublime and Beautiful,* London, 1756, pp. 200–1.
3. *Biographia Litteraria,* 1817.
4. *Notes to Lessing's Laokoon,* 1826–27.
5. See J. J. Rennes, *Bowles, Byron and the Pope Controversy,* Amsterdam, 1927.
6. These were, for Bowles, also a part of nature and superior in poetic quality to external nature.
7. The phrase is Cazamian's: *Histoire de la littérature anglaise,* Paris, 1924.
8. Among examples of this prose literature treating natural revelation, which continued down to and after Paley, note the following:

Thomas Jackson, *Treatise of the Divine Essence and Attributes,* 1628.

Samuel Parker, *Tentamina physico-theologica de Deo,* 1665.

Stephen Charnock, *Discourses upon the Existence and Attributes of God,* 1682.

John Edwards, *Demonstration of the Existence and Providence of God,* 1696.

Samuel Clarke, *Demonstration of the Being and Attributes of God,* 1705.

William Wotton, *The Omnipresence of God, an Argument of his Divinity,* 1720.

John Wilkins, *Principles and Duties of Natural Religion,* 1722.

William Wollaston, *The Religion of Nature Delineated,* 1724.

Samuel Colliber, *An Impartial Enquiry into the Nature and Existence of God,* 1735.

Moses Lowman, *Argument to Prove the Unity and Perfections of God, a Priori,* 1735.

—— Barr, *A Summary of Natural Religion,* 1736.

Phillips Glover, *The Argument a Priori, Concerning the Existence and Perfections of God,* 1737.

Benjamin Heath, *An Essay towards a Demonstrative Proof of the Divine Existence, Unity, and Attributes,* 1740.

Henry Knight, *The Being and Attributes of God Demonstrated,*
1747.

Richard Jack, *Mathematical Principles of Theology; or, the Existence of God Geometrically Demonstrated,* 1747.

Anon., *Introduction to the Religious Study of Nature,* 1749.

William Paley, *Natural Theology,* 1802.

9. The phrase is Drennon's. See above.

10. Edith C. Batho, *The Later Wordsworth,* New York, 1933, Chapter III.

INDEX

A

Addison, Joseph, ix, 6, 21, 22, 23, 59, 112, 143, 220, 223
Adrian, Cardinal (Hadrianus Castellensis), 5, 6
Aetna, 194
Aikin, Arthur, 176, 182–83
Aikin, John, 23, 88–89, 110, 124, 144–49, 150, 151, 153, 176, 181, 182, 190, 201, 202, 217, 234, 236
Aird, Thomas, 191, 241
Akenside, Mark, xi, 23, 58, 68, 73, 86, 111–13, 116, 121, 131, 146, 155, 160, 162, 205, 209, 217, 234
Alamanni, Luigi, 5, 23
Aldington, John, 79
Alexander, Caleb, 222
Alison, Archibald, 57
Alken, Samuel, 243
Allen, John, 198, 201
Alley, Jerome, 121
Allston, Washington, 132, 237
Alves, Robert, 132, 237
Amadis de Gaul, 99
Anderson, Robert, 73, 83, 110, 233
Andrews, Robert, 221
Anglesea, Arthur Annesley, 1st Earl of, 24
Animal Biography, The, 181
Anson, George, Lord, 57
Anstey, Christopher, 118
Anstey, John ("John Surrebutter"), 118–19
Apollonius Rhodius, 14
Aratus, 3, 12, 13, 15, 16, 17, 22, 23, 32, 48, 53, 221, 222, 223, 226
Arber, Edward, 230
Arblay, Madame d', 145
Aristotle, 8, 9, 12, 13, 14, 17, 20, 22, 28, 48, 53, 62, 211, 225, 226, 227
Armstrong, John, 23, 43, 68, 108, 109–10, 110–11, 115, 116, 122, 228
Arnold, Matthew, ix, 206
Artis, E. T., 186
Art of Architecture, The, 228
Art of Candle Making, The, 96
Art of Love, Paraphrased from Ovid, The, 227

Art of Poetry, The, 228
Ash, Charles B., 228, 242
Ashmole, Elias, 5
Atkins, Henry, 204, 242
Atkinson, Joseph, 242, 243
Aubin, R. A., 193, 196, 241
Ausonius, 144, 194
Austin, J. L., 228
Austin, William, 4, 225
Autumn, 131
Autumnal Reflections, 184

B

"B., J.," 227
"B., O.," 151
Bacon, Sir Francis, 62, 93
Baillie, Joanna, 180, 191, 241
Baker, George, 242
Baker, Henry, 45, 85, 234
Bakewell, Robert, 57
Baldi, Bernardino, 5
Balfour, Alexander, 187
Banks, James, 223
Banks, Robert, 243
Barbauld, Mrs. Anna Letitia, 23, 124, 131, 146, 185, 236
Barclay, Alexander, 4, 33
Barga, Pietro Angelio da, 6
Barker, Thomas, 5
Barnes, William, 187
Barr, — —, 244
Barrington, Daines, 124, 144, 146, 150, 238, 239
Barrow, Isaac, 19
Barton, Bernard, 187
Batho, Edith C., 245
Bathurst, William, 223
Beattie, James, 116, 166, 221
Beaumont, Lady (wife of Sir George), 73
Behn, Aphra, 27, 220
Belfour, John, 92, 222
Bell, John, 73, 110
Benson, William, 220
Bentley, Richard, 54, 215
Bentley, Samuel, 131, 237
Berchoux, Joseph, 119–20, 222, 223
Berghem, Nicolas, 93
Berners, Dame Juliana, 4, 224